HOLY REBEL

Fight the good
Fight,
Holy Rebel !
I Tim 6:12
Pastors Jodd & Kelly

Holy Rebel: Armed with Truth, Stand Your Ground, and Rebel Against Hell's Agenda.

Copyright © 2022 Todd and Kelly Hudnall

This manuscript has undergone viable editorial work and proofreading, yet human limitations may have resulted in minor grammatical or syntax-related errors remaining in the finished book. The understanding of the reader is requested in these cases. While precaution has been taken in the preparation of this book, the publisher and author assume no responsibility for errors or omissions, or for damages resulting from the use of the information contained herein.

This book is set in the typeface *Athelas* designed by Veronika Burian and Jose Scaglione.

Paperback ISBN: 978-1-955546-24-9

A Publication of *Tall Pine Books*
119 E Center Street, Suite B4A | Warsaw, Indiana 46580
www.tallpinebooks.com

| 1 22 22 20 16 02 |

Published in the United States of America

HOLY REBEL

ARMED WITH TRUTH, STAND YOUR GROUND,
and REBEL AGAINST HELL'S AGENDA.

TODD *and* KELLY
HUDNALL

"In Holy Rebel, my friends, Todd and Kelly Hudnall, have written not so much a book but a manifesto, a call to a roaring spiritual resistance to the demonically induced control centers and ideologies boasting their dominion over our souls, families, churches, cities, and nations. This is an all-out confrontation to the church of compromise and acquiescence in the face of the Powers. Rat a tat punching paragraphs of penetrating Bible truth and their authentic experience drive home the urgency of engagement and a return to repentance, revival realities, and cultural reformation. The book rejects the counsel of despair. It is the roar of the Lion of Judah who has overcome, rising in the church. It's an Elijah/Jezebel showdown. To the victor goes the soul of the nation."

LOU ENGLE,
Intercessor, Author, and the visionary co-founder of *The Call*

"Nothing makes my heart leap more than when I find brothers and sisters in the faith who understand the times we are in, and who know what God is asking of them, and more than that, who exhort others to the battle. So it is a great joy to know Todd and Kelly Hudnall, and to heartily endorse their vitally important book, HOLY REBEL. It is a stirring invitation to join the great adventure for which we were born!"

ERIC METAXAS,
Author of *Bonhoeffer* and *Letter to the American Church*
Host of the *Eric Metaxas Show*

"This book is fire! While reading, I got so excited, I shouted 'amen' on almost every page. If ever there was a time for the Church to boldly preach biblical truth and stand tall for moral truth, it is now! This is not a time for passivity. This book will wake you up to your Kingdom calling; my heart was enflamed with faith and passion to be a holy rebel for a Kingdom of God revolution. Using the whole Bible—from Old Testament prophets to the New Testament church, Todd and Kelly Hudnall have captured the essence and purpose of biblical leadership. Holy rebels are men and women who are not intimidated into silence or fearful of persecution. They are on fire with the love of God, the truth of scripture, and won't back down from a fight. I challenge you to read this book and let the Holy Spirit make you a holy rebel of love and boldness."

DR. STEVE HOLT,
Founder, Senior Pastor of
The Road @ Chapel Hills, Colorado Springs, Colorado

"I've never started an endorsement by quoting 1950's rocker Jerry Lee Lewis, so please pay attention, 'There's a whole lotta' shakin' goin' on' (Hebrews 12:26-28). The pandemic has had us shaking, the economy has had us shaking, inflation has had us shaking, critical race theory has had us shaking. Cultural aberration from biblical standards has had us shaking, mass shootings have had us shaking, cancel culture has had us shaking, gender neutrality confusion has had us shaking. But all the shaking reveals what can't be shaken... the kingdom of God (Hebrews 12:28). So, what is the answer and how do we get there?"

In your hands is an invaluable and indispensable tool called Holy Rebel. In this revolutionary book Todd and Kelly Hudnall have shown the answer in a rebel of a different kind. This is not a call to a hatred of those who believe differently, but a call to the reestablishment of God's Word... to *cancel* cancel culture with the truth, that can truly bring freedom and redemption.

I am always excited to be a part of anything Todd and Kelly are a part of for the kingdom. They always share great insight and truth that impact our times. We are in the greatest war of our lifetime and my friends Todd and Kelly have drawn up a prescription for victory in this moment of time. Rebel against the devil... yes! Rebel against the philosophy of a wayward culture... yes! Rebel against lethargy in the church... yes! Read Holy Rebel and see truth reestablished in America. It is time to speak the truth in love (Ephesians 4:15). It's time for revival!"

RON MCINTOSH,
International Speaker and Author

"Years ago, I heard a seasoned man of God who is now in heaven, talking about preachers. He said that he heard three types of messages in his life. Some come from the intellect and reach other people's intellect. Others come from the heart and touch people's hearts. But the most impactful messages are those that come from a person's life and impact lives. This book, Holy Rebel by Pastors Todd & Kelly Hudnall, is a message that comes from their lives. They believe it and live it. This book is a battle cry to summon an army of believers to advance the kingdom on their knees."

MARK COWART,
Senior Pastor of *Church For All Nations, Colorado Springs, CO*

"Todd and Kelly Hudnall embody the theme of their book, Holy Rebel. Over the years, they have taken a stand for biblical truth and against evil. They have courage, a commodity that seems to be in short supply these days. Their new book provides insight into the spiritual battle we're facing in America and how the people of God can prevail over the darkness. Allow me to go a step further. When I first met them decades ago, I immediately tried to hire them. Why? When you read the book, you will see why. They are a power couple. Powerful in the Spirit. Listen to them. You will not regret it."

Dr. Jim Garlow,
CEO, *Well Versed*

"It has been my pleasure to have a wonderful relationship with Todd and Kelly Hudnall for many years. First, when they moved from Kansas to Lufkin, Texas, where they became lead pastors to a congregation that became a megachurch with a ministry that reached thousands through the means of television and the local church ministries. Later, I visited with them when they became the lead pastors of a great church in San Diego, California. And more recently I have visited with them at Radiant Church in Colorado Springs where they serve as the lead pastors of a very active congregation that meets in three locations."

It is my joy to recommend this up-to-date book that is definitely 'on-target' with a message that is a must for all conservative patriots to read. If ever there was a time for 'holy rebels' to stand up, speak up, and join up with many others who will seize the present opportunities to radically change our nation for good and for God, it's now!

I strongly suggest that you read the first chapter and the eleventh chapters as soon as you can. Of course, you will want to read all of the chapters but get ready to be challenged and stirred in your thoughts and spirit to arise to the call for service to your country and to your Lord for 'such a time as this!' We are 'more than conquerors' ... let's prove it! Righteous Rebels, arise and shine!"

Vic Schober,
Former District Superintendent of the
North Texas District of the Assemblies of God

Dedicated to our children Faith and Luke Hudnall
Two of the most amazing Holy Rebel warriors we know
And to their generation (Gen Z)
May they rise up to partner with Heaven
In a holy rebellion against the agenda of Hell

To our church family
Radiant Church in Colorado Springs
We are truly blessed to pastor a church of
Holy Rebels who are passionately following Jesus
Together with us

To Jack Shultz
For loving us, believing in us, for being our
Chief armor bearer
And partner in this holy mission

CONTENTS

FOREWORD

THERE IS NO record in the Bible of God telling David to kill Goliath. It was Goliath's blasphemy that informed David to act. For David, it was a foregone conclusion that something will be done about it.

Psalm 119:126 mirrors that foregone conclusion: "LORD, it is time for you to act, for these evil people have violated your instructions."

Any believer who is waiting for special instructions before rebelling against the wholesale desecration of our nation can be considered a part of the desecration.

The greatest burden I bear is to watch the devil flooding our nation with evil while the church is ignorant of her role in stopping it—and of her authority to stop it.

Fallacies abound. We are told that if we are not nice it will reflect badly on the Gospel. Yet, in our tent crusades it is the clarity of moral preaching that is winning souls.

We are told to leave politics out of the pulpit. Such a towering misnomer! First of all it is no longer politics—it is evil. Second of all, silence in the face of evil is itself the highest form of politics.

A burning question is a question that must be answered as fast and as forceful as putting out a house fire. The Psalmist asks, "If the foundations are destroyed, what can the righteous do?"-Psalm 11:3

Holy Rebel emphatically and practically answers the burning question. Within these pages you will become "urgent in season and out." You will be fired up, then equipped, and finally directed to your sacred role in defeating evil in America.

Above everything else this book is about God's secret weapon: the local Church. I have always believed that the local church was supposed to be the most fiery and effective weapon in God's arsenal.

Think about it. No true evangelist is against the local church. The mass soul winner is constantly thinking of where they will direct the souls who are saved in their outreach.

Satan is most terrified by the fact that this book is proven to be real because the principles in this book have built a mighty church. Radiant Church is living proof of every word of this book.

This growing miracle family defies all the rules of church growth. And why not? They are Holy Rebels.

Fasten your seat belt. Theory is about to be replaced by reality. Compassion is about to take on muscle. The wheat and the chaff will be separated. The sheep and goats will go their separate ways. Let's go get our country back.

MARIO MURILLO
Evangelist

CHAPTER ONE

JESUS: THE FIRST HOLY REBEL

"He was counted among the rebels" (Luke 22:37 NLT)

THE CRUCIFIXION WAS near, Jesus carefully explained to His disciples what was about to take place. Many prophetic passages were about to be fulfilled. Jesus told them, "For the time has come for this prophecy about Me to be fulfilled: 'He was counted among the rebels.' Yes, everything written about Me by the prophets will come true" (Luke 22:37, NLT).

This holy prophecy Jesus refers to is in the book of Isaiah. "I will give Him the honors of a victorious soldier because He exposed himself to death. He was counted among the rebels. He bore the sins of many and interceded for rebels" (Isaiah 53:12, NLT).

Jesus was counted among the rebels. He was not counted among the reformed, the accepted, the politically correct, or the cultural elite, and not even counted among the religious leaders of His day. Our Lord and Savior, Jesus Christ, was "counted among the rebels." Yet, Jesus was not an ungodly rebel like the two men hanging on crosses on each side of Him. Though He did not sin, Jesus was still counted among the rebels. Jesus was a Holy Rebel. He rebelled against hell and the forces of darkness to bring freedom and redemption to all who would receive Him as Lord. He came as a holy rebel to initiate a holy rebellion against the power of Satan and to defeat him finally.

When hearing the word "rebel," we immediately think of criminals, insurrectionists, or insubordinate people choosing to go against the tide. Most rebels are argumentative, always looking for a fight, and filled with hatred towards others or the system. Jesus was a rebel of another kind, and as His followers, we are called to be rebels of a similar kind in our time.

Over the past decade, I have grown more concerned about the exponential rise of evil, wickedness, darkness, and immorality. The prophet Isaiah foretold that a time would come when good would be called evil and evil would be called good. We live in that time when those who live holy lives of purity and righteousness are considered an insufferable blight on humanity. The current culture is systematically working to marginalize, cancel out, silence, and destroy every person who desires to live according to God's Word. Jesus told us this would happen.

A MESSAGE FROM THE PRAYER CLOSET

Several years ago, the Holy Spirit gave me a prayer mandate for these times. I had shut myself up, alone with God in the prayer closet. I wept and interceded on behalf of this generation of youth and children who are growing up in gross darkness. Through many tears, I agonized over the precious children and youth who are being indoctrinated with hell's agenda in every facet of society. The perverted, demonic messages are constantly flowing into them through public education and much of its literature. The relentless flow of immorality and wickedness is being propagated through entertainment, music, and media. Many churches and pastors today have traded the truth of God for a lie. They have become man pleasers rather than God pleasers and they are conveying a confusing message that leads to bondage rather than freedom. They are blind guides leading the blind.

Tragically, today's youth carry the weight of ungodly distortions of truth generated by technology. They have become trapped, enslaved, and dominated by the conveniently disguised devices that release a constant flow of messages meant to separate them from the God who loves them and trap them in Satan's web of lies. While mourning over this situation, I cried out, "Lord, we don't know what to do, but our eyes are on You! Please show us what to do and show us how to pray specific, targeted prayers for this generation during this time of gross darkness."

Deep, intercessory prayer continued to pour out of me like an unstoppable force until a holy stillness came over me. God's presence seemed tangible in the closet that day, and I knew I must be silent as I waited to hear Him speak. What I heard Him say took my breath away and changed my life and prayers forever. In His still, small, powerful voice, He spoke, and I will never forget it. God's message was clear, as I heard Him say, "Pray for a holy rebellion to be awakened and stirred in the hearts of My people and this generation of youth. Pray that they will rebel against hell's agenda of darkness and reject the evil and perversions with My weapons of righteousness, holiness, and truth."

That prayer mandate was given to me years ago, but I continue to pray it daily. As you read this book, I pray that you will join us in this holy rebellion against hell by praying this prayer over yourself, your family, the church, the nation, and especially over today's youth. The war against evil forces begins on our knees, in our prayer closets and war rooms, with prayer and intercession. We dare not march into the battle without first engaging in prayer, seeking God's wisdom and counsel. Never consider entering a war without first spending time in "the secret place" with God as your Commanding Officer. He who dwells in the secret place of the Most High shall abide under the shadow of the Almighty (Psalm 91:1-2).

WE ARE AT WAR

I will never forget the day that our four-and-a-half-year-old son was playing alone in his room, and he came running to me to tell me that God had spoken to him. When your four-year-old son tells you God spoke to him, you are all ears. I remember it well because I was mopping the floors in the kitchen, and when he said those words, my cleaning came to an abrupt halt. I got down on his level, looked him in the eyes, and asked, "What did God say to you, Luke?" He replied in his sweet, raspy little voice, "He said that there was going to be a war, and He wanted me to fight in it." Then he ran back to his room to play.

While he went back to playing, I fell to the floor, amazed and in awe at the words he had heard. My heart was racing as I pondered it. I asked the Lord what it meant and what kind of war it was? That year was 2012, and, at that time, a war that God would call Luke to fight in seemed foreign and hard to imagine. Yet, I knew that God had spoken to him. Luke is fifteen at the time that I'm writing this, and he still remembers that day well and what the Lord spoke to him.

Today, the undeniable reality is that we are at war, and, like it or not, it is my reality and yours, and it is the truth of all humanity. This is not a political war as many deem it; it is in fact, a war between good and evil, light and darkness, truth and lies, and freedom versus slavery. We must realize that God is calling all of us to fight in this battle in this hour; God's not just calling Luke. Often, a four-year-old can hear the voice of God more clearly than many adults.

The Lion of the Tribe of Judah is roaring across this land. "A Lion has roared! Who will not fear? The Lord GOD has spoken! Who can but prophesy" (Amos 3:8)? The King's holy roars are shaking His church and awakening His sons and daughters. However, many are sleeping through this time of war and do not want to be awakened. The comfort of living in denial and doing business as usual feels familiar and safe. The call to war requires sacrifice, change, and self-denial and means we must abandon the old wineskins (Mark 2).

We are called to be like mighty warriors trampling the enemy (Zechariah 10:5 NIV), and weapons are required for the battle. So, we must take up our spiritual weapons that are not carnal but are mighty through God in demolishing the enemy's stronghold (2 Corinthians 10:6). Like our son Luke, you have been drafted into His army.

God is undoubtedly speaking today, yet many of His appointed ones choose to ignore His voice. Denial is consent, accepting the reality of what is happening all around them and doing nothing to fight against it. Unaware of the threats we face, many are sleeping through hell's furious attacks on people's lives and the nation's freedoms, pretending there is no battle, and everything will be okay. This is a divine warning: There is no hope if the church ignores this crisis and complies with hell's agenda through its silence. Not tomorrow, but now, is the time to rise and resist hell's plots with righteousness and holiness. Now is the time to unveil the truth and expose the enemy.

Satan and his minions have always fought to silence the voice of Christ's followers concerning political and cultural issues. He knows that if pastors stand up and speak up about the truth of hell's devious plots, then the church will follow, and the enemy's plans will be aborted. Do not be misled, for the kingdom of darkness will fight fiercely to keep Christians blinded, paralyzed, and silent to the truth. Ignorance is not bliss when fighting against a formidable foe. The battle we fight against hell's army is not a walk in the park. It requires commitment, insight, courage, and spiritual strength.

One convincing trick of the enemy is to persuade people that this war is only "political" and that pastors should remain silent by staying out of politics. We must be clear in our position and confront the lie face-forward with our voices, making it clear that our spiritual battle is not about "politics." It is a fight between light and darkness, the duality of good and evil which results in life or death, the succession of lies or the victory of truth, and finally, the choice between slavery or freedom. In the end, it is the great battle between heaven and hell, and the battlefield is on earth where we are the soldiers in God's army.

SOMEBODY DO SOMETHING

If those who have been entrusted with God's truth remain silent and do not get involved, then our nation's blood will be on our own hands. We must contend for truth and not be misguided in this crucial time. God will most certainly hold His people accountable for doing nothing, saying nothing, and for not standing in this hour. Almighty God has drafted each of us into this battle, fighting the good fight of faith as His holy rebel warriors. A.W. Tozer said it well, and his words are valid for us today: "You are a soldier of God. And the quicker you realize it, you will drop your toys and pick up your weapons."

While typing these words, I am reminded of the words of the prophet in Isaiah 6:8, "Also I heard the voice of the Lord, saying: 'Whom shall I send, And who will go for Us?' Then I said, 'Here *am* I! Send me.'" Ability without availability will not win the war, so make yourself available to God and go to the battle with Him

With every passing generation, God searches for and seeks those who will answer the call. He continues to search for those who will stand up like Isaiah and do something in their day and for their generation. God told Jeremiah that he was called as a prophet to the nations, but Jeremiah argued that he was young and could not speak (Jeremiah 1:6, 7). So, God said, "Do not say, 'I am a youth.' For you shall go to all to whom I send you, and whatever I command you, you shall speak" (verse 8). God's concluding words are powerful for this generation. "Brace yourself, Jeremiah! Stand up and say to them whatever I tell you to say. Don't be terrified in their presence, or I will make you [even more] terrified in their presence. Today I have made you like a fortified city, an iron pillar, and a bronze wall. You will be able to stand up to the whole land. You will be able to stand up to Judah's kings, its officials, its priests, and [all] the common people" (Jeremiah 1:17-19, GWT). That is God's Word to this generation: stand up, speak up, do what God says and go where He sends you without excuse.

A LIFE-CHANGING MOMENT

In 1994, a young American father took his 11-year-old daughter to Israel. He wanted her to see the country and understand the unique bond between Israel and America. He knew that there was no way she would understand what was so unique about this country if she did not realize what the Jewish people had been put through and how close they were to annihilation.

He took her to Yad Vashem, the world Holocaust remembrance center. He wrestled with the possibility that his young daughter would be overwhelmed by the graphic nature of what she would see. So, he decided to take her through the center, but he would lead her out if it became too much.

Their journey was arranged chronologically, so the first thing visitors would see was how children (just like her) were separated and then isolated by having the star of David sewn on their clothing, not to be honored but to be ridiculed and humiliated. The little girl was shocked that somebody would do this to a child, but the shock continued and intensified as they went through the part of Yad Vashem that depicted the Warsaw ghetto and the Nazi concentration camps. She saw the horrors inflicted upon the Jewish people who were herded like animals into that hideous environment.

Then the little girl arrived at the pictures and depictions of the artifacts from the Nazi death camps. At that moment, when the little girl saw those pictures, she fell silent, staring in disbelief as she read the captions under each photo.

When the little girl came to the end of her visit to Yad Vashem, there was a guestbook where people could record the date, their name, and from where they came and a space for comments. She reached into her daddy's pocket, grabbed a pen, and started writing her name and address, then paused for a moment.

Her dad was looking over her shoulder to see what she might write to see if she really understood what she had experienced. As the father looked over his eleven-year-old daughter's shoulder to see what she would write, he saw her write five words that he would never be forgotten: why didn't somebody do something? That's all she wrote, and the little girl did not say a word for four hours, but the father knew that his little girl understood very clearly what we all must come to understand as well.

Now you hear the rest of the story. The father was Mike Huckabee, and his little girl was Sarah Huckabee Sanders. This story impacted my life when I heard Governor Mike Huckabee share this story several years ago.

YOU CAN MAKE A DIFFERENCE

One person can make a difference, and everyone should try. You may not be in Israel or at Yad Vashem, or the Holocaust Museum, but I hope and pray that you understand how necessary it is for us all of us to be somebodies who are willing to do something. Somebody must be willing to stand against hell's wicked intent and fight for what is right. The time for a holy rebellion is now. We must rebel against hell's agenda today before it's too late. The church must awaken and engage in this holy rebellion before a similar fate is carried out upon our own children.

THE PLIGHT OF THE PERSECUTED CHURCH

Barbaric is a term describing well the plight of modern-day martyrs. The estimates of the number of martyrs per year vary but all of them are heartbreaking. The Center for the Study of Global Christianity has extensively researched Christian martyrdom, both historical and contemporary. They estimate that between 2005 and 2015, there were 900,000 Christian martyrs worldwide — an average of 90,000 per year.[1]

In their 2021 annual report, The World Watch List (WWL) stated, "Every day, 13 Christians worldwide are killed because of their faith. Every day, 12 churches or Christian buildings are attacked. And, every day, 12 Christians are unjustly arrested or imprisoned, and another five are abducted."[2]

Tertullian, one of the great early church fathers, said that the blood of the martyrs is the seed of the church. The early church grew in an environment of persecution. According to Open Doors, the listed nations contain 309 million Christians living in places with exceedingly high or extreme levels of persecution, up from 260 million in last year's list. Like the early church, they are growing in a culture of persecution and death.

It is tragic and inexcusable that Christians in the free world do nothing through intense intercession or support of them in any way. You and I are called to do something. We can begin by praying daily and partnering with groups like the American Center for Law and Justice, The Nazarene Fund, Open Doors Ministries, Voice of the Martyrs, and others who are somebodies doing something

REPENTANCE REQUIRED AND ACTION EXPECTED

We must repent for our lack of concern, prayerlessness, and inaction concerning the persecuted church. We are one body, made up of many members worldwide, and when one member suffers, we all suffer. This is why, at Radiant Church, we pray regularly for the persecuted Church, and we encourage you to pray daily and ask the Lord to show you how to stand up, pray, give, and make a difference. God is calling us to be holy rebels and to rebel against the powers of darkness through awareness, prayer, giving, and fighting for the freedom of all people, everywhere, to worship God.

Grief still strikes me deeply when I think about the pastor who rebuked me for alerting American Christians to the brutal atrocities happening to Christians in other nations. This pastor scolded me and told me that Christians in the West could not emotionally handle this information. He told me I needed to back off from alerting people in America because it was too much to comprehend and made them painfully uncomfortable.

Stunned amazement, shock, and horror paralyzed me for a moment as I allowed his rebuke to sink in. Honestly, I could not believe my ears. The first thing that came to my mind was, "I wonder if he would say the same thing if Isis was hunting him and his family? I wonder how he would feel if it was his children whose heads were being severed from their bodies and kicked down the street?"

Unfortunately, too many American Christians live in a cloistered world separated from persecuted Christians who have suffered greatly, with many tortured and killed because of their love for Christ. What little they have heard does not begin to explain the horrific violence and oppression being conducted against Christians today. Without a doubt, our persecuted brothers and sisters are asking the question, "Why doesn't somebody do something?"

God has strategically arranged multiple divine appointments for our family to spend time with many of our persecuted brothers and sisters. We have had the great honor of personal, in-depth, private conversations with persecuted Christians from other countries. We have listened to their personal stories of persecution, threats, being hunted down by terrorists, imprisoned, beaten, and tortured for their faith. The horrifying accounts of losing friends and family members who are modern day martyrs are gut-wrenching. The Christians we have met with were miraculously delivered from the demonically driven terrorists. While some of them have fled from the terror to America, many are not liberated, and they desperately need our prayers and support today.

I wish I could share all the inspiring stories that these modern-day heroes of the faith have endured. A few years ago, God providentially arranged for us to experience the sobering conviction of hearing from three pastors of underground churches in Iraq and Cuba. Their life stories of modern-day persecution and what they have endured for standing firm in the faith is harrowing, to say the least.

These courageous saints live in countries where their lives, families, and their churches are in constant danger because of their faith in Christ. One of the pastors of an underground church in Iraq spoke to us, and his words cut through my own soul like a knife. He cried out in desperation to the American church and directly to American pastors, calling us to repent and turn from our apathetic and complacent Christianity. There are few things that are more humbling than having a persecuted Christian from an Islamic nation tell you that you need to repent for your pathetic state of apathy and complacency. He spoke these God-inspired words that pierced my heart and continue to stir my soul today, "The church in America is guilty of only doing what you want to do and justifying it."

He directly confronted those of us in the American church for doing what is convenient, culturally acceptable, and what fits comfortably into our schedules without too much sacrifice. God's fire and holy passion consumed the Iraqi pastor's entire being as he continued to confront the lukewarm American pastors in the room. I cannot tell you how others in the room were impacted by our dear brother's admonition, but he had my full attention. I knew I was guilty as charged, and I repented with weeping and deep sorrow over my own sinful, apathetic state. God used him to bring down fire from heaven to burn up the apathy and the carnality in my life.

The Lion of the Tribe of Judah is roaring over His people today to wake up and understand that there is a world around us in desperate need. Whether or not we hear it audibly, the cries are coming from around the world, much like the cries of the Jews in Nazi Germany, "Why doesn't somebody do something?" Today, if you choose to be silent and play it safe, backing away from the current battle against hell's agenda, then it may be your child or grandchild who looks at you one day and asks, "Why didn't somebody do something?" Please stop for just a moment and allow the Holy Spirit to speak to you personally about your part in this battle and how you are to fight for your persecuted brothers and sisters today.

THE NEXT GENERATION OF MARTYRS

Recently, a dear friend told me about a bone-chilling accusation made by her young adult daughter. My friend and her daughter had gone to a prayer meeting with a group of Christian women. These women had been meeting regularly for years to pray for the nation. Upon leaving the meeting, the daughter broke down and began to weep. Her mother asked her what was wrong. Through tears of anguish and frustration, she expressed her turmoil over the fact that these women have prayed and prayed, but they had done nothing to stand up and speak against the wicked agenda that was threatening to strip us of our freedoms completely. She concluded by stating that their refusal to stand up and do something to fight against the agenda of hell in America has set her generation up to be martyred.

Our lack of passion, voice, and involvement against this evil force destroying our nation and our world may lead to the persecution and martyrdom of our children tomorrow. Are you willing to be silent and do nothing? I pray not. My hope, my prayer, is that you will hear the Lion of Judah roaring over you, upon you, and through you, in this hour. My prayer is that you are awakened to the reality of this war, and you are ready to join us in this good fight of faith. Join the holy rebellion and rebel against the forces of hell with us, with God's weapons of righteousness, holiness, and truth. We all need to be in it to win it.

THIS IS A JOB FOR SUPERMAN

Superheroes continue to be extremely popular in our culture. The Marvel Cinematic Universe series is the highest-grossing film franchise with total worldwide box office revenue of 22.93 billion U.S. dollars. "Avengers: Endgame" was Marvel's highest-grossing movie with 2.8 billion dollars in global revenue. Some may be asking, "Why the craze over fictional superheroes?" The explanation is evident; everybody everywhere knows we are in a crisis. Our nation and our world are in distress and desperate need because we are in deep, deep trouble.

We all desire a hero to come and fix our messed-up lives and our messed-up planet. Where is Superman when you need him? The world is looking for a superhero who will swoop down, land in the middle of the chaos and destruction, and rescue those held captive by the evil powers of darkness, wickedness, corrupt leaders, and the demonically driven terrorists around the globe. This impossible turmoil cannot be remedied by a human being; this is a job for a Superhero.

People worldwide realize that somebody needs to do something, but they don't know what to do. There is a global cry for a rescuer. That Rescuer came two thousand years ago as the first Holy Rebel. Jesus is the only real Superhero, and His power is divine power, ultimate power with all authority in heaven and earth. But He has shared that authority with us. In Luke 10:19, Jesus said, "Behold, I give you the authority to trample on serpents and scorpions, and over all the power of the enemy." This holy rebellion could only be fought and won by the only real Superhero. He was counted among the rebels who rebelled against the evil powers and rose victorious, and now He has given us authority to enforce His victory on the earth.

The saddest indictment against the church in America today is that we would rather watch fictional, make-believe Superheroes on the big screen while eating popcorn, drinking soda, and reclining in comfort – then going back to our lives of safety and ease while we make excuses and rationalize the fact that we are doing extraordinarily little or nothing at all to rebel against hell and make a difference.

It's time for somebody to do something. It's time for the church to awaken, rise up, and shine forth in this world of darkness. There should be no more hiding in the shadows. Fellow Christians, stand up and stop shrinking back in fear of man and intimidation. The hour is urgent, and the time is now. Cowardly silence is not an option. God is calling you to join His holy rebellion against the forces of evil that threaten to kill, steal, and destroy. You were born for this. You are somebody who has been created, called, and chosen by God to stand up and do something.

CHAPTER TWO

THE CLASH OF KINGDOMS

D URING FORMER PRESIDENT Obama's keynote address at the "Call to Renewal" conference, he declared, "Whatever we once were, we are no longer just a Christian nation. We are a Jewish nation, a Muslim nation, a Buddhist nation, and a Hindu nation, and a nation of nonbelievers."[3]

The former President's principal argument was that rather than being defined as a Christian country, we had become a religiously pluralistic nation. Yet this statement uncovers something far bigger. In America's past, though we often fell short of biblical values, we at least held the same sense of right and wrong, and we collectively based our morality on scriptural teachings.

In a general way, the American culture was a Christian culture, which held values derived from the Bible. God's Word informed our national conscience. Societal sins in America were overcome by appealing to the Scripture. The greatest abolitionists prior to the Civil War appealed to the Word of God as they called for the elimination of the evil of slavery. Dr. Martin Luther King Jr. led the charge to end the sin of racial segregation and injustice by proclaiming the words of the Old Testament prophets.

That day has passed, and Christianity has become a subculture within a broader secular, pagan, and anti-biblical culture. Yet, we are not called to be a subculture. Instead, we must take up the mantle of being Holy Rebels who are radically counter-cultural. We are part of God's kingdom and are called to embrace and expand His kingdom culture, which directly oppos-es the current dominant American culture. Holy Rebels counter the sec-ular culture by being tenaciously committed to Jesus Christ, to His king-dom, and to the truth of God's Word.

Good public policy is important for the flourishing of our society. Yet, it's critical we understand that the battle for the soul of our nation is not about partisan politics. It is not about the donkey or the elephant. Rather, it is about the Lion of the Tribe of Judah and His kingdom. It is about the holy versus the unholy, righteousness versus unrighteousness, justice ver-sus injustice, biblical values versus godless ideologies, and the kingdom of God versus the satanically inspired kingdoms of this world (Matt. 12:26).

THE COSMIC CONFLICT

The fifth chapter of Joshua contains a fascinating account that explains our allegiance. The children of Israel are preparing to invade the land of Canaan that God had promised them and to recover it from the wicked, perverse, and corrupt nations that were dwelling there. Joshua is given an encounter with someone many scholars believe to be a pre-incarnate vis-itation of Jesus Christ. Initially, He identified himself only as a military fighter, and Joshua asked, "Are You for us or our adversaries?" The re-sponse he hears from the Lord is not what he expected. Jesus does not say that He is for them or against them; He simply says "No." Joshua was think-ing about the situation the wrong way. The Lord explains, "As Commander of the army of the Lord I have now come" (Josh. 5:14). Now recognizing who the stranger is, Joshua falls on his face to the earth and worships Him, say-ing, "What does my Lord say to His servant?" Dr. Tony Evans paraphras-es the Lord's response as, "Joshua, I did not come to take sides, I came to take over."[4] That is true for us. We often conceive our situation the wrong way. The question is not whose side the Lord is on, but who is on the Lord's side. God's side is always the side in alignment with the truth of His Word.

If you are not familiar with the biblical understanding of the clash of kingdoms, this chapter of the book may be the most difficult to grasp. This is a theological study containing a Biblical mystery but don't let it over-whelm you. I encourage you to fully engage your mind and ask the Holy Spirit to illuminate these truths, because they provide a critical founda-tion to the book. In comprehending them you will be better equipped to step into your calling as a Holy Rebel and to destroy the works of darkness.

To understand this cosmic conflict, we must go back to Genesis 1-3, where we find a record of humanity's beginning. God created the heavens and the earth, making human beings as the pinnacle of His creation. He made man and woman (Adam and Eve) in His image and gave them stewardship of the kingdom of God on earth (Gen. 1:26). God was the king of the universe, but He made humankind vice-regents on earth. They were kings on earth, in submission to the Great King, who was God.

He gave the first couple dominion of the earth to subdue it, not for their purposes, but for God's purposes and glory. The tempter, the old serpent known as the devil and Satan, told them that if they rejected God's rule and declared themselves independent of God, they would be *as* God (Gen. 3:1-5). Adam and Eve believed the lie, and through voluntary treason forfeited their position as vice-regents. They surrendered to the lie of the serpent, who was the original unholy rebel, and joined his rebellion.

The Apostle Paul taught that sin entered the world through one man, Adam (Romans 5:12). He was our federal head, which means what happened to the first man affected those following. Just as decisions of our parents and grandparents affect us, Adam's destiny became our destiny. When Adam lost his dominion, we all lost our dominion. God's kingdom rule through humanity was subverted.

Since Adam's original sin, every human being has in essence agreed with Adam that we should be "as God." We can call our own shots and live life as we choose. Because of the fall, Paul calls Satan "the god of this age" (2 Corinthians 4:4) and "the prince of the power of the air" (Ephesians 2:2). Jesus also called Satan "the ruler of this world" (John 14:30). The Apostle John tells us that "the whole world lies under the sway of the wicked one" (1 John 5:19).

When the original couple believed the serpent's lie and rebelled against God, all creation was plunged into darkness. In Ephesians 2, Paul wrote of humankind as being dead in our trespasses and sins, walking according to the course of this world and the prince of the power of the air. We are driven by the lust of our flesh, fulfilling the desires of the flesh and the mind, and being by nature the children of wrath (Ephesian 2:1-3). God, however, had a plan and purpose that He revealed on the day humanity fell.

THE ASCENDANCE OF THE SEED

God announced that a Rescuer was coming through the seed of the woman who would crush the head of the serpent and restore humankind's dominion (Gen. 3:15). The rest of the Scripture explains that God would circumvent the normal means of conception, and through the womb of a virgin, He would come and crush Satan's rule over humanity and redeem the universe. This begins a major theme in the biblical narrative of Satan endeavoring to destroy the offspring before God's plan can be fulfilled. Throughout the Old Testament, Satan attacks the redemptive plan of God, but God always counters and prevails over the enemy. It is like a cosmic chess match where Satan makes His move, but God's counter-move brilliantly outsmarts His opponent.

A major character in this cosmic drama is Abraham. God tells Abraham he is a carrier of the seed that will bless all nations (Gen. 12:2-3). Through his descendants, God establishes the Hebrew people and eventually the nation of Israel. Through Israel, God will establish His kingdom rule. And whoever their judge, ruler, or king was, he was only to be a representative under God, carrying out God's rule. The nation of Israel never lived up to its calling, but they saw something greater coming.

King David was Israel's preeminent ruler. However, the prophets said his rule and his kingdom were only a shadow of the real kingdom that was coming. The ultimate Anointed Ruler would come from the seed (or offspring) of David (2 Sam. 7:12-16). And, from that time forward, the Rescuer of humanity — the seed who crushes the serpent's head — became known as the Messiah. The Hebrew people awaited such a kingdom and for the Messiah, who would be the king of that kingdom.

Despite Israel's rebellion against God and their subsequent division, scattering, and captivity, the Lord was faithful to His promise and sent their Rescuer in the person of Jesus. Yet, when God's Messiah came, they rejected Him because they willfully misunderstood what the kingdom was meant to be. They envisioned it as a political and military kingdom. In the minds of most of the Jewish people, the Messiah's arrival would mean the blood of their Roman oppressors would run in the streets, and Israel would become the world's dominant nation. However, Israel's expectation was not God's plan.

THE MESSIANIC HOPE

When you open your Bible to the first verse of the New Testament, you read Jesus was the Son of Abraham and the Son of David (Matt. 1:1). In this simple genealogical fact, you discover the fulfillment of the ancient messianic hope, as it substantiates that Jesus was the seed of promise. Jesus is the seed of the woman, not the seed of the man, because He is born of a virgin. He was both the promised seed of Abraham and of David. When the angel announced the coming of Jesus to Mary in Luke 1:33, the angel said, "And He will reign over the house of Jacob forever, and of His kingdom, there will be no end."

God sent a forerunner of the messianic seed, and his name was John the Baptist. John announces: "Repent, for the kingdom of heaven is at hand!" (Matt. 3:2). Then, Jesus is baptized by John and driven by the Spirit of God into the wilderness where that old serpent, the devil, tempts him. Paul calls Jesus the last Adam, and, like the first Adam, Satan tempts Jesus, but instead of it being in a lush, perfect garden, it is in a barren, dry wilderness. The grand temptation was an offer to shortcut the cross and to be given the kingdoms of this world.

In Luke 4:5-7 we read, "Then the devil, taking Him up on a high mountain, showed Him all the kingdoms of the world in a moment. And the devil said to Him, 'All this authority I will give You, and their glory; for this has been delivered to me, and I give it to whomever I wish. Therefore, if You will worship before me, all will be Yours.'"

THE KINGDOM OF GOD HAS ARRIVED

Adam had delivered to Satan the authority and dominion of the earth. Yet, rather than rule under the authority of God, Satan governs as an evil overlord. Satan offers to give Jesus dominion and authority over the kingdoms of this world if He surrenders and worships Satan. Jesus rejects this temptation and two others. While Adam fell through disobedience, Jesus defeated Satan through obedience to His Father. He was the first man who ever perfectly obeyed the Father. When this happened, the entire demonic world was alerted that a man had defeated Satan.

The new king had come, and the kingdom of God appeared. Satan and his malevolent kingdom were given notice that a new king had arrived to devastate Satan's kingdom and liberate those bound by his demons (Acts 10:38). Jesus was at war with the devil's kingdom to reverse the curse and every consequence of the fall. Blind eyes saw, deaf ears heard, lame legs walked, and those in bondage were liberated. It was a thrilling new day. The kingdom of Heaven was breaking through demonic walls of resistance. The long-awaited Messiah had come. It was the in-breaking of the activity of God on earth. In Matthew 12:28 Jesus announced, "If I cast out demons by the Spirit of God, surely the kingdom of God has come upon you." Miracles were evidence of the arrival of a glorious new kingdom.

It was a new kind of kingdom you could not enter without rebirth. Jesus explained unless you are born again, you cannot experience the kingdom of God (Jn. 3:3). Yet, instead of humanity submitting to God's king, they arrested Him and determined to crucify God's Rescuer. Jesus had to stand before Pilate. Governor Pilate was a representative of Rome, which was the ruling kingdom of that day. Pilate looked at the battered man standing in front of him, and Jesus appeared so insignificant with a crown of thorns on his head and a body that was lashed and bleeding. Pilate asked Jesus, "Are you a king?" Jesus said, "My kingdom is not of this world." "If it were, my followers would fight." Every kingdom has an army and fights physical battles, but not this kingdom because it is a different kind of kingdom. In this kingdom, out of love, you die for your enemies. His kingdom operates in the world but is not of this world.

Pilate presented Jesus to the Jewish mob and declared, "Behold your king." They said, "We have no king but Caesar." The Jewish crowd represented all of humanity in rejecting their Creator King. So, Jesus was crucified and buried, but death could not hold Him, and Jesus rose from the dead to bring about a new kingdom that would someday topple every humanly constructed kingdom (Dan. 2:44).

THE CONQUERING KING

As the last Adam, Jesus rose from the dead and regained the dominion and authority that the first Adam had lost. Keys represent authority, and Jesus stripped Satan of the keys he had usurped. In Revelation 1:18, the exalted and glorified Jesus declared, "I am He who lives, and was dead, and behold, I am alive forevermore. And I have the keys of Hades and of Death."

Paul explained what happened that day when, speaking of Jesus, he wrote: "Having disarmed principalities and powers, He made a public spectacle of them, triumphing over them in it" (Col. 2:15). Jesus regained all rule and authority by overcoming the Cosmic Interloper, Satan. Jesus Christ is now King of Kings and Lord of Lords, and the kingdom of God has come. But, if the kingdom of God has come, why do we not see all the promises of the kingdom fulfilled? The reason we are not seeing it is because of the nature of the kingdom.

In Romans 10:9, Paul wrote that if we believe in our hearts that God raised Jesus from the dead and surrender to Him as King, we enter the kingdom of God. Colossians 1:13 describes the believers as being delivered from the power of darkness and conveyed into the kingdom of the Son of His love. Instead of upending the political order, God's kingdom has upended the spiritual order. God transferred those who believe in Jesus out of the kingdoms of this world into the kingdom of God. Yet, it is not a physical kingdom, but a spiritual kingdom. In Luke 17:21 Jesus said, "For indeed, the kingdom of God is within you." If you have surrendered to King Jesus, the kingdom of God has come into your own individual life.

THE KINGDOM PARADOX

In Romans 14:17 Paul tells us the kingdom of God has come in the Holy Spirit. Though the kingdom is here, we live in a profound paradox, for it is here but still yet to come. Paul teaches us that though we are in this kingdom now, we won't know the fullness of the kingdom until we inherit a life that does not decay (1 Corinthians 15:50). Peter announces that those in the kingdom now still have an everlasting kingdom to look forward to (2 Peter 1:11). Today we live in the tension of a kingdom that *has* come but is *yet* to come.

The author of Hebrews explains this tension in Hebrews 2:8. Speaking of God the Father subjecting all to Jesus Christ he writes, "You have put all things in subjection under his feet. For in that he put all in subjection under him, he left nothing that is not put under him. But now, we do not see all things put under him."

This verse can be confusing. It tells us all things are subjected to Jesus—nothing is *not* subject to Him — yet we do not see all things subject to Him. George Eldon Ladd explains this mystery in writing, "The kingdom is here but not yet."[5] God's kingdom is both a present reality and a future hope. The kingdom has been inaugurated but not yet consummated. We see this again in Romans 16:20, where Paul writes, "And the God of peace will crush Satan under your feet shortly." While we await the kingdom to come, we walk in a foretaste of kingdom promises, just not yet in fullness.

A day is coming when Jesus will establish His millennial kingdom. The kingdom of God now is a preview of what will be. What Jesus will enforce universally in that day He now enforces *in part* through the body of Christ. That is why Christians are concerned about our earth and the current problems of humanity. It is not some ethereal belief. As Christians, Jesus calls us to carry out His kingdom will and purpose now until He comes again.

Someday, even the millennial kingdom will be swallowed up by the eternal kingdom, and we will rule and reign with Christ forever, which was God's original intention in Eden (Rev. 20:6, 22:5). Currently, He mediates His kingdom rule through the subjects of His kingdom, the church. God brought His kingdom will to the earth through Old Testament believers like Abraham and David. The Lord used the early church to demonstrate His kingdom in the book of Acts. Now in our time, God wants to use us as His kingdom representatives, fulfilling His will on earth today.

THE CHURCH AND THE KINGDOM

God has called the church to expand Christ's spiritual kingdom. By the authority we have in Jesus and the Spirit's power, we are to advance God's kingdom rule. That's what the followers of Christ did in the book of Acts. We see it in Jesus' kingdom commission to His church.

Matthew 28:18-19 tell us that after His resurrection, Jesus came and spoke to his disciples, saying, "All authority has been given to Me in heaven and on earth. Go therefore and make disciples of all the nations." Jesus did not say, "All authority has been given to me... so I'm going to go." He said, "All authority is given to me, so *you* go." He took His authority and entrusted it to His church. Jesus went *up* so the disciples could go *out* as His representatives. God's original purpose was that His people would be His vice-regents under Him. That authority and commission has been restored by Jesus Christ in His church.

In Matthew 16:18, Jesus said, "I will build My church, and the gates of Hades shall not prevail against it." The word church is the Greek word EKKLESIA, which means a called out legislative assembly of citizens.[6] In the Greek and Roman culture of Jesus' day it spoke of a governmental or judicial body that ruled. We are called out, as representatives of Jesus Christ to legislate the kingdom of God on the earth by actively carrying out God's kingdom agenda. We are on a mission to infiltrate our world and transform it through the love of God and the kingdom power and authority of Jesus (Lk.13:20). Jesus said, "And from the days of John the Baptist until now the kingdom of heaven suffers violence, and the violent take it by force" (Matt. 11:12). It is not for the timid or the passive. We are to be heaven's governmental representatives, kingdom warriors, and Holy Rebels.

When Christ came, He enforced God's kingdom rule and dominion. Now He entrusts that responsibility to His church. He told us to pray, "Your kingdom come. Your will be done on earth as it is in heaven" (Matthew 6:10). So much of heaven's will is not being accomplished on earth. Instead, the Satanic government of Hell has been ravaging our nation and our world. The hindrance of the gospel to unreached people groups, the severe persecution of believers by hostile governments, and the lack of food and clean drinking water to large population groups are all contrary to the will of God, and the church is praying and working to bring a change. The assault on biblical marriage and the advancement of all forms of sexual perversion is not the will of God. The promotion of gender confusion and the mutilation of young children on the altar of the LGBTQ agenda is not God's plan. The promotion of racism and racial division is not the heart of heaven. The crisis at our southern border that results in a flood of life-destroying fentanyl and methamphetamine into our country, the rape and abuse of women, and the trafficking and abuse of children breaks God's heart. Millions of babies being killed in abortion clinics is not what Heaven wants. Government leaders who mandate oppression and evil are opposing the agenda of Heaven for earth. As God's EKKLESIA we have been called out to use our influence and our spiritual weapons to push back against the forces of hell and to use our spiritual authority to help advance the kingdom of God — to see His will be done on earth as it is in Heaven.

We look over the carnage of this sin-sick, demon-infested world and recognize this is not God's will. Jesus is telling us to pray for the violent overthrow of demonic spiritual strongholds and a transformation of the hearts of men and women to experience righteousness, peace, and joy in the Holy Spirit. It is an invitation to advance God's kingdom will on earth, looking forward to its ultimate fulfillment in a new heaven and a new earth. It is a kingdom *now* that is looking forward to the eternal kingdom that *shall be*.

In Revelation 11:15, the Apostle John foretells of a day when "there were loud voices in heaven, saying, 'The kingdoms of this world have become the kingdoms of our Lord and of His Christ, and He shall reign forever and ever!'" Until that time, the church is to advance this spiritual kingdom. Of course, only God can build His kingdom, but we are given the privilege of participating with Him. The book of Acts is about the expansion of the kingdom, and we are to continue the work.

Like the early church, we can become vice-regents of the King, helping enforce the kingdom of God on earth now, until He comes back to bring the kingdom in its fullness. You do not have to be a helpless spectator when you are to be a powerful participant, demonstrating the kingdom of God on earth. Of course, this is not some sort of physical militia or religious jihad but the kingdom of God breaking into our lives, invading our souls, and transforming our entire way of living.

SEEK THE KINGDOM, NOT TEMPORAL THINGS

In Matthew 6:33, Jesus said, "But seek first the kingdom of God and His righteousness, and all these things shall be added to you." This verse comes in the context of worry, like worrying about what you are going to eat, drink, and wear. We can enjoy things and do what we can to protect and secure items of value in our life. Yet, if our greatest value and devotion is for the kingdom, we will not live in fear, worry, and anxiety over losing what we know is temporary and relatively insignificant.

Our problem is that we treasure things that cannot last, setting our hearts too much on this world. We tend to find our identity and security in what is only temporary. Jesus challenges us not to put our treasure in what the world can take away — for no disaster, catastrophe, crisis, or cancel culture can take away your treasure if your treasure is not in this world. Your heart and treasure, your identity and security are to be rooted in Christ and His kingdom. You can live above worry and fear when you transfer your devotion to the kingdom. If you make God's kingdom your true priority, the things you worry about, and fear will not seem so significant anymore. It is a completely different way to live. Instead of making the focus of our lives on personal happiness, pleasure, achievement, the approval of the world, safety, and security, live with a kingdom mindset. When you are living for eternity, you become more concerned about the kingdom of God rather than your temporary existence.

OPPOSING KINGDOMS

Right now, there is a clash of kingdoms. The kingdom of God and the kingdom of Satan are in opposition. As representatives and administrators of God's kingdom we are participants in this battle. Whether we want to be in this cosmic war or not is irrelevant. We are in it. Like Adam and Eve in the Garden, the Lord has also entrusted us with the stewardship of our families, churches, and the citizenship of the nation we live in. We will be held accountable for that stewardship (Matt. 25:14-30, 1 Cor. 4:2), and we are called to occupy until our Lord returns (Lk. 19:13). The Lord has given us His power, authority, and presence to engage in this kingdom conflict.

Of course, this war is not the Creator God and the creature Satan battling each other on equal footing. In the book of Job, Satan had to ask permission to assault Job's life and was given limits on what he could do (Job 1:10-12, 2:4-6). God has Satan on a leash, and often the leash seems long and the boundaries wide. But never forget, ultimately "the devil is God's devil," and God's omnipotence contains the adversary and sets clear parameters for him. Someday, God will pull the devil's leash and will draw him in once and for all, but until then, we must contend with this adversary.

Through the death, burial, resurrection, and ascension of Jesus, Satan was thoroughly and completely defeated. Yet this defeated foe still operates as God's adversary, seeking to disturb His kingdom. At the end of World War II, following Japan's surrender, the battle still raged in areas of the South Pacific. Though already officially defeated, some Japanese soldiers had not received the word and were still waging guerrilla warfare. Though the outcome was decided, the fighting was not over. Still, the bullets wounded, and their mortars killed, young American soldiers.[7]

In the same way, our enemy was officially defeated, and the outcome was decided, but he continues to fight. Even though Jesus defeated our enemies, they will not be eternally under our feet until Christ returns. Now it is the responsibility of His church to enforce Satan's defeat. We are not going out to achieve a victory; rather, we are going into the battle *from* a victory. We are enforcing Christ's victory. God's people will be in a war with the powers of darkness until our Lord returns. Though Satan's ultimate fate has been sealed, he is still fighting, and unless we realize it and respond appropriately, we may become one of his victims. It is essential to know how to stand against him and serve in this epic battle.

A key to confidence and victory in the fight is understanding our authority in Jesus and standing in His victory. In 2 Corinthians 2:11, Paul tells us not to let Satan take advantage of us by being unaware of his tactics. Jude 1:9 tells us that even Michael the archangel did not come against Satan in his authority, but said, "The Lord rebuke you!" We will only be successful in defeating the devil to the degree that we live under God's authority. When under authority, you realize you are not big enough or strong enough to handle things yourself, but we were given the authority of Jesus Christ.

On a busy rush hour afternoon, if I went to a major intersection and started directing traffic, few people would pay attention, but if I went out with a police uniform and a badge, they would suddenly begin following my direction. That's because they would recognize that I had the authority to direct the traffic. We cannot combat the powers of darkness on our own, but, as followers of Jesus, He gave us authority.

When commissioning His disciples, Jesus "gave them authority to drive out evil spirits and to heal every disease and sickness" (Matthew 10:1). In Luke 10:19, Jesus told his disciples, "Behold, I give you the authority to trample on serpents and scorpions, and over all the power of the enemy, and nothing shall by any means hurt you." As with his original disciples, it is also true of us, but we must follow the instruction of James in James 4:7 and "submit to God." Then we can resist the devil and he will flee from us. We submit to God first, and then, in His authority, we can resist the devil.

There is no question about the outcome of the cosmic battle between the forces of God and evil. In 1 John 4:4 the Apostle John writes, "You are of God, little children, and have overcome them because He who is in you is greater than he who is in the world." Satan's destiny is sealed. Despite any apparent short-term gains, he is in for an eternal defeat. Through the victory of the finished work of Christ, Satan and his demons have been utterly defeated for eternity and only have a lake of fire to look forward to. No matter how difficult times may seem, followers of Jesus have strong internal confidence in Christ's victory.

I heard a story about a man and his wife walking through a mall. They strolled into a pet store and browsed through it. They walked past a talking parrot who said, "Hey, mister, you're dumb and ugly, and so is your wife!" The embarrassed store owner apologized and explained, "We got him six months ago, and he just does this." The store owner grabbed a large pair of leather work gloves and slapped the parrot silly with feathers flying. He took the gloves off and again offered his apologies. As the couple began to leave, the parrot squawked, "Hey, buddy!" The man shot back, "What?" as if to dare the bird. The parrot said, "You know what!" When we feel battered and beaten, life gets really difficult, and it seems our enemy is winning the day, we can stand in the confidence of our victory in Christ. And when the enemy whispers, "What makes you think you're winning?" we can say, "You know what!" The finished work of Jesus is our confidence.

CHAPTER THREE

NEVER FORGET

"Only be careful, and watch yourselves closely so that you do not forget the things your eyes have seen or let them fade from your heart as long as you live. Teach them to your children and to their children after them" (Deuteronomy 4:9 NIV).

THOSE OLD ENOUGH to remember will never forget the 9/11 terrorist attacks in America on September 11, 2001, as they launched coordinated attacks on the U.S. using airplanes as weapons, killing nearly three thousand individuals unaware of what would happen on that day. The nation, gripped with shock and horror, watched the tragic footage of planes crashing into the buildings, fire, smoke, crumbling towers, people jumping out of windows to their death, others trapped inside and buried alive. Stunned, we all sat around our television screens as the horrific scenes ran continuously. The traumatic events of that day seemed too awful to be true. A major shift took place in America on 9/11. We collectively experienced what seemed to be a terrifying nightmare from which we never awakened. The lingering visions of those days became a tragic wake-up call for America, but America didn't wake up.

Recently, I wept again as I watched, remembered, and listened to gripping footage of that day which we vowed to never forget. The recordings of voice-mail messages sent by the victims to their loved ones whom they were leaving behind affected me profoundly. Especially heartbreaking was the message left by a woman to her husband and children, moments before the plane she was on crashed. One can only imagine the cries of desperation, panic, and fear of those trapped inside the inescapable crumbling towers after the planes had struck their targets. The words of one man watching the destruction that day have continued to replay over and over in my head: "This is a whole new kind of war." Each day I wake up realizing all over again that everything has changed. We are in a war, and it is a whole new kind of war. Ignorance or denial of this war will prove to be devastating and deadly.

The terrorist attacks on 9/11 were a very visual assault, and the entire world watched in horror. The tragedy that day, coupled with other battles that are continually waging all around us, begins in the unseen spiritual realm. Therefore, the spiritual realm is where the war must be fought and won first.

God's Word explains that our world is currently under the sway of the evil one. The Apostle John describes the conflict clearly: "We know [for a fact] that we are of God, and the whole world [around us] lies in the power of the evil one [opposing God and His precepts]" (1 John 5:19, AMP). The evil one and those who have partnered with him have engaged in a full-on, hardcore, unholy rebellion against God and His truth and against His faithful followers. At first glance, it can feel overwhelming and alarming —until we remember who God is. We must never forget Who God is.

NEVER FORGET WHO GOD IS

Life can be hard, tragic, and at times feel unbearable. I know this very well and have experienced it personally. During a season of intense spiritual warfare in my own life, I became deeply distressed and utterly exhausted from the battle. Once again, my heart seemed shattered by the demonically inspired plans of the evil one. Naturally, I did what I always do when unholy attacks from hell hit me and I'm suffering from the blows. I found the only cure for a wounded soldier is in running to our commander-in-chief, who is also our Father. As I walked through our neighborhood, the pain in my heart was too intense and the cries came flooding out of me. Uncontrollable tears were streaming down my face. "Abba, Father..." I cried out, "Why is it so hard? Why is the battle so relentless? Why are we constantly fighting against these demonic attacks and agendas?" I continued to weep as I asked Him for answers.

Then it happened. God spoke, and everything changed. Things always change when God speaks; your perspective changes, your heart changes, your attitude and emotions even change. I heard God speak powerful, life-giving words I'm convinced He wants you to hear today. His words were unmistakable and crystal clear, "Those who follow Me the most passionately are the most fiercely hated by hell. But I AM with you. And I AM The Lord." Before you read any further, please take a moment to re-read those words slowly and let them sink in deeply and change your perspective. These words are for every Holy Rebel warrior who is passionately pursuing God's kingdom purpose. The battle is real, and the warfare is relentless. Yet, He is with you, and He is The Lord.

Those words are forever burned into my heart and my soul as a Holy Rebel warrior serving faithfully in His army. When you submit and commit your life to God, hell fiercely hates you. That day, the fountain of tears immediately ceased; it felt as if He breathed His life-giving breath into my soul and revived my spirit.

Praises instantaneously burst out of my mouth like rivers of living water that I couldn't hold back, even if I wanted to. God turned my mourning into dancing. Circumstances didn't change, and the battle wasn't over. But the realization that we are so fiercely hated by hell because we are one with the Father, Son, and Holy Spirit brought forth joy unspeakable and full of glory.

No matter what happens in your life — whether it be what's happening in your family, your nation or your world— never forget who God is. God is God. Jesus alone is The Lord who is unbeatable, unshakeable, unconquerable, unstoppable. He is the Alpha and the Omega, the Beginning and the End. Jesus is the victorious one who cannot and will not be defeated. God is your Father when you receive Jesus as your Lord and Savior. He is with you and will never leave you nor forsake you. Now it is time to pause for a moment and take time to give God praise for these glorious truths.

KNOW HIM, LOVE HIM, OBEY HIM

Make it your highest goal and ambition to know Him intimately. Be a God chaser. Run after Him with all your heart, soul, mind, and strength. Know Him personally, like Abraham, of whom it is written that He was a friend of God (James 2:23). Follow Him fully, like David, of whom it is written that he was a man after God's own heart (Acts 13:22). Today, decide to be a person who seeks after God with all your heart, for you will find Him (Jeremiah 29:13). Run to the secret place of the Most High God, every day, several times throughout the day (Psalm 91:1).

If you do this, He will be your refuge, your fortress and your deliverer in every situation you face. If you fail to do this, you will be left vulnerable to the enemy's schemes and strategies. God's Word tells us it is the truth that will set us free and keep us free.

God longs to gather you and draw you close to Him, like a mother hen, drawing her chicks close under her wings. However, He will not force us or enslave us against our will. That's how hell operates. The devil and his fallen angels seek to enslave, control, dominate, and oppress people. Our heavenly Father lovingly calls us and draws us because He longs for us to come near to Him. Then He waits for us to respond to His love and run to Him for protection. The only way to be genuinely protected in this battle is to stay close to Him. Make it your goal to get as intimately close to God as possible. This is a goal you will never regret.

My daily ambition is to draw near to Him. I desire to be so close to Him so that I can hear the whispers of the still small voice of my Father. My constant obsession is to know Him more intimately, follow Him more closely, and abide in the shadow of His wings — safe, secure and protected (Psalm 91:1).

I pray you will make this your highest ambition and greatest obsession. There is no safer place in the universe than close to our Heavenly Father, in His Presence, protected and kept by His grace.

SATAN IS THE TERRORIST OF ALL TERRORISTS.

Satan is the terrorist of all terrorists who works tirelessly to get us to forget who God is. Deception is his primary weapon against us. If he can deceive us, he can steal the truth from us, seeking to kill God's plan for us through doubt, fear, and intimidation, thus destroying our true identity and divine destiny. We must rebel against hell's strategies by using God's weapon of truth. Never forget who God is.

1 Chronicles 29:11 reminds us of who God is: "Yours, O Lord, is the greatness, the power and the glory, The victory and the majesty; For all that is in heaven and in earth is Yours; Yours is the kingdom, O Lord, And You are exalted as head over all."

Thinking about God and who He is fills us with hope, courage, faith, and expectation even amid the darkest nights and deepest valleys. When the enemy is coming in like a flood on every side, and our situation looks, feels, and sounds hopeless, remember who God is.

When one of Nehemiah's brothers informed him of the devastation of Jerusalem and the distress of those who survived, he prayed to God, "I pray, Lord God of heaven, O great and awesome God, You who keep Your covenant and mercy with those who love You and observe Your commandments" (Nehemiah 1:5). Looking at the mess in front of him seemed daunting and impossible. Then he remembered who God was and declared out loud the greatness of his God.

Maybe that's where you are right now. You look at your life with its circumstances, family matters, your pain, and whatever else you face may appear hopeless. But like Nehemiah in his day, we must rise up in our day and rebel against hell's unholy agenda against God, His truth, His people, including our families and our nation. God always has a plan of deliverance, victory, and restoration. Never forget who God is, for He has a plan for you, your family, your church, your nation, and for the crisis in our world.

We who are called by God's name are God's answer for a world in crisis. His plan for us is to rebel against this present darkness through humility, repentance, prayer, and seeking His face (2 Chron 7:14). As crazy as it may sound, His people are His solution. Politicians are definitely not the answer. Science is not the answer. Nor is liberalism, socialism, Marxism, and any other 'ism'. Religion is not the answer. A lukewarm, compromising, apathetic church is most certainly not the answer.

God's answer is a revived church. Revived Christians who are not "woke" but awake and are the only hope for a world in crisis. Believers who are on fire with holy passion from heaven. Christians who are biblically uncompromising, full of faith and the Holy Spirit. This is the army God is raising up in this hour. He is calling you to be a part of this army of Holy Spirit-filled, empowered, faithful, on-fire for God, holy rebel warriors.

In one of his "Give Him15" posts, Dutch Sheets said, "A rebellious culture enabled by a lukewarm church has allowed hell to make great progress in our nation. But today, we grab hold of our covenant with You. We stand on the fact that You keep covenant and mercy to a thousand generations (Deuteronomy 7:9). We reach back into our history, declare our faith in You, and decree that we will once again be a light to the nations. We will once again be a strong voice of the gospel and freedom to all the nations of the earth."

Dutch continues, "On the other hand, the giants opposing You are in covenant with Satan and his kingdom, whom You have defeated and stripped of his authority. So, in the authority of Your name, we decree that the giants of unrighteous government, false religion, pride, murder, and immorality will fall. They will no longer succeed in ruling this nation. Jesus will be exalted. Yahweh will be honored. Revival is here and coming. America shall be saved."[8]

The only hope for this nation and the nations of the world is the true church of Jesus Christ. We are God's answer to our nation's crisis. Therefore, we must never forget who God is. And we must never forget who we are.

KNOW YOUR TRUE IDENTITY

"But you are a chosen generation, a royal priesthood, a holy nation, His own special people, that you may proclaim the praises of Him who called you out of darkness into His marvelous light" 1 Peter 2:9 (NKJV). Your true identity as a follower of Jesus is that you are not of this world. You are an ambassador of heaven representing God here on earth, standing against hell and all of its darkness for the sake of the lost.

You are among the called-out ones.
Child of God, that is who you are, never forget it.
Stop living like you are still in darkness.
Stop living like you are still of the world.
Stop acting like the dark world that you live in.

You are called out of darkness into His light, so deny yourself, take up your cross and follow Jesus. You are called to be a Holy Rebel, like Jesus. Never forget that every person is a rebel of one kind or another. There is no neutral ground between heaven and hell because every human being is either partnering with hell in its unholy rebellion against God and His truth or submitted to God and partnering with Him in a holy rebellion against the powers of darkness and the forces of evil. Jesus clarifies this in Matthew 12:31 "If anyone is not with me, then he is against me. He who does not work with me is working against me."

The author of Hebrews 13:8 reminds us that Jesus Christ is the same yesterday, today, and forever. He does not change, and His truth does not change, but people change, cultures change, governments change. When people, cultures, governments, and religions change, demanding that the church change with them, we must remember who we are.

We are followers of Jesus Christ, the first Holy Rebel. Jesus did not change to fit the cultural, political, or religious norms of His day. Jesus did not conform to the world or to the world's way of thinking, nor shift His message or His methods to please people. Our Lord and Savior lived to please only One, His Heavenly Father. He was not moved or influenced by people, even His own family members. As sincere followers of Jesus today, we must stand firm in Christ and His unchanging truth. We must choose each day to deny ourselves the path of least resistance. We must choose to follow Jesus and rebel against the God of this world while avoiding the broad way that leads to destruction.

The enemy of your soul comes to steal your true identity. God calls you His own, chosen ones, sons and daughters of the King. God calls you "oaks of righteousness to display His splendor" (Isaiah 61:4). Those whose trust is in Jesus Christ as Lord have been washed, cleansed, and made righteous with the righteousness of Christ.

Satan comes to convince you that you are not enough. And he's right. Yet God says that His power is made perfect in your weakness. The enemy of your soul comes to oppress you with guilt, shame, and condemnation. God calls you holy, blameless, and beyond reproach because of the blood of His Son. God says that there is no condemnation to those who are in Christ Jesus. Hell's demons come to attack you with mental torment and lies, saying you are worthless, insignificant, and without value. But God calls you fearfully and wonderfully made with a divine destiny and an eternal purpose.

Every Holy Rebel warrior must solidify in their heart who they are in Christ. Never forget who God says you are. The lies of our enemy can be so convincing, feeling so powerful and paralyzing. Rebel against hell's lies with God's truth about who you are in Christ. It requires submission to God and His word and absolute resistance against the deception of the evil one. The only way to rebel against this hellish tactic is to take up your sword of the Spirit and carry it with you every day. Stand upon God's truth. Enforce God's truth. Decree and declare what God says about you and the powers of darkness must flee.

KNOW YOUR CONDITION

As Holy Rebels, we must know God, know our true identity, and know our current condition. More than common sense, it is wisdom to assess and evaluate where we are and understand how to proceed. Because of an unholy resistance coming against God's people, Nehemiah saw their fear and then spoke to the nobles and officials and the rest of the people, saying, "Do not be afraid of them; [confidently] remember the Lord who is great and awesome, and [with courage from Him] fight for your brothers, your sons, your daughters, your wives, and for your homes'" (Neh 4:14, Amp).

Have you ever had someone come to you and tell you, "I have good news and bad news; which do you want first?" Well, I believe that was the case with Nehemiah as he considered the bad news about their condition, and then Nehemiah looked to God, who had the good news about the situation.

BAD NEWS AND GOOD NEWS

It reminds me of a true story from about twenty-three years ago when Todd and I were pastoring in Texas. We lived in the parsonage next to the church, which was very convenient, but it also left us vulnerable to some interesting situations. Todd was going to fly to Atlanta for a Promise Keepers Conference, but moments before he was to leave, he came to me and said, "Honey, I have some good news and some bad news. Which do you want to hear first?"

Pausing for a second to process the question, I decided on the bad news first. I needed to know my condition (the bad news) because ignorance is not bliss. I needed to be aware, alert, and prepared. So, this is how the scenario played out: Todd says, "Well, the bad news is that a police officer just came to tell me they apprehended a guy from Mexico who had a gun and a map to our church. This man (who was obviously oppressed and driven by demons) says he is coming to kill the false prophet." Definitely bad news to hear that a demonized man with a gun and a map to our church is coming to kill "the false prophet."

Next Todd says, "But the good news is that the police have picked him up, and they have him under psychological examination." Okay! I would consider that good news. He is in custody, so no worries. However, Todd continued, "But the other bad news is that they can only hold him for twenty-four hours since he hasn't actually perpetrated a crime." So, we're back to bad news again.

"But the other good news," Todd gently explains, "is that the police will periodically patrol the church grounds and property to make sure things are okay." Then Todd prayed for me, and he prayed for the unknown, self-proclaimed assassin, and he prayed that God would send his angels to keep me safe. He kissed me, said goodbye and left to catch his plane.

There I was, all by myself, dealing with this news I had been given. Todd would be in Atlanta for several days, and I would be home alone with a delusional, would-be killer who was sent on an assassination mission to our church. This was not good. Like Nehemiah, I assessed my situation and then considered my options. I could have just sat there in fear and waited like a helpless victim who had no power against this evil plot. Honestly, fear tried to consume me, but I know who my God is, and I know who I am. I know that greater is He who is in me than this crazy guy who is of this world and driven by darkness. So I prayed in the Spirit and in the understanding (1Cor 14:15). Then I went to work on executing a plan.

I washed our two ninety-pound German Shepherds and brought them in the house with me. Next, I called friends who had plenty of guns, and they loaded me up with guns and ammo. I cannot help but laugh as I recall the details of this event. So, as I went to bed that night I was prayed up, had the doors bolted shut, both dogs in bed with me, and a loaded gun next to the bed. Therefore, I knew my condition and was aware, watchful, prayerful, alert, and ready for battle. No demon or plan of hell was going to prevail on my watch.

Now, let's look at our current conditions today. The bad news for us today is that it feels like, looks like and sounds like our nation and the world have been hit by multiple terrorists and assassins. It feels as though the forces of hell have struck and our nation is crashing and crumbling like the twin towers. If you sense that, then you are likely experiencing shock and awe over what is happening in your own life today. The bad news seems to come from every angle, and when you think it cannot get worse, more bad news hits you and brings you to your knees.

The spiritual battle has intensified for every one of us. And we are seeing the manifestation of that battle escalating every day. We see it in our nation, states, cities, schools, and in our families and it looks impossible. Like Nehemiah, we look at the mess all around us, and from a natural standpoint, it appears to be hopeless. Yet, like Nehemiah, we must stand up and fight.

EVERYTHING HAS CHANGED.

"Everything has changed, and you will never do ministry the same." God spoke those words to Todd and me several years ago following a prophetic vision. Todd and I were in our basement, crying out to God in prayer and deep intercession. Having entered into deep, travailing prayer for our nation, God's presence filled the room. We could feel a supernatural shift taking place in the spirit realm. The shifting we felt was not a good shifting. We were both physically affected by this experience, with our bodies trembling.

Then I saw a vision of a portal opening in the sky over America. Out of that portal came hordes of demons. It was terrifying. I heard the Lord speak these words that have never left me: "Everything has changed. You will never do ministry the same." Since that day, that vision, and that prophetic word, God has been shifting us to be prepared for the battle we are all in today.

It is imperative that we all understand that everything's changed, and we will never do life the same. We must wake up, understand the condition we are in; stand up against the armies of hell that have been advancing against us; and fight for our sons, our daughters, our families, and our nation. We cannot continue with business as usual, or church and Americanized Christianity as usual, or we are doomed.

On September 2001, the terrorists struck America, and it was a major wake-up call. Yet, once the rubble was removed and cleaned up, America went right back to business as usual. I'll never forget that day. Our large worship center in Texas was filled as people ran to the church seeking refuge, answers, hope, and peace amid the great fear that terrorists had struck in every heart. That horrific event woke people up for a moment, but America quickly returned to her backslidden state, back to her idols, back to her pride and her defiance against God and His truth. America — and the church in America — went right back to business as usual, spiritually speaking— ignoring this wake-up call to repent, humble ourselves, and return to God.

For years, Rabbi Jonathan Cahn has been warning America to repent, humble themselves, turn from their wicked ways and pray before it's too late. Rabbi Cahn has spoken prophetically of the striking similarity between the rebellious Israelites and today's rebellious America.

Like Israel, America began as a nation dedicated to God and blessed by God. Yet, like the nation of Israel, America grew spiritually complacent and apathetic. America moved away from God, turning from the God who blessed her. We pushed God out of our culture, drove Him out of our government, eliminated His truth, and banned Him from educating our children.

A quote from Cahn's book, *The Harbinger*, is sad but rings true: "As God was expunged from American life, idols came in to fill the void; idols of sensuality, idols of greed, of money, of success, comfort, materialism, pleasure, sexual immorality, self-worship, self-obsession. The sacred increasingly disappeared, and the profane took its place."[9]

God warned them (Israel) and us (America), "Woe to those who call evil good and good evil". That word "woe" is the most severe warning that can be given, to repent before it's too late. Because it will not go well for those who call evil good and good evil. America has become a nation that celebrates, propagates, and mandates what God calls evil — and condemns, cancels, and destroys what God calls good.

Rabbi Cahn has righteously stated of rebellious Israel and rebellious America, that what they had always known to be holy, they now profane. Cahn elaborates, "Everything was now upside down. What they had once known as right, they now saw as outdated, intolerant, and immoral. And what they had once known as immoral, they now championed and celebrated as sacred. They had transformed themselves into the enemies of the God they had once worshiped, and the faith they had once followed until the very mention of His name was banned from their public squares. And yet in spite of all this, He was merciful and called to them, again and again."[10]

But just as God called Israel then, He calls to us today: Turn! Repent! Come back! Come back! Be saved from destruction! He sent prophets to wake them up, and He called them back from the sin that would enslave and destroy them; but they hardened their hearts and rebelled against God. So, the nation was brought into the first stage of judgment. Sadly, this is our current condition in America today. But God is a God of mercy, and He calls out to us three times in Isaiah chapter nine, telling us that even in His anger, His hand is stretched out still. "For all this, His anger is not turned away, but his hand is stretched out still. Therefore, the Lord shall have no joy in their young men, neither shall have mercy on their fatherless and widows: for everyone is a hypocrite and an evildoer, and every mouth speaketh folly. For all this, His anger is not turned away, but his hand is stretched out still" (Isaiah 9:12, 17 KJV).

In the King James version of Hosea 4:6, God warns: "My people are destroyed for lack of knowledge: because thou hast rejected knowledge, I will also reject thee, that thou shalt be no priest to me: seeing thou hast forgotten the law of thy God, I will also forget thy children."

He will forgive us if we turn back to Him. It begins with you and me, His people, humbling ourselves before Him, seeking His face, praying, and turning from our wicked ways. God is righteously angry at sin because He is holy, just, and good. A good God and Father must judge sin. Sin is hell's rebellion that always leads to destruction, bondage, and, ultimately, death. God is love, so He must hate the sin that destroys those whom He loves, but His hand is stretched out still. Reach out to Him today in humility and submission. Draw near to Him, and He will draw near to you. His hand is stretched out still to all who will receive Him. His hand is stretched out to offer His mercy, grace, forgiveness, and restoration. Run to Him.

———— CHAPTER FOUR ————

THEATRE OF WAR

WITH THE OUTBREAK of the Coronavirus in March of 2020, President Donald Trump declared he was a wartime president battling an invisible enemy.[11] As followers of Jesus Christ, we are all wartime people in an invisible war. It is a conflict of which most of the population is unaware. This war is not against a virus but against an unseen spiritual foe, a spiritual battle that profoundly affects the physical world.

The theatre of this war is first and primarily waged on an internal battlefield requiring a daily decision to submit our lives to Jesus Christ and live a victorious life over the desires of the flesh. The Scriptures remind us of the constant challenge of crucifying our flesh by reckoning ourselves dead to sinful desires, intentionally setting our minds on Christ, living according to God's Word, and walking in the power of the Holy Spirit (Galatians 5:24, 2:20, 5:16, Romans 6:6-7, 11-12; 8:3-6, and Colossians 3:2). But there is also an external war. In Ephesians 6:13-18, Paul divulges a set of spiritual armor that equips us for the fight, but first he describes why the armor is necessary.

> "Put on the whole armor of God that you may be able to stand against the wiles of the devil. For we do not wrestle against flesh and blood, but against principalities, against powers, against the rulers of the darkness of this age, against spiritual hosts of wickedness in the heavenly places" (Ephesians 6:11-12).

Paul makes it clear that we are in a fight. The Greek language indicates the battle in which we are engaged involves "hand-to-hand combat."[12] But it is not against a visible opponent. Instead, our battle is against an unseen adversary in the spiritual dimension, which Paul identifies as the devil. Most Americans consider him a metaphor or a mascot, but when observing the horrific evil and senseless inhumanity that occurs in our world, clearly there is a malevolent force at work on the earth.

There was a time in our nation when the operation of this dark power was largely covert. Yet, as our culture became increasingly pagan and progressively opposed to biblical truth, its actions became more blatant and obvious. This force of evil is what the Bible calls satanic, and it regards the devil as a real and significant spiritual being.

According to the Scriptures, Satan is not simply a force, but is a personal spirit with a mind, will, and emotions. Every New Testament writer refers to Satan. He is mentioned in 19 of the 27 New Testament books. The authors would neither want us to be ignorant of the dark spiritual realm nor to become obsessed with it. Rather, we are to keep our focus on God, but have an awareness of our invisible enemy, of his damaging influence, and of his cunning tactics (2 Corinthians. 2:11).

THE ORIGINAL UNHOLY REBEL

While God is the Almighty, omnipresent, all-knowing Creator, Satan is a limited, *created* being lacking divine attributes, because God created him. Some refer to him as "God's devil," meaning that God will play on the devil's stage, using Satan to fulfill His divine plan. When I was in elementary school, my mother regularly passed out gospel tracts containing the message of salvation. These tracts depicted spiritual warfare by showing God on His celestial throne and Satan on a demonic throne. As compelling as the tracts may have been, they gave Satan something he never had: a throne.

There is only one throne in the universe, because there is only one solitary sovereign ruler, Almighty God. Satan's counterpart in the spiritual realm is not God, for God has no rival. Rather, the devil's peer is the archangel Michael, as depicted in Revelation 12:7-8.

God created Satan as one of His high-ranking angelic beings. Isaiah prophetically wrote that Satan's original name was Lucifer, or "Shining One" (Isaiah. 14:12-16). In Ezekiel 28, the prophet refers to Lucifer as the "king of Tyre," a dazzling creature gifted with outstanding abilities as a musician and entrusted with great responsibility (Exodus 28:12-13). Instead of being humbled by the exalted position God granted him, and using his gifts to honor God, he arrogantly used his freedom to rebel against his benevolent Creator (Ezekiel 28:13-16, Is. 14:12-16). Lucifer's fall came through his pride.

In a culture that celebrates a pride that defies God, followers of Christ must take the countercultural mindset of humility. Otherwise, we can soon behave like the original unholy rebel. The overconfident Lucifer convinced one third of the angels to join him in his rebellion (Revelation 12:9). The Shining One became Satan, and God pulled Satan down, along with his rebellious followers, from their original favored positions and cast them out of heaven (Isaiah 14:15, Revelation 12:9, Luke 10:18).

These fallen angels ended up as disembodied demonic spirits, making up Satan's wicked spiritual forces. As a created being, Satan has the same limitations as other angelic beings. Though the devil is superior to humans in his capabilities, unlike God, he is not present everywhere and can only be in one place a time. While God accomplishes much of what He does through His church and His angels, Satan carries out his purposes through surrogate minions because he has limitations. Satan is not omniscient. He does not know what we are thinking or anything pertaining to the future outside of what God has revealed.

Satan, however, is an intelligent being who watches us and can predict what we are thinking and what is coming. Hebrews 2:16 (Berean Literal Translation) says, "Because the fallen angels made the wrong choice, they no longer experience redemption. For if God did not spare the angels having sinned, but having cast them down to Tartarus, in chains of gloomy darkness, delivered them, being kept for judgment." Some of these fallen angels violated God's established boundaries (Genesis 6:1-2, 4), so the Lord has already incarcerated them in Tartarus, a compartment of hell (2 Peter 2:4, Jude 1:6). Yet, the vast majority of demons are currently engaged in the spiritual battles we face. The ultimate fate of Satan and all fallen angels is the eternal lake of fire (Matthew 25:41, Revelation 20:1-3, 10).

Satan and his demons are spiritual beings and do not have physical bodies, but they can oppress, occupy, and even possess the bodies of people and animals (Matthew 8:28–34). Much of the ministry of Jesus involved casting evil spirits out of the demonized (Matthew 8:16, Acts 10:38). People sometimes have unusual strength and suffer a great deal of torment at the hands of demonic spirits. One demonized man in the Bible lived like an animal, cutting himself, and was out of his mind because of the demons (Mark 5:1-20 and Luke 8:26–39). In another case, demons possessed a young boy, causing him to throw himself into fire or water (Mark. 9:14-29). Jesus delivered both of them from their oppression. The demon-possessed man in Luke 8 was so strong that he could break chains and shackles, and nothing could hold him. In the book of Acts, one demonized man assaulted seven men, stripping them naked and severely injuring them (Acts 19:13-19).

SATANIC LIES AND DECEPTION

The name Satan, used fifty-two times in the Bible, actually means adversary or opponent. Satan is the ultimate adversary of humanity. He desires to render you ineffective as a follower of Christ, to make your life miserable, and to terrorize your soul. Peter tells us to be sober and vigilant in dealing with our adversary. We must not take our enemy lightly or flippantly. We must not ignore him, underestimate his power, or overestimate his involvement. For example, if we view Satan as responsible for all that goes wrong in our lives, we overestimate his involvement, and we lose focus of his actual strategy and attack methods, rather than being vigilant, alert, and watchful.

In Ephesians 6:11, Paul sounds the clarion call "to stand against the schemes of the devil." The Greek word *METHODEIA* for "schemes" implies an orderly and logical arrangement or strategy, usually to achieve an end purpose.[13] Satan's scheming, crafty actions, and artful designs have method and purpose, for his aim is to mislead the immature who are not grounded in Christ. Charles Spurgeon has the following cautions regarding our adversary, the devil. "He will attack you sometimes by force and sometimes by fraud. By might or by sleight, he will seek to overcome you, and no unarmed man can stand against him. Never go out without all your armor on, for you can never tell where you may meet the devil. He is not omnipresent, but nobody can tell where he is not, for he and his troops of devils appear to be found everywhere on this earth."[14]

Some of Satan's key strategies are lies and deception. In John 8:44, Jesus told the gathered crowd that Satan does not hold to the truth, "for there is no truth in him. When he lies, he speaks his native language, for he is a liar and the father of lies." Satan's lies deceived the original couple, Adam and Eve, and blitzed humanity by enticing them to believe the lie that, independent of God, they would be their own gods. Ever since the Garden of Eden, the devil has ensnared humanity in a web of lies. _

When Paul addresses Satan as the god of this world, it is in the context of blinding people's minds from the truth (2 Corinthians. 4:4). He blinds people to God's truth that can set them free from lies and deception. In our country, truth has been assaulted and left for dead. The prophet Isaiah spoke of a time like ours, when in Isaiah 59:14 he declared, "... Truth has stumbled in the streets." The lies and deception of Satan have violently mugged truth. In utter confusion, our culture asks the same question as Pilate did before Jesus' crucifixion when he asked, "What is truth?" People think ultimate truth is unknowable or nonexistent.

We are told that people must define truth for themselves. The common phrase is, "What is true or right for you may not be true or right for me." Truth becomes relegated to how you feel about something. This misconception extends to denying clear, undeniable, and even biological realities. It is the time in which we live. The world's educational systems, in league with the Washington elites, Hollywood media moguls, Silicon Valley social media giants, and Madison Avenue advertising agencies, systematically teach this deceptive understanding of truth.

You will be mocked, ridiculed, and even vilified if you proclaim the Bible's absolute truth. Yet, if you bring the philosophy of relative truth to its logical conclusion, it completely falls apart. The rich oppressing the poor, the powerful crushing the weak, tyranny, genocide, rape, and cold-blooded murder are unquestionably wrong actions. Yet, if there is no standard of truth, no one has the authority to say so. Despite this untenable conclusion, our society still insists there is no absolute truth. What is good and right has been turned on its head, and we have become a confused society full of contradictions.

We are currently living in a society in which it is common for people to call perversion normal, to call wrong right, and to declare foolishness to be wisdom. The dominant culture in America has abandoned truth. Yet, amid the satanic ethos of lies and deception, Jesus declares in John 14:6, "I am the truth." In a world of lies, Jesus came as "THE truth." In John 1:17, the Apostle John states that "truth came through Jesus Christ." The truth took on flesh and blood and walked among us.

Sadly, humanity rejected the Truth and crucified Him, wholly ignorant that Truth went to the cross and died to free us from the lie. But Truth stubbornly rebelled against death, and He rose from the dead to reign (Psalm 89:14) and to pour out the Holy Spirit, who Jesus identified as the Spirit of Truth (John 14:17, 15:26, 16:13). Jesus promised that the Spirit of Truth would guide us into all truth (John 16:13), empowering His disciples to walk in the truth (3 John 3:3) and to proclaim the gospel of truth (Colossians 1:15). First Timothy 3:15 defines the Church of Jesus Christ as "the pillar and ground of the truth." Followers of Christ must be people who reject lies and live by the truth.

By rejecting the truth of God and the rule of His Son, people open themselves up to satanically inspired deception and delusional lies. Revelation 12:9 foresees a day when Satan will deceive the entire world. In 2 Timothy 3:13, Paul warned us of a time coming when "evil men and impostors will grow worse and worse, deceiving and being deceived." We live in such an era, where people appear to be under an evil enchantment, blinded by deception, only partially alive, under the control of a delusion (Isaiah 59:10). In 1 Timothy 4:1, Paul wrote to his young spiritual son, "The Spirit clearly says that in latter times some will abandon the faith and follow deceiving spirits and things taught by demons." Satan inspires false religions and deceptive teachings that lead humanity to destruction. Sometimes it comes as truth taken to an erroneous extreme, but God provided us with truth that is true for all people, at all times, in all places, and He calls us to ground our lives in that truth.

SATAN IS LIKE A LION

> "Be sober, be vigilant; because your adversary the devil walks about like a roaring lion, seeking whom he may devour" (1 Peter 5:8).

Lions prowl around, stalking their prey, looking for an opportunity to pounce. This king of beasts has soft paws, allowing him to sneak up on his prey. Satan and his demonic forces are sneaky, creeping around in undetected silence. While the target is unaware, he observes, seeking the right time to attack. That is how those of the demonic realm operate. They seek openings when we are vulnerable and in weak moments. We must remember that we have an enemy stalking us in those times and circumstances. Lions do not chew their food; they devour their prey, swallowing them in chunks.

As a roaring lion, Satan desires to devour our joy and peace, our family and health, our testimony, and, most of all, our relationship with Christ. Lions are also nocturnal, for hunting at night allows them to use their incredible night vision to attack. When compared to humans, lions have significantly more *rod cells* (photo-receptive cells in the retina of their eyes that enable night vision) than *cone cells* (which provide greater color vision). Lions have around twenty-five rod cells to each cone cell, while humans have about four rod cells to each cone cell. This contributes most to the lion's impressive nocturnal vision. These large cats can see six to eight times better than humans in low light conditions.[15] Satan is a nocturnal predator, so if we are involved in dark activities, we are most likely to become a target of Satan. In Ephesians 5:8-15, Paul warns believers not to participate in the useless deeds of darkness.

I heard pastor and author Jimmy Evans discuss lions being para visional.[16] That means, if you are sitting in a truck, lions see you and the vehicle as one. To them, the truck and all sitting in it are one massive animal that is too large for them to attack. The lions cannot see you individually and will leave you alone. Yet they will kill you if you stand up in the truck.

It reminded me of when I was in Kenya on safari, and the guide told me, "Under no circumstances stand up in the truck!" He was trying to keep me from potential devastation. Being part of a local church body is our truck. An animal by itself becomes easy prey for a predator, and the same is true for followers of Christ. How interesting it is that studies have found, during the COVID pandemic, that the people who attended church regularly were among those who maintained the best mental health.[17]

Lions love to intimidate and strike terror in the heart of potential prey with the sound of their roar. Historian and author David Barton shares a fascinating analogy of responding to the satanic roar.[18] He explained the lion is the king of the beasts, and, when the male lion roars, his voice terrifies animals all across the savanna. His roar can carry for five miles and causes the weak and the powerless to run in fear. Yet, the real danger is with the quick and fierce females. While the male lion roars at one end of the savanna, the female hunters will wait silently at the other end to attack the fleeing prey. When the male lion roars, the unsuspecting victims run in the opposite direction of the roar. They flee into the trap of the female lions, who await to attack and devour. Rather than run from the roar, the greatest possibility of survival is to run to the roar.

Satan and his demonic forces are powerful and dangerous. Rather than run from them in fear, Holy Rebels must advance in the authority of Christ by the power of the Holy Spirit. Equipped with God's truth, we must run into the roar to fulfill the will and purpose of God for our generation.

Many people live deeply fear-filled lives, consumed with real and imaginary phobias, so the enemy employs our fears to his advantage. It seems our entire society is living in fear of cultural bullies. These deceptive bullies exploit politicians, CEOs of large companies, and society at large for their nefarious purposes.

Instead of running from what causes fear, Holy Rebel warriors need to run into it, to make a difference for Christ and stand for truth. The Russians did not resist Lenin's takeover, nor did the Germans oppose Hitler's rise to power. We must have the courage to stand against totalitarianism and evil. Remember, our battle is a spiritual fight. Submit to God and resist the devil, and he will bolt from you in the blink of an eye (James 4:7). We must act now because light always overcomes darkness. Truth overpowers and disables lies. As Holy Rebels, we must have the courage to run toward the roar as we shine the light of God's love and wield the truth of His Word.

THE ENEMIES' METHODS OF ATTACK

When Paul remained in Athens, he was anxious for the church at Philippi. He dispatched Timothy, because he was worried about the Tempter deceiving them and was concerned that his work might have been in vain (1 Thessalonians 3:5).

Typically, temptation comes through our selfish desires (James 1:14), but temptation also comes from demons who watch us, know us well, and know what might draw us away from God (1 Chronicles 21:1). The devil tempts us in order to entrap and destroy us, yet temptation can be God's opportunity to test and strengthen our faith (James 1:13, Lk. 22:31). Every believer will face temptation. The devil tempted Jesus in the wilderness, but He overcame all the Tempter's mental attacks (Matt. 4:1).

During Jesus' temptation in the wilderness, He demonstrated how to defeat the tempter. "Now when the tempter came to Him, he said, 'If You are the Son of God, command that these stones become bread.' But He answered and said, 'It is written, "Man shall not live by bread alone, but by every word that proceeds from the mouth of God"'" (Matthew 4:3, 4). Yet, even after the tempter's defeat, we are told he left Jesus until another opportune time. This incident shows us you can overcome Satan's temptations, but he will return to tempt at another time. Never forget to counter every temptation with the Word of God, which is active and powerful (Hebrews 4:12).

Satan tempts us by implanting thoughts in our minds. One of our adversary's primary weapons is an accusation. The title "devil" (*DIABOLOS*) means "accuser" or "slanderer."[19] Revelation 12:10 calls him "the accuser of our brethren, who accused them before our God, day and night." Zechariah 3 provides a glimpse into the invisible realm, where Satan accuses Joshua, the High Priest, of the nation's sins. The book of Job unveils what happens in the unseen realm, where Satan constantly accuses the saints in the Court of Heaven. In the narrative, Satan accuses Job of only serving God for what the Lord did for him.

The Accuser will remind God of your failures, shortcomings, and sins. Thankfully, 1 John 2:1 reminds us of our advocate before the Father, Jesus Christ, the righteous One who is our defender. As you read Job's story, you can also see how Job accused God of being unfaithful and unfair, and Job's friends accused Job of unrighteousness and committing injustice. Behind the scenes, it is obvious Satan is at work polluting minds with his lies. He works the same way in our lives.

Another name for our enemy is the destroyer (1 Corinthians. 10:10, John 10:10, Exodus. 12:23, Revelation. 9:11). Satan and his dark forces seek to destroy. They destroy families, churches, and nations — corrupting moral standards, disrupting societal order, and bringing chaos and devastation. The Apostle John refers to Satan as the evil one. He is evil personified (John. 17:15 and 1 John. 5:18). Another of the devil's titles is "Beelzebub" (Luke 11:15, 18-19), which means the "Lord of the Flies," or what the Jews understood as "the God of Filth." Similarly, his demonic cohorts are "unclean spirits" (Matthew 10:1). When there is a fly infestation, they bring corruption and destruction. Satan is a corrupter. If we become involved in filthy thoughts, caught up in pornography, use filthy language, have offensive morality and ethics, the Lord of the Flies, the God of Filth, has entrapped us.

In Daniel 10, it appears Satan assigned demonic forces to certain areas and regions of the world (Daniel 10:12-13). The Bible does not go into detail, but it appears this text unveils a demonic hierarchy, organization, and strategy (Ephesians. 6:12). In military terms, Satan has a well-defined and well-organized global command and control structure.

HOLY ANGELS

But the word of God makes clear that there is another well-organized and far more powerful angelic army that is arrayed against Satan's evil forces – God's holy angels. Throughout Scripture, God is referred to as the Lord of Hosts. In the New Living Translation, this name is translated as the Lord of Heaven's Armies.

The Bible mentions angels nearly three hundred times with various titles such as "sons of the Mighty" (Psalms 29:2), "sons of God" (Job 1:6; 2:1; Psalms 29:1; 89:6), "holy ones" (Psalms 89:19), "princes" (Daniel 10), and symbolically as "stars" (Revelation 12:4). Regardless of the number, angels appear throughout Scripture from Genesis to Revelation (Gen. 3:24, Revelation 20:1).

Angels drove Adam and Eve out of the Garden of Eden and were mediators in bringing the law from God to Moses. They were prominent in the life and ministry of Jesus, from the announcement of His coming to His birth, throughout His earthly ministry, in the garden before His crucifixion, and after His resurrection and ascension. When reading the book of Revelation, you see angels who are active in the judgments brought on the earth during the time of tribulation. Angels will heavily populate heaven throughout eternity.

God created angels before humans (Colossians 1:16, Job 28:4,7). They do not procreate (Matthew. 22:30), yet they are innumerable (Daniel 7:10, Hebrews12:22, Job 25:3-4). They are awesome in appearance (Matthew 28:2-4). They do not always have wings, but they fly (Daniel 9:21). The Bible is clear that angels are not worthy of worship, and it forbids the worship of angels (Colossians 2:18, Hebrews 1:4, Revelation 19:10, 22:8), but angelic beings are extravagant in their worship of God (Nehemiah 9:6).

The Scripture teaches God created every angel to be good (Genesis 1:31), though one third eventually fell in the rebellion of Lucifer (Revelation 12:9). It is encouraging to realize there are far more angels than demonic spirits. In 2 Kings 6, the King of Syria sent a great army with chariots and horses to the city of Dothan to surround Elisha's residence. The servant of Elisha frantically called out, "Alas, my master! What shall we do?" We can feel the same way when we recognize the vast demonic horde that is formed against us. What Elisha told his servant is true for us. "Do not fear, for those who are with us are more than those who are with them" (2 Kings 6:16). Elisha prayed, "Lord, open his eyes that he may see," and the young man saw the mountain full of horses and chariots of fire all around Elisha. He saw God's angelic host working on their behalf. I pray we will have a revelation of the great angelic forces available to us as we pursue God's plan and purpose for our lives.

Like human beings, angels have personalities (Ezekiel 28:12, 1 Peter 1:12, Luke 15:7). In religious art and popular culture, angels are typically depicted as beautiful, petite women or cute cuddly babies. In many of the appearances of angels in the Bible they look nothing like that. People who saw them nearly passed out in fear of them (Luke 1:12-13). Angels are incredibly powerful (Psalm 103:20). Their capabilities are awe-inspiring. One angel could roll a four-ton stone away from the grave of Jesus (Matthew 28:2). Another single angel held off the entire Egyptian army all night long (Exodus 14:9). A single angel killed seventy thousand men during a plague (1 Chronicles 21:14-15), and another slew one hundred and eighty-five thousand Assyrian soldiers (2 Kings 19:35).

During the tribulation, God will dispatch four angels to hold off the winds from blowing on the planet. Angels are awesome in power, and the Scripture portrays them as flawless, sinless, immortal beings. They also apparently have their own unique language (1 Corinthians 13:1). Though all of this makes them superior to humans in many respects (Psalms 8:3-5), redeemed humanity has a superior Kingdom position (1 Peter 1:12). The Scripture teaches that one day believers will judge angels (1 Corinthians 6:3). Yet, angels are not jealous of humans since they rejoice when a prodigal comes home to Christ (Luke 15:10).

God created angels to serve His purposes, including ministering to Christ's followers (Hebrews 1:14). One should always be sociable to strangers because Hebrews 13:2 (NIV) tells us you never know when you might be entertaining angels unawares. It certainly happened to Abraham and Sarah when three visitors arrived at their tent, informing Sarah she would have a child in her old age. We learn they were two angels and a pre-incarnate appearance of Christ. The Lord commissioned the two angels to go on to Sodom and Gomorrah to bring judgment, and the men of Sodom assumed the angels were human beings.

I have a friend named Gene Lee who years ago started a business and was doing a lot of work in Houston, Texas. His company was struggling and having trouble making ends meet. One day, while speaking to a worker at a McDonald's restaurant in downtown Houston, he spotted a happy homeless man cleaning up outside the diner. Gene asked the man if he could buy him lunch, and the man accepted, so they went into the McDonald's and ordered. Gene handed him his lunch, and the man said, "God bless you." Gene replied, "He certainly does." The man then said, "No, you don't understand; He is going to bless you today," and then he promptly walked out of the restaurant.

Gene was a little taken aback by the encouragement imparted by the man's words. He quickly recovered and immediately followed the man out to invite him to sit down and eat with him. Yet, when he stepped outside the store, the man was nowhere to be seen. It was as if the person had disappeared. That day in the mail, Gene received an unexpected check for past work he had done that covered all of his unpaid bills and kept his company afloat. His company grew and succeeded beyond his wildest imaginations. That day was a turning point for Gene, and he always wondered if he had entertained an angel without knowing it.

ANGELIC WARS

Satan and his evil spirits make war with God's holy angels in the epic battle for the souls of men and women. Like it or not, cosmic powers have entangled us in this war, and we must learn how to follow the Lord as our commander-in-chief. As we do, the Lord of Hosts will dispatch angels on our behalf. You could call them God's secret agents who take their marching orders from Him. Though we do not see them, they are active and so subtle we may write their activity off as coincidence, but we must recognize what is occurring in the spiritual realm and how we can participate in this cosmic conflict.

We get a glimpse of this conflict in Revelation 12:7. "And there was war in heaven, Michael and his angels waging war with the dragon. The dragon and his angels waged war, and they did not prevail, and there was no longer a place found for them in heaven" (NASB). With his fallen angels, the dragon, who is Satan, warred against God's holy angels. One of the clearest pictures of these wars is in Daniel 10, where Michael the archangel broke through demonic opposition to allow the angel Gabriel to deliver a message to Daniel. The angel's key to victory in the skirmish was Daniel's prayer and fasting (Daniel 10:1-13).

The Bible gives us a slight glimpse into these angelic wars, and it is unwise to over-speculate or to bring too much of our imaginations into it. It's enough to know that angelic wars are happening and how to affect them.

Angelic wars occur in the realm of the Spirit, as the Lord's angels are at war to fulfill God's Kingdom purposes. Sometimes those purposes include judgment. In Psalm 78:49, the psalmist identified the source of the plagues visited upon Egypt as "angels of destruction among them." In the Scriptures, there are many incidents in which angels acted as agents of divine judgment when God's people sinned or when their enemies sinned against them. In Genesis 19:11, angels struck the perverse men of Sodom with blindness, and in Acts 12:21-23, an angel of the Lord struck down evil king Herod and brought about his gruesome death.

Throughout Scripture, we see angels delivering messages from God. In Hebrews 1:14 (TLB) we read, "For the angels are only spirit-messengers sent out to help and care for those who are to receive his salvation." We derive the word "angel" from the Greek ANGELOS, meaning "a messenger or envoy who is sent."[20]

In a dream, an angel told Joseph to marry his pregnant fiancée Mary, for she was miraculously "with child" and would give birth to the Son of God. An angel appeared in another dream a second time, warning them to go to Egypt. In Luke chapter 1, we find the angel Gabriel appearing to Mary to announce that she will give birth to Jesus. In that chapter, the angel Gabriel appeared to Zacharias to let him know that he and his wife Elizabeth, who had infertility issues, would soon become parents. When Zacharias did not believe, the angel made him mute until after the child's birth.

In Acts 27, the sailors did not listen to Paul, and the ship sailed into a horrific storm. When conditions seemed hopeless, Paul announced to those on board the vessel, "For there stood by me this night an angel of the God to whom I belong and whom I serve, saying, 'Do not be afraid, Paul; you must be brought before Caesar, and indeed God has granted you all those who sail with you'" (Acts 27:23-25). An angel gave him a message, and it came to pass just as the angel had told him.

The messages angels bring will often include a direction. In Judges 13, an angel tells a woman she will have a son, who we now know was Samson. In verse eight, her husband, Manoah, asks God to send the angel back to instruct the couple on how to bring up Samson. The Lord answered Manoah's prayer, and the angel returned with instructions.

In Acts 8:26, Philip is part of a powerful move of God's Spirit in Samaria, where miracles are occurring, people are coming to Christ, and believers are being filled with the Holy Spirit. Amid the extraordinary events, an angel speaks to Philip and tells him to leave the revival and go to the desert region of Gaza. It seemed like an unreasonable request, which may be why God sent an angel to deliver the message. Philip does not hesitate. Upon hearing the angel, he leaves for Gaza, where he leads an Ethiopian official to Christ. Many historians believe he was the first to bring the gospel message to Africa.

In Acts 10, Cornelius has an open vision of an angel who instructs him to call for Peter, who was staying in Joppa, to come and share the gospel with him. He obeys, Peter responds, and the house of Cornelius is both converted and filled with the Holy Spirit. Notice in both cases that the angel did not preach the gospel to those needing to hear, but angels were the connectors delivering a word to human messengers who would reach them. Other than during the tribulation, God does not give angels the privilege of preaching the message of Christ (Revelation 14:6). God seems to have reserved that task for human followers of Jesus.

There are many Bible stories of angels communicating with men and women. Kelly and I have had angels speak to us in dreams. The most memorable was when Kelly and I received a call to pastor our current church. Like Philip in Samaria in Acts 8, we were in the middle of a move of God at the church we pastored in Texas when the Lord profoundly dealt with Kelly and me about going to Colorado Springs to a specific church. During the process, I fell into a trance and saw a vision of Kelly and me standing on a dock. An angel came down from heaven in a chariot, stopped several feet from us, and yelled, "I can't make the connection, so pray in the Spirit." As the angel told us, the connection did not happen, but we kept praying in the Spirit until we became the church's pastors six years later.

God uses angels to meet our physical, emotional, and spiritual needs. In 1 Kings 19, an angel fed Elijah when he was on the run from Queen Jezebel after his great contest with the false prophets of Baal. Even more memorable is the incident when Jesus confronted and defeated Satan in the wilderness. The Lord had fasted for forty days before this, so when "the devil left Him," Jesus was hungry, and an angel came and ministered to his need (Matthew 4:2, 11).

After Jesus went through His grueling emotional experience in Gethsemane, an angel appeared. Luke 22:43 says, "Then an angel appeared to Him from heaven, strengthening Him." Angels strengthen and assist us in enduring challenging times, as happened with Jesus in the wilderness and the garden. The angels bolstered him but did not deliver him from the situation. Following Christ does not exempt us from difficulties; we still face problems, disappointments, and even death. Yet God's grace enables us in those dark hours. Sometimes God sends His angels to help get us through with greater strength and stability. I saw an interview with John Kilpatrick, the pastor who led the Brownsville Revival in Pensacola, Florida.[21] He told the story of an angelic experience he had when he was fifteen. John was part of an ongoing evening prayer service, and on a Sunday evening, seventeen people gathered for the meeting. The pastor had experienced severe resistance and problems in the church and announced to the prayer group that he was planning to leave the church. There was some sorrow at the meeting, but as they were all praying, the church's locked doors flew open, and everyone saw two angels walk into the room, march to the front, and stand at attention like rugged warriors.

Then, both angels walked through the church and out of the building. Everyone was overwhelmed and astonished, and the word got around the church and the community. At the next Wednesday evening service, every pew in the church was full, resulting in a dramatic change in the church's atmosphere and a transformation of the ministry. According to Kilpatrick, the appearance of these angels brought a spiritual redirection with fresh spiritual vibrancy in the church. God uses angels to meet our needs.

Another assignment of angels is escorting Christ's followers to heaven at death. Jesus explains this in the parable of the rich man and the beggar Lazarus. In the story, Jesus said that the beggar died and was "carried by the angels to Abraham's bosom" (Luke 16:22).

I had godly grandparents, and, when I was still in elementary school, my grandfather contracted cancer. We went to see him and my grandmother one weekend. After we left, my grandma said, "It's too bad that they had to leave, and we're by ourselves again." My grandpa said, "Emma, we're not alone." My grandma replied, "What do you mean? There is no one else here." He said, "Don't you see them, the angels? They are sitting around me." That night, he went home to be with Jesus. I believe he peeked into the other dimension and saw the angels prepared to escort him to heaven.

The last aspect of angelic activity we will address is their work in guarding, protecting, and delivering believers. Psalm 34:7 tells us, "The angel of the LORD encamps all around those who fear Him and delivers them." The angel's purpose is not to protect all people from all calamities, but to intervene in assuring the accomplishment of God's kingdom purposes.

In Exodus 14:19, we read how the angel of God watched over Israel as they left Egypt. Genesis 18 provides us with an account of angels protecting Lot's family from danger in Sodom and Gomorrah. 2 Kings 6 tells us the story of God's angels surrounding Elisha and his servant to protect and guard them. The book of Daniel gives us the stories of an angel (or it may have been a pre-incarnate visitation of Jesus) protecting three young men from a fiery furnace (Daniel 3:23-28) and stopping the mouths of lions that would have killed Daniel (Daniel 6:22).

In Acts 12, we read about an angel who rescued Peter from prison. What is interesting is that after Peter got out and went to the home of Mary, where people were praying for his release, these followers of Christ refused to believe God had answered their prayer. When the servant girl Rhoda insisted Peter was at the door, they said, "It must be his angel." Evidently, the early Jerusalem church believed that followers of Christ had angels assigned to them. It is obvious God gave Peter such an angel who delivered him from prison.

Sometimes angels do the miraculous, and sometimes it does not seem so miraculous, but angels are on assignment to protect us. In Matthew 18:10, Jesus said to "Take heed that you do not despise one of these little ones, for I say to you that in heaven their angels always see the face of my Father who is in heaven." Based on this verse, some believe (as Billy Graham did) that each of us has a guardian angel assigned to watch over us and protect us throughout our lives. I do not know that we can make a strong scriptural case for this idea, but I am confident God will, at times, provide us with angelic protection.

Years ago, on a cold winter's evening, I was driving down a busy road in Topeka, Kansas, when I hit a patch of black ice and lost control of my car. All I had time to do was call out, "In the name of Jesus, Lord, help me." Miraculously, my car swerved in and out of traffic as if an expert driver were steering, but it was not me. I had no control. As I approached a red light, I called out to God again, and my car slid to the left around the corner, just as the light turned red, and I headed to my destination. I believe it was angelic protection. I can just imagine a big angel holding onto my back bumper and steering the car through that traffic. What is certain is God will sometimes protect His people with angelic involvement.

I finish this chapter with one final important warning concerning angelic visitations: If you have such an angelic experience, praise God for it, yet do not seek it. In 2 Corinthians 11:14, Paul tells us, "For Satan himself transforms himself into an angel of light." Throughout history, people claiming angelic encounters have birthed false religions and some of hell's greatest heresies.

I've shared extensively about angels because we want you to be aware of these incredible creatures God commissions to assist Holy Rebels in the battle. In the chapters ahead, you will see that as we pray and declare God's Word (Ps. 103:20, Gen. 24:7), as we follow the Holy Spirit in obedience to the Scripture (Ps. 91:11), and as we worship the Lord (Ps. 8:2), angelic activity will naturally occur to assist us in fulfilling the Lord's will and purpose in our lives. Remember the words of Elisha, "Do not fear, for those who are with us are more than those who are with them."

——— CHAPTER FIVE ———

SATANIC STRATEGY

WITH THEIR CITY under siege, welcome news arrived in Sicily. Harald "Hardrada" Sigurdsson, the Viking warlord and eventual King of Norway, was on his deathbed.[22] For the Sicilians, this was a hopeful turn of events. Harald was a relentless military leader known for ruthless brutality. With this powerful warlord's death, it was possible Sicily would be spared. A few weeks later, a representative from the Scandinavian forces came bearing updated news and an unexpected request. They declared warlord Harald was dead, and the enemy army petitioned that the town give their leader a proper Christian burial inside the city's walls.

In a display of great compassion, hoping it would serve as a gesture of goodwill to their invaders, Sicily agreed to the request. They conditioned the agreement upon the enemy bringing no weapons into the city. The next day a Scandinavian honor guard of trained warriors marched toward the town, carrying on their shoulders an enormous coffin containing Harald's fully armored body. Wearing their religious robes, the priests reverently watched as the procession moved to the opened gates of the city. To the shock of the Sicilian onlookers, Harald suddenly and violently burst out of the casket with his sword swinging. His death was a ruse, and the coffin concealed a stash of weapons for Harald's soldiers.[23]

The armed Scandinavian warriors brutally assaulted the citizens of Sicily, showing no mercy as they looted and pillaged the city. Harald conquered through lies and deception, taking advantage of the Sicilians' naïve compassion. As in this medieval historical account, Satan has a strategy of lies and deceit designed to bring destruction and devastation.

God threw our adversary, Satan, out of heaven. Now, Satan aims to diminish the glory of God by continuing to pursue his own glory and by destroying God's image-bearers. His greatest opposition is the church of Jesus Christ. The devil will use disguise, deception, lies, misdirection, and division to conquer and destroy us. In this effort, he uses what Ephesians 6:11 calls "wiles." The Greek word *METHODEIA* for wiles means strategies, schemes, tactics, and well-crafted trickery, which applies to the devil.[24]

In 2 Corinthians 2:11, Paul tells us that Satan can take advantage of us if we are ignorant of his devices. It is, therefore, imperative that we become familiar with Satan's strategies of war. The devices and strategies of Satan are first seen in Genesis chapter 3:1-13. In this passage, we discover the devil's method of disguise, deception, lies, misdirection, and division. The author refers to Satan as "the serpent."

DISGUISE

Genesis 3 introduces us to Satan, "Now the serpent was more cunning than any beast of the field which the Lord God had made" (Genesis 3:1).

Some believe the devil came to Eve by possessing a serpent. If so, he came disguised as something other than what he truly was. Others understand "the serpent" as a metaphor for Satan's character and nature. In either case, other passages of the New Testament are clear that the serpent was Satan (2 Cor, 11:3, Rev. 12:9 and 20:2). Serpents are subtle, stealthy, hard to detect, and dangerous, and that is Satan in his subtlety. He did not come to Eve as something to be feared, questioned, or run from. The serpent was much too cunning for that. Satan will not show up in our lives with a red suit, pitchfork, horns, and cloven hooves. Paul tells us Satan can transform himself into an angel of light (2 Corinthians 11:14).

I have heard testimonies of Satan or demons appearing to persons in malevolent brilliance, but that is not typically how our enemy disguises himself. When he comes to us, he will not appear in demonic splendor or as a hideous monster. Rather, he will come as a social influencer, an entertaining movie, a fun-loving friend, a concerned relative, an interesting university professor, or a woke pastor.

In the book of Revelation, as John unfolds the events of the tribulation, he writes: "Then I saw another beast coming up out of the earth, and he had two horns like a lamb and spoke like a dragon" (Revelation. 13:11). One of the most obvious symbols in the book of Revelation is Jesus as the lamb. Yet, here a beast is portrayed as a lamb who looks so empathetic, caring and appears to be Christlike, but he speaks like a dragon. This lamb is really the false prophet who promotes the Antichrist through religious deception. He is persuasive because he appears spiritual. Satan can camouflage himself in disarming and appealing disguises.

This story of the devil's stealth is played out in Job's life. Satan aims to entice Job to curse God (Job 1:11, 2:5). Then Job's wife encourages her husband to "curse God and die" (Job 2:9). Satan persuaded Job's wife to become the provocateur, inciting Job to sin. In Matthew 16, we find a similar scenario, in which Jesus foretold that in Jerusalem, He would suffer and die, but would be resurrected from the dead (Matthew 16:21). In response, Peter audaciously rebuked Jesus, saying, "Far be it from You, Lord; this shall not happen to You." Jesus recognized Peter had become the unwitting voice of the devil, so He turned and said to Peter, "Get behind Me, Satan! You are an offense to Me, for you are not mindful of the things of God, but the things of men" (Matthew 16:23). Jesus' chief disciple had become the well-meaning but misguided tool of the devil. Satan speaks to us in various ways, yet his voice is often hard to detect as coming from the enemy of our soul. That is why we must discern the voices we hear based on God's Word.

DECEPTION

In Genesis 3:1, the serpent speaks, and he says to the woman, "Has God indeed said, 'You shall not eat of every tree of the garden'?" The serpent's opening salvo was, "Has God indeed said?" The first maneuver of Satan is always to attack the Word of God. It is with questions such as these: "Are you sure God said that?" "How do you know?" "There are so many interpretations of Scripture, so how can you possibly be sure?" Our enemy will attempt to get us to doubt God's Word. Anything you see or hear challenging the credibility of Scripture is satanic.

And the woman said to the serpent, "We may eat the fruit of the trees of the garden; but of the fruit of the tree, which is in the midst of the garden, God has said, "You shall not eat it, nor shall you touch it, lest you die'" (v. 2, 3).

Eve got into a conversation and then an argument with the Adversary.

I have learned it is never a successful strategy to get into a debate with the devil. He has been at this a long time and is an expert debater. When we do, he can create doubts in our minds about God and the truth of Scripture. If you have doubts concerning what God has said, doubt your doubts. Do not doubt the Word of God. Instead, follow the instructions of James in James 4:7: "Therefore, submit to God. Resist the devil, and he will flee from you." Eve did not do this. Instead, she conversed with the devil.

Eve did not accurately explain what God said. God said they could freely eat from the trees of the garden. The Lord was saying, "You can have everything you want, except for one." However, Eve omitted the word "freely." This omission diminishes the generosity of God and obscures the reality of the situation.

Notice how Eve said they could not *touch* the fruit from the tree of the knowledge of good and evil. God never said that. He did tell them they could not *eat* from it, but He said nothing about touching it. She also changed "you will surely die" to "lest you die," lessening the severity of the consequence of disobeying. What we see illustrated are liberalism and legalism. Liberalism takes away from the Scripture, while legalism adds to the Bible. A liberalist will say God does not actually mean that or it no longer applies to us today. In the New Testament, the Sadducees were liberalists who did not believe in the supernatural or the resurrection.

On the other hand, the legalist will agree with what God said and add to it. In the Gospels, the Pharisees were the legalists who added rules and regulations to what God had said. The enemy does not care if we are a liberalist or a legalist, so long as we pervert or oppose the truth of God's Word. The message is clear; do not add to or subtract from the Bible.

A national survey recently found that nearly 70 percent of self-professed "born again" Christians disagree with Jesus' words in John 14:6, where He proclaimed, "I am the way, the truth, and the life. No one comes to the Father except through Me."[25] They are pretending Jesus said, "I am not the only way to God," or, "I am one of many ways to the Father," but He didn't say that. The Apostle Peter affirmed the words of Jesus in Acts 4:12, when he declared to the Jewish council: "Nor is there salvation in any other, for there is no other name under heaven given among men by which we must be saved." If we compromise this truth, as many do, we fall for deception.

These believers have fallen for the deception of pluralism. They accept the popular idea that many ways lead to God. The Apostle Paul predicted this trend of denying the truth of Scripture. In 1 Timothy 4:1, Paul writes, "The Spirit clearly says that in latter times some will abandon the faith and follow deceiving spirits and things taught by demons." Satan inspires false religions and false teachings that lead humans to destruction. Paul calls Satan the god of this world who blinds people's minds from the truth (2 Cor. 4:4). In Revelation 12:9, we read that a day is coming when Satan will deceive the entire world.

One awful deception today is gender dysphoria and gender fluidity. Among young people, it has become a popular fad to be fluid about your gender. This craze started because a small fraction of people in our society felt disconnected between who they think they are and their biological reality. A biologically male person feels, deep down inside, that he is a female trapped in a man's body, or a biologically female person, who, deep down inside, feels she is a male in a female body. According to biology and human DNA, males are males and will always be males; females are females and will always be females.

No number of medications or surgeries will change that. Even more significantly, from the first chapter of the Bible, it says, "So God created man in His own image; in the image of God, He created him; male and female He created them" (Gen. 1:27). Gender is not a social construct but is God's design for humanity. God created us male or female, and that is sacred. Rejecting our God-given gender is the equivalent of rebelling against our Creator.

To fix this problem, our society instructs these confused people to deny the truth and embrace their feelings. The LGBTQ+ community encourages them to have hormone treatments to block their development, and physical surgery to alter their appearance. That is not how we handle other cases when people's feelings contradict their reality.

Anorexia is a good example.[26] Those with anorexia are so upset with their bodies that they cannot see the truth. Anorexics can be on the borderline of starvation, look at themselves in the mirror, and see fat bodies. No rational, caring person would say, "Though you are extremely thin, you see yourself as obese. So, let's get you on a low-calorie diet plan, hire a trainer, and significantly increase your exercise. I will fully support you in your desire to lose weight."

Instead, we say, "Your brain is deceiving you. Let's align your thinking so that you can see yourself according to reality, and you can live a healthy life." We have a society that is told to live by feelings. The Scripture is clear;

we must live according to the truth as believers. Instead of trying to manipulate reality to align with our feelings, we must tell our feelings to line up with the truth.

Alexander Solzhenitsyn was a well-known anti-communist dissident. Just before his exile to the west, Solzhenitsyn published a final message to the Russian people titled, "Live Not by Lies!"[27] The title arose from the reality that under communism, the Marxist elites ordered the population to live contrary to what was the truth. Yet, they were fearful of challenging the lies. Solzhenitsyn equated "lies" with ideology, the illusion that human nature and society can be reshaped to predetermined specifications. And his last word before leaving his homeland urged Soviet citizens as individuals to not cooperate with the regime's lies. Solzhenitsyn wrote, "Even the most timid can take this least demanding step toward spiritual independence. If many march together on this path of passive resistance, the whole inhuman system will totter and collapse."[28]

We live in a similar environment today. It is imperative that we overcome our fears, live not by lies but align our lives to the truth, even in the face of bullies who oppose us and attack us for our stand.

LIES

In the Genesis narrative, we read, "Then the serpent said to the woman, 'You will not surely die" (Genesis 3:4). The serpent's statement directly contradicts the actual Word of God. In Genesis 2:16, the Lord had said, "In the day that you eat of the tree of the knowledge of good and evil you shall surely die." Lying is not only a tactic of the devil; it is at the core of his character. Jesus explained that to the duplicitous religious leaders of His day:

> "You are of your father the devil, and the desires of your father you want to do. He was a murderer from the beginning and did not stand in the truth because there is no truth in him. When he speaks a lie, he speaks from his own resources, for he is a liar and the father of it. But because I tell the truth, you do not believe Me" (John 8:44-45).

Satan is a liar, so when we listen to the devil, we are listening to lies. They are thoughts filled with demonic deceit. If we believe them, his lies will enslave us. It is also important to realize that with a cunning stroke of deception, rather than speaking in the third person, Satan will often speak in the first person, fooling us into thinking these are our thoughts. This is a list of what his lies sound like.

- God doesn't really love me, or I wouldn't have all these problems.
- I'm not good enough.
- I can't change. I'll always be a loser.
- I am worthless. No one could ever love me.
- I've done too much wrong. God could never work through my life.
- I will never be free.
- There is no hope. I might as well give up.
- Everyone would be better off if I didn't exist.

We know it is Satan's voice when the voice we hear contradicts biblical truth. The only way to deal with satanic lies is to counter them with God's truth. That is how Jesus responded to satanic attacks in the wilderness (Luke 4). With every lying temptation the adversary hurled at Him, Jesus countered with the truth of God's Word, declaring, "It is written" (Luke 4:1-13).

In his usual fraudulent trickery, the serpent said to Eve, "For God knows that in the day you eat of it your eyes will be opened, and you will be like God, knowing good and evil" (Genesis 3:5). The adversary attempted to seduce Eve with questions about God's character by sowing seeds of doubt in her mind regarding God's goodness. The trap was set, and she fell prey to the serpent's scam. Eve was quickly persuaded to believe that God's motives were selfish. That the Lord was depriving her of something that would be beneficial for her, and that God did not have her and Adam's best interests in mind.

God creates boundaries and sets guidelines for our security and well-being, but Satan, the snake, will tell us the opposite. Once we question the goodness of God, it becomes easier to disobey the will of God. Also, notice how the serpent minimizes the consequences of the rebellion and exaggerates the benefits of the sin. That is how Satan always operates.

The Evil One will make sure you understand the potential pleasure and excitement of an adulterous affair, but purposely fail to mention the possible loss of your marriage, family, and reputation. He will not explain how promiscuity can cause sexual disease, an unwanted pregnancy, and emotional scars. Rather, Satan ignores the consequences of sin while always promoting the potential benefits and immediate gratification of rebellion.

Encased in this lie of Satan is the grand temptation resulting in the disastrous fall of man. The first couple rejected God, abandoned His rule, and declared themselves independent of God, with the promise of becoming gods themselves. This is the creature's attempt to rebel and cast off the Creator, which was Satan's original sin that had him cast from heaven. In Isaiah 14:14, Lucifer himself defiantly proclaimed, "I will be like the Most High!" As Satan did in his original rebellion, so he convinced Adam and Eve to declare through their actions, "We shall be as God!"

MISDIRECTION

> "So, when the woman saw that the tree was good for food, that it was pleasant to the eyes, and a tree desirable to make one wise, she took of its fruit and ate" (Genesis 3:6).

Through his usual chicanery, Satan took Eve's eyes off God, away from His Word, and shifted her focus to the tree and the fruit. This is Satan's tactic of misdirection. He shifts our focus from Jesus and His Word to something else. Usually, it is something we believe will meet a need God is not presently meeting. Though God had freely given them everything they could ever want, in the act of misdirection, the serpent enabled them to see the one thing they did not have.

In 1 John 2:16, the Apostle John writes, "For all that is in the world—the lust of the flesh, the lust of the eyes, and the pride of life—is not of the Father but is of the world," which correlates perfectly with Genesis 3.

- The lust of the flesh— "She saw it was good for food."
- The lust of the eyes— "It *was* pleasant to the eyes."
- The pride of life— "A tree desirable to make one wise."

Satan always assumes he can stir up our flesh, passions, and pride to pursue what God has forbidden. The lust of the flesh and the lust of the eye make us take our eyes off God and to focus them on our own desires, happiness, and fulfillment. Pride is the most dangerous because it allows Satan's deception to be incredibly effective. Pride led to the fall of Lucifer, resulting in his becoming Satan. The sin of pride made "being like God" attractive to Adam and Eve. It is pride that causes people to reject the truth because they get the idea that they know better than God. The sin of pride tells us we deserve and should have what we do not have. It is pride that makes us feel self-sufficient and that we do not need God, virtually denying God's existence.

Satan's concoction of lies made Eve so focused on what she did not have that she lost sight of all she had and, therefore, lost everything. He also employed the same strategy on King David in 2 Samuel 11. David had it all: a relationship with the true God, great fame, tremendous power, abundant wealth, and a big family. Yet, Satan misdirected David to the one thing he did not have: Bathsheba. The number of people who have fallen into this same trap is innumerable. You can appear to have it all, but instead of concentrating on what you have and thanking and praising God for it, the enemy tricks you into focusing on something you do not have. It feels like it is the one thing that will meet your need and fulfill your life.

"She also gave to her husband with her, and he ate" (v. 6). It makes you wonder what Adam was doing this whole time. God instructed him to tend and keep the garden, so when he saw the serpent attempting to deceive his wife, he should have driven the snake out of the garden. Instead, he did nothing.

To do nothing is an awful sin to commit, because it brings suffering to those close to you. Many have credited the amazing German theologian and Nazi dissident Dietrich Bonhoeffer with these words: "Silence in the face of evil is itself evil. God will not hold us guiltless. Not to speak is to speak. Not to act is to act."[29] Though Bonhoeffer is probably not the actual source, these words align with his life, as well as with Scripture and the original sin of Adam.

In Robert K. Hudnut's 1971 book, *A Sensitive Man and the Christ,* he makes a case that even a sensitive man must act when the need arises. "Caught between the establishment and the radicals, caught between the colleges and the kids, caught between the generations, caught between the Athenian and Corinthian, sensitive men dare not be silent. Not to speak is to speak. Not to act is to act. To do nothing when a house is burning is to do something. It is to let the country burn."[30]

During a time when the Apostle Paul could have been intimidated by the opposition, "the Lord spoke to Paul in the night by a vision: 'Do not be afraid, but speak, and do not keep silent'" (Acts 18:9). I believe the Lord is saying the same to His people today.

Adam stood idly by while his wife was tempted, confused, and deceived. Adam's responsibility was to take dominion, then say and do something. We must not think that, while great evil is going on, we will be fine, as long as we do not participate. God calls us to take a stand, speak up, and act against evil. Sometimes we pray and wait for God when He is waiting for us. That is because there are realms in which God gives us authority and the responsibility to act. Some things do us little good to pray about unless we are willing to be part of the solution. It is not enough to pray that our children will be more obedient unless we impose loving discipline. Instead of simply praying about a problematic employee, the employer also needs to confront their actions.

Since Adam did not take responsibility and operate in his authority, silently watching, it ultimately led to Adam falling into the same sin. In I Timothy 2:14, Paul says, "Adam was not deceived, but the woman being deceived fell into transgression." God gave the original instructions about the tree to Adam. He knew the truth better than Eve did, therefore knowing that it was his responsibility to drive out the serpent. Yet Adam stood by without interrupting Satan's deception. Satan misled Eve, but he did not deceive Adam, who knew the truth, saw the error, and still rebelled against God by eating the fruit.

Maybe Adam accepted her actions and then participated in her sin out of a false love for her and a misguided tolerance for her behavior. He knew she was believing a lie. He knew the consequences. Yet, because he claimed to love her and did not want to lose her, he accepted her sin and then joined in it himself.

Husbands and fathers, we must rebel against hell's lies and be the spiritual leaders in our homes. We must know the Word. We must communicate and live out the Word of God, the truth, to our families. We are responsible to make sure our wives and children do not fall into temptation and the deceptive snare of the enemy. Do we know what our kids are being taught in school? Do we know what they are watching on television and on the Internet? Too many Christian parents forsake the responsibility of guarding their kids' hearts and neglect their calling to make sure they are being taught the Word of God (Deut. 6:6-7). Then, when the enemy deceives their children and they fall into a life contrary to Scripture, though the parents know what is right, they end up accepting it, like Adam did, "out of love for their kids." These parents actually have the greater sin.

Verse 7 reads, "Then the eyes of both of them were opened, and they knew that they were naked, and they sewed fig leaves together and made themselves coverings."

Adam and Eve felt the cumbersome guilt and shame of rebellion against God. The world as they knew it had now fallen into corruption and disarray. By their fruitless efforts, they endeavored to cover their sin. This is like people today who think some humanistic philosophy or utopian theory will fix the world. Whether it be liberation theology, critical race theory, or some other Marxist ideology or extreme environmentalist crusade, none of these human inventions can deal with sin or eradicate the world's problems.

The answer to the world's problems is not what man can do to fix it. Rather, it is what God has done through the cross of Jesus Christ. Fig leaves are artificial attempts to hide what we cannot change. In the Genesis account, the answer is found in the shedding of the blood of an animal to cover Adam and Eve, which prophetically pointed toward Jesus, God's Rescuer, who would make everything right again.

"And they heard the sound of the Lord God walking in the garden in the cool of the day, and Adam and his wife hid themselves from the presence of the Lord God among the trees of the garden" (v. 8). God created Adam and Eve for a close, intimate relationship with Him. Yet, notice how they ran and hid from God, with whom they had previously walked and talked. "Then the Lord God called to Adam and said to him, 'Where are you?'" (v. 9).

God never asks a question for His information, for our God is all-knowing. He asks us a question to bring confession and repentance.

"So, he said, 'I heard Your voice in the garden, and I was afraid because I was naked, and I hid myself'" (v. 10-11). The Lord always calls us to come into the light and confess our sins. But Satan's intention is for us to run into the dark and hide our sins.

"And He said, 'Who told you that you were naked? Have you eaten from the tree of which I commanded you that you should not eat?' Then the man said, 'The woman whom You gave to be with me, she gave me of the tree, and I ate'" (v. 11-12)

Instead of confessing and repenting of his sin, Adam took it like a man and blamed his wife. The art of blame-shifting became a way of shifting Adam's culpability to Eve and God. Adam was saying, "Really, it's Your fault, God; it's the woman You gave me. When it was just You and me, everything was all right."

DIVISION

By causing Adam and Eve to doubt God's Word, Satan instigated division between the original couple as well as with God. Whenever we choose to ignore God's Word, we create division, and division makes us more vulnerable to the enemy.

In John 17:21, Jesus prayed His disciples would be one, but before this prayer (in verse 16), He asked the Father to sanctify His followers in the truth, for God's Word is truth. That is because God unites His people through the Word of God, and when some will not submit to the Scripture, it causes division. When people turn and reject God's truth, then division is inevitable (Luke 12:51-53).

Agreement with God's Word creates unity, and the more committed the body of Christ is to God's Word, the more united we become. Thus, Satan's cunning strategy for dividing us is to persuade believers to depart from God's Word. Amos 3:3 posed this question, "Can two walk together unless they are agreed?"

There was a time when our nation was more united by our general agreement with biblical values, but the further our country drifts from the truth of Scripture, the greater the division believers will encounter in the broader culture. Also, the more the culture rejects God's Word, the more despised, hated, and persecuted the church will become (John 15:24). "And the Lord God said to the woman, 'What is this you have done?'› The woman said, "The serpent deceived me, and I ate'" (v. 13). Eve was more in touch with what happened and far more honest than Adam. Satan deceived Eve, and she sinned against God. It is time the church recognizes the cunning acts of Satan's lies, which deceive us and compromise our convictions, leading us to sin against the Lord. We cannot expect to honor God and be the salt and light of the earth when we walk in lockstep with the mindset and values of the world.

The antidote to falling into the sin of the original couple is to engage in a ferocious, tenacious, and uncompromising commitment to the truth. This is our holy rebellion against hell's strategy of deception and lies. It will require saturating ourselves in God's Word. We must *hear* (Rom. 10:17), *read* (Deut. 17:19), *study* (2 Tim 2:15, Acts 17:11), *meditate* (Josh. 1:8), *memorize* (Ps. 119:11), *pray* (Dan. 9:1-3, Acts 4:24-26), *declare* (Jer. 23:28-29), *believe* (2 Cor. 4:13, 1 Thess. 2:13), and *obey* the Word of God (James 1:22, Rev. 1:3). There must be absolute fidelity to the truth of Scripture. Our thoughts, motives, and actions must be compared to the words in the Bible and what we read, hear, and see, requiring it to be discerned according to the Scripture. We must be people of the book, fully devoted to God's truth. Our greatest weapon against the strategy of hell is the weapon of truth.

CHAPTER SIX

GOD'S HOLY FIRE

"Then the fire of the Lord fell and consumed the burnt sacrifice, and the wood and the stones and the dust, and it licked up the water that was in the trench. Now when all the people saw it, they fell on their faces; and they said, 'The Lord, He is God! The Lord, He is God!'" (1 Kings 18:38-39)

THE HOLY REBEL'S strategy in our rebellion against hell's agenda requires God's holy fire. Like Elijah, we must have the fire of God upon our lives, consuming us for His glory. God's Holy fire is not optional, it is mandatory in this battle.

We are truly blessed to be surrounded by amazing fire-baptized men and women of God in our lives. The Lord has brought a great deal of wisdom to us through His servants. Todd and I have learned to seek God first and make His Word the highest priority in our lives while also listening carefully to what He says to us through other leaders, mentors, and prophetic voices. We have so much to learn from others, and God strategically places people in our lives to help lead, guide, and direct us. God sent Elijah to mentor, guide, teach, and train Elisha. Elisha honored the prophet and thus positioned himself to receive from the man of God. Elisha's attitude of humility and respect for Elijah made him eligible for a double portion of the anointing of God. This is an important principle for each of us.

The moment we think we know it all and we don't need the counsel of others we become disqualified for the double portion. We have much to learn and glean from godly leaders that the Lord brings into our lives. When we stay humble, open, and attentive to their wisdom and counsel, we are positioned for more of His anointing, blessing, and power. Pride, however, will block us from receiving all that God has for us. Therefore, ask Him for godly leaders, pastors and teachers who carry His fire; and then thank Him for them. Walk in humility and honor towards them. This will position you to receive all that God has to impart to you.

Mario Murillo is one such leader God has connected us with, and we thank God for him. He spoke to us recently about Elijah and the fire of God on Mount Carmel. As he shared this insight, it was as if God was speaking directly to us through Mario's voice. He spoke of God's fire falling upon Elijah's sacrifice. God's fire demonstrated His Divine power, and it affirmed Elijah's life of uncompromising surrender and obedience. Similarly, when we live our lives in total abandonment to God—and rebelling against the forces of hell—His holy fire falls upon our hearts, affirming our lives of obedience as well. As Mario spoke, I could feel the fire of God increasing in my heart and I knew God was speaking to me personally through this man of God. Treasuring every word, I became more determined to live in such a way that His holy fire would continually burn and be manifest in my life.

We must desire and acquire the fire of God upon our lives, our families, and our churches. A Christian without the fire of God burning in his or her soul is not okay. A church without the fire of God is not okay. A church without God's fire is not a biblical church; it is a religious institution. One of our neighbors told Todd recently that every time he talks to either of us, he senses God's presence and feels like a fire is ignited in his soul. When the fire of God is burning in someone's heart, it is apparent in his or her life and it will spread to others who desire it as well. We must set our hearts on fire with God's holy fire every day so that others will see us burn for Him. That fire in us draws others to the God who sends the fire.

To be clear, it is obvious when a person is on fire for God and when he or she is not. A dear woman came forward in a recent church service to have me pray with her to receive Christ. She explained to me very matter-of-factly that she had been to several churches, seeking for what seemed real. Then she explained that when she comes to Radiant, she can feel God's presence. Then she said, "There's something different here. When I watch the people singing praises to God, I can tell that you really know God, and I want to know Him like you know Him." What she was sensing and experiencing was the fire of God burning in the hearts of passionate followers of Jesus. She was drawn to that fire and desired to acquire that fire herself.

ACQUIRE THE FIRE

"At each and every sunrise, you will hear my voice as I prepare my sacrifice of prayer to you. Every morning I lay out the pieces of my life on the altar and wait for your fire to fall upon my heart" (Psalms 5:3 TPT).

God desires to set every heart ablaze with His holy fire. Still, He will not override our will, our flesh, and our ambitions. He responds to the heartfelt cries of His children in prayer. If you want His holy fire in your life, consider praying like this: Lord, I need Your Holy Fire burning in my heart every day. I do not want to live without it. I need Your fire to purify me, my passions, desires, and purpose. I lay all the pieces of my life upon the altar today. Lord, I wait for Your fire to fall upon my heart and consume me for Your glory. Burn up everything in me that is not of You, Lord. Send Your fire upon my life to empower me to live an uncompromising life of obedience and surrender to You. Amen.

First, we must acknowledge our desperate need for God's fire in our lives. We must have the fire of God burning in our hearts, in our churches and in our homes. God's holy fire is not optional, it is mandatory. Religion rejects and downplays the fire of God. Pride opposes the belief that you must have the fire of God burning in your heart. The reason for this is that the kingdom of darkness is terrified of Holy Spirit, fire-baptized followers of Jesus. Therefore, the powers of darkness strive continually to extinguish the fire of God or keep us from His holy fire. The fire of God upon His people is as terrifying to hell today as it was on Mount Carmel in Elijah's day. Satan knows very well that without the fire we lack the power to fulfill God's mission and calling.

Dutch Sheets shared a prophetic dream that Gina Goldstein had concerning the church. The message for the church from that dream is very important for us today: "God has come to reignite the church with Pentecostal fire so that our lives and message will be presented with a demonstration of the Spirit and power. Then the world will see and know that He is God." Gina also related a word that another minister had received from the Lord, "I made the church the way I wanted it and now I want the church the way I made it." She continued with this mandate: "Make no mistake... the true church that Christ birthed is not intended to be a weak entity sitting in hiding, hoping to hold on until He returns. He formed us to be a glorious church filled with and operating in the power of His Spirit. We are called to be filled with His fire and clothed in His glory. The church must be marked and known by the demonstration of His awesome might. That was His intention from the very beginning, and He is now bringing the church back into alignment with His original intent. Out from that church will emerge carriers of the fire. He will work through them to initiate the awakening revival that brings us back into alignment with His original intent."[31]

YOU'RE GOOD

Christianity without God's fire is not good. Todd and I, and our kids had just returned to Colorado from a trip to North Carolina. When we arrived in Denver, we were hungry, so we stopped at a conveniently located chain restaurant a short distance from the airport. There weren't many people in the restaurant; however, once we were seated we couldn't seem to get anyone to wait on us. After a very long time, a server finally approached our table. Unfortunately, it went downhill from there.

We gave her our orders, and then she disappeared. We waited and waited, but there was no sign of her. We were very thirsty, so when she came quickly through the dining room, we tried to get her attention. She saw us waving for her attention and without even stopping to see what we needed, she nodded at us and said, "You're good." We looked at each other in stunned amazement. I asked Todd and the kids, "Did she just say what I think she said?" They nodded affirmatively, that we all heard the same thing. I wanted to tell her in a very nice but convincing way that we were not good. We were tired, hungry, and thirsty and after 30 minutes, we were still waiting for water.

She eventually served our drinks, and then we waited and waited for our food. When the food finally arrived, they had forgotten Luke's meal. Again, we waited and waited... and when Todd, Faith and I had finished our meals, Luke's dinner still had not come. Again, we tried to flag her down to tell her that Luke still didn't have his food. Once again, without stopping or slowing down to see what we needed, she blew us off and in a very condescending tone she said, "You're good." By this time, I was about to blow a gasket. I was not good. And I was astounded that she continued to insist that we were good when we were not receiving the service, food, and drink that we had come for and paid for. This restaurant advertised great food and excellent service and we came expecting that.

We had never experienced such awful service at a restaurant in our lives. It was unbelievable, and we were not good. Yet she kept arrogantly insisting, "You're good." It seemed that she thought if she kept telling us we were good without our food and drink, that we would eventually accept it and be fine with it. We were served a partial portion of what we had asked for and were told, "You're good". This felt like another episode of the 1960s television series: *The Twilight Zone*. I almost expected Rod Serling to come sauntering into the room, cigarette in hand, to tell us, "You have just entered the Twilight Zone".

We left the restaurant bewildered, disappointed and hungry because they did not deliver or serve as they had advertised. The Holy Spirit spoke to me about this bizarre experience and how this is exactly what happens in many churches today. Many churches announce they are a Christian church and follow Jesus. They are open for business, people are busy, running, working, and serving. They may even have large crowds showing up each week. However, they are often withholding or refusing to give the people what they really need. Their guests come in spiritually hungry and thirsty, hoping to have their deepest longings fulfilled.

Imagine with me (in the tone of Rod Serling's voice) a room filled with hungry guests sitting, waiting, and watching the busy workers coming in, going out, and moving about the room with the appearance of accomplishing a glorious mission. When the waiting guests are served, they are grateful, but then realize that there is something missing. They receive the partial portion with gratitude, but when they raise their hands to ask for the missing piece (as with Luke's dinner) they are told, "You're good." When these questioning parishioners insist that there's more, they are told again and again, "You're good."

This is happening in many churches and God is "not good" with this. When the church gives partial portions of the Word of God while withholding, denying, or unhitching from the whole, it's not good. Churches that offer God the Father and Jesus the Son, but reject, quench, and block the Holy Spirit are not good. Those who claim to be Christian organizations but deny the fire and the power of God, are not good. In 2 Timothy 3:5, we are warned about those who have a form of godliness but deny the power of God, or the fire of God. We are instructed clearly in verse 5, "And from such people, turn away!"

A partial portion of what God has for you is not good. Having a form or an appearance of Christianity but denying His fire and His power in demonstration is not good. The fire of God is necessary in each of our lives to bring glory to His name. Sadly, many decide to leave the Holy Spirit out, put the fire out, and just serve what they deem is best, telling the people emphatically, "You're good." Religion always rises against—and in place of—the Holy Spirit and His fire. Many respected ministers today choose to quench the Holy Spirit and put out any fire because it's uncomfortable, uncontrollable, and inconvenient. All the while, they keep telling you, "You're good". Without the fire of God, we are *not* good, and we know it.

We hunger for more. We desire more. Reading the Bible, we scratch our heads and ask, why aren't we on fire like these early church disciples? Why don't we see the fire and the power of the Holy Spirit in our lives today? Those are appropriate questions to ask. The answer is clear: you have been denied the truth about God's Spirit, His fire and His power that is available for you in this day and in this time. So go ahead and ask for more. Run from people who lack the fire of God and tell you that "you're good" without it. Without the fire of God that comes with the empowerment of the Holy Spirit, we are not experiencing true Christianity. We have been led into the cold, dead, dry bondage of religion. Jesus came to set us free from this and to send the fire of the Holy Spirit upon our lives.

DO NOT SETTLE FOR LESS

Regularly, we have people from around the nation who reach out to us in desperation. They see and hear what God is doing in our church and in other churches that are ablaze with the fire of God. They see it, hear it, and feel it in the messages, the worship, and the praises of His people. When hearts are ablaze with His fire, you can hear the roars of praise coming from His praise-filled warriors. Recently, a member of our media-tech team was mixing the sound for our worship service at Radiant. Following the service, he said that the roar of praise coming from the congregation was so loud he had a difficult time mixing the sound for the worship team and band. The fire of God burned so hot that the loud praises of His people were louder than the worship leaders. When you are on fire for God, you are not silent. The prophet Jeremiah said God's Word was like a fire shut up in his bones that could not be contained. Because of that fire, Jeremiah could not keep quiet.

Passionate followers of Jesus know that there's more and they long for the fire of God in their churches. Hungry for more, they set their own hearts on fire for God but then they go into churches where the fire of God is quenched. They attend services that are slick, entertaining, and very comfortable for the person who doesn't want the fire of God. They leave thankful for the portion they received but still hungering for what is missing.

God's fire is falling today to consume and burn within the hearts of those who are hungry for more. Denomination has nothing to do with this. God's fire is in the heart of every person and church that is fully surrendered to Him and desperate for His holy fire. We urgently need the fire of God to burn up and destroy the bonds of lukewarm "Christianity." Radiant is a church that desires and longs for the fire of God to fall upon every heart. We will not settle for less. This is what the church has been mantled for and therefore, this is what we contend for. We are called to be carriers of His fire and to see it spread across the nation and around the world. So, when religious people try to convince you that you're good without the fire of God, remember 2 Timothy 3:5. Run from dead, lukewarm religion and run into the holy fire of God. The Holy Spirit is speaking clearly right now. Do not settle for less in your own life. And do not settle for less in a church.

A MESSAGE TO SINGLES

This is an important message for single men and single women also: don't settle for less in a husband or in a wife. Set yourself on fire with the fire of God and keep His fire burning in your life. Then pray for and wait for God to bring you a spouse who has the fire of God in their life.

Todd and I celebrated 31 years of marriage this year. We met in church (a church on fire) where we were both passionately following Jesus, and His fire was burning in our hearts. Todd told our daughter Faith recently, "God knew your mom had to have a radical, passionate, spirit-filled, fire-baptized husband because she would have been miserable married to someone without God's fire."

When I became a Christian and before meeting Todd, I would occasionally date, and I could tell right away if they had the fire of God or if they "were good" without it. If the fire of God was missing and there was no desire to acquire His fire, it was over. There was no reason to pursue a relationship any further. When I met Todd Hudnall, immediately I saw the fire of God in him.

Science tells us that fire attracts fire. When you place two candles together, the flames draw in cold air from below and around them and create heat. While one burning candle produces light and heat, two burning candles together create a much greater source of heat, light, and power. Deuteronomy 32:30 states that with God as our Rock, one can put a thousand to flight, but two can put ten thousand to flight. When two fire-baptized followers of Jesus come together with God as our source, His power is exponentially increased for His glory.

PURIFYING FIRE

"So because you are lukewarm (spiritually useless), and neither hot nor cold, I will vomit you out of My mouth [rejecting you with disgust]. Because you say, 'I am rich, and have prospered and grown wealthy, and have need of nothing,' and you do not know that you are wretched and miserable and poor and blind and naked [without hope and in great need]," (Revelation 3:16-17 AMP).

These are the words of Jesus and must be deeply considered and embraced by every follower of Christ. He lovingly, clearly, and firmly says to us: if you are lukewarm (lacking His fire), if you claim you are just fine without His fire, you are wrong. Jesus makes it clear that lacking His fire is not good and then He tells us what to do in verses 18-19: "I counsel you to buy from Me gold that has been heated red hot and refined by fire so that you may become truly rich; and white clothes [representing righteousness] to clothe yourself so that the shame of your nakedness will not be seen; and healing salve to put on your eyes so that you may see. Those whom I [dearly and tenderly] love, I rebuke and discipline [showing them their faults and instructing them]; so be enthusiastic and repent [change your inner self—your old way of thinking, your sinful behavior—seek God's will]."

We must ask for and allow God's fire to purify us. His purifying fire is necessary to burn away all that would hinder and hold us back from having hearts on fire for Him. Chuck Pierce, in his book, *Rekindling the Altar Fire,* writes: "God uses us as instruments of His glory only after purifying us and refining us with His fire, awakening our spirits and renewing our lives to truth. Breaking the chains of sin and burning down our egos." Jesus is calling on each of us to come to Him and ask Him for the pure spiritual gold that comes only from the refiner's fire.

Have you ever heard people talk about cold, dead churches and refer to them as the "frozen chosen"? Well, that's exactly what happens when the fire of God has gone from a church or from a person's heart. There was a man in our church who was once on fire for God. He wrote songs, played instruments, used his voice and his life to honor God and carry God's holy fire. He was a firebrand for God. However, sadly, somewhere along the way he stopped kindling the fire of God. The enemy came into his life so subtly, through an adulterous woman that Proverbs warns so severely against. Satan used that woman to put out the fire of God in that man's soul. His soul burned for a woman who was not his wife; and you cannot have God's fire and the fire of wickedness at the same time. Sin is like a heavy, wet blanket thrown upon the fire of God in a person's soul. Satan uses seduction and sin like a fire extinguisher in the Christian's life.

Sadly, that man never returned to lay out the pieces of his life on the altar and wait for God's fire to fall upon his heart. His marriage was destroyed, and his wife and his kids were devastated. The last I heard from him, this man who, at one time, had the fire of God burning in his soul, had given himself over to sin and his life was destroyed.

Recently, in prayer I received another vision from the Lord. I saw a wall of fire that formed a circular hedge around the church. The orange and red blazing flames were high and forming a perfect circle. Great peace and comfort overwhelmed me as the Holy Spirit assured me that when we run to His holy fire, we are protected from the destruction of hell's unholy fires. Then I saw a young woman step out of the flames and walk away. I knew this woman was a passionate follower of Jesus and my heart was deeply troubled as I watched her walk away. The Holy Spirit revealed to me her heart that was like a white, burning, hot coal. Yet, as she walked away from His fire, her heart grew cold, hard, and black. Grief stricken, I cried and prayed that she would turn back and be restored to her former state of burning for Jesus.

A CONSUMING FIRE

Hebrews 12:29 says that our God is a consuming fire. If you will wait upon the Lord daily, surrender your life to Him, lay the pieces of your life on the altar, and cry out for His holy fire to fall upon your heart, you will be protected from hell's destroying fire. Run to Him and allow His holy fire to consume you for His glory.

We have lived through some horrific fires in the state of Colorado and experienced the reality of a consuming fire. Fire can start very small and then quickly grow, increase, and consume everything in its path. Dear friends and members of our church Bruce and Joy Reasoner lost all their earthly possessions in a major forest fire several years ago. The Lord was with them through that fire, and they clung to Him through the devastating loss. We all watched how He so lovingly and faithfully carried them and restored them. His grace is sufficient for us, and He is with us when we walk through the fire.

A short time ago, I was driving toward our neighborhood where there was a lot of smoke from a fire. Evacuations were beginning, and police cars were blocking streets so that no one could go in that direction. As I began praying about these fires, the Holy Spirit spoke to me, "What would you do if your house and your possessions were lost in a fire?" I replied, "Well, it would be very hard and very painful, but this world is not my home and my joy and hope is not in my possessions." Then I began quoting Isaiah 43:2, "When you walk through the fire, you will not be burned; the flames will not consume you." I literally quoted those verses from Isaiah and said, "Lord, as long as You are in the fire with us, we will not be destroyed."

A few hours later, I received a phone call and was told that church members Angie and Adam Rutowski's home was surrounded by a massive fire. They sent a frightening picture of the mammoth flames encircling their home. The photo painted a very ominous reality that looked inevitable. We began praying and alerted our prayer ministry team to pray, and God performed a miracle.

Angie was trembling as she Face-Timed us. She walked around their property showing us the burn from their neighbor's house, the field, and everything consumed in its path right up to their home. What we saw next was astonishing. It was as if someone had drawn a line about 15 feet out all around their home, the building next to the house, and their propane tank. The massive flames had burned everything around and up to them and were stopped. We were in awe of what the Lord had done and how He had protected them, their home, their outbuilding, and their propane tank from the fire. We praised Him and thanked Him for His amazing hand of protection and intervention.

This is a powerful picture of us and an important reminder that we will all go through "the fire" in this life. We will all go through hard things and hell will try its very best to take us out. But as long as we kindle the fire of God in our hearts and keep it burning brightly, our God, Who is a consuming fire, will be with us and we will not be destroyed. When you are consumed by Him, you will not, and cannot, be destroyed by the evil one. The only way to fight hell's destructive fires is with God's holy fire.

LIGHT IN THE DARKNESS

"The Lord went before them by day in a pillar of cloud to lead the way, and by night in a pillar of fire to give them light, so as to go by day and night" (Exodus 13:21). His fire lights our way in and through the darkness. Without His fire, the darkness will continue to infiltrate our hearts, our homes, our churches, and the earth.

Darkness is increasing as we draw near to the day of Christ's return. A church without the fire of God will not prevail against the darkness of culture and society. When the fire of God is absent, the people cannot see through the darkness, and they will stumble and fall into the snares of the enemy. Without His fire lighting up the night, the darkness becomes all that they can see. When this happens the darkness becomes what they are familiar and comfortable with. Therefore, they compromise and embrace the darkness.

Without God's fire, we lose our way. A teenager in our congregation shared her horror over the views of her classmates in a high school sociology class. This young freshman was attending the first class of the year and what she experienced was heartbreaking. The teacher engaged the students in a lively discussion about different people groups and their beliefs and values. When the spirited teens discussed Christianity, their perspective was alarming. The student from our church was horrified when the overwhelming attitude in her peer group was that Christianity was a joke. One student boldly stated, "We know the Christians in our school, and they aren't any different from the rest of us; so why would we need Jesus?"

When the fire of God is in a student's heart; it is evident in their life and others can see the difference. When there is no fire, there is no passion and where there is no passion, there is no light. Therefore, those in darkness look at them and see only a reflection of darkness. When there is no difference between the life of a Christian and the life of an unbeliever, there is no light to lead them to Christ. We must have the fire of God in our lives, lighting up the darkness and pointing the way to Jesus. A Christian without His fire is a Christian without His light; and without His light, we will be consumed by the darkness. The world must see the light of God shining in our lives into the darkness. We must have His fire to light up the night and lead people to Him. Hunger for His fire. Desperately desire, draw near, and let His fire consume you for His glory. His fire in you will keep you armed, engaged, and protected in the fight. The fire keeps you going when the battle intensifies.

CHAPTER SEVEN

BATTLE READY

IN THE YEAR 480 B.C., a massive Persian army of 300,000 soldiers invaded the nation of Greece. Only 300 Spartan warriors guarded the narrow pass of Thermopylae. They alone stood in the way of the destruction of Athens and the future of Western Civilization. The conflict was vicious and bloody. In the end, the Persians won the battle but for three days the overwhelmingly outnumbered Spartan warriors fought with such strength, courage, and sacrifice that their valor inspired the entire Greek nation. This moral victory led to the Greeks ultimately winning the Greco/Persian war.[32]

Historians consider the Spartan warriors the bravest, fiercest fighting force in ancient Greece and one of the most prepared armies in history. Military experts of that day considered a single Spartan warrior to be more valuable in battle than several soldiers from any other state. The Greeks had such absolute confidence in their army that they did not build a wall around their city, claiming their warriors were their wall.[33]

The key to the superiority of Sparta's warriors was their extensive preparation. At seven, a Spartan boy was required to enter a rigorous state-sponsored military preparation program called the Agoge. The Agoge instructed the trainees on duty, discipline, and endurance. During the training, the Agoge subjected them to a grueling schedule, austere conditions, and constant physical competition.[34] They were born, bred, and arduously trained for fighting. When forced into combat, these warriors were battle-ready.

WE ARE WARRIORS

As fire-baptized followers of Christ, we also must prepare for battle. Today's American culture stands in direct opposition to every biblical value we hold, and we must respond to it by being tenaciously committed to the Word of God. When we are, hell will hammer us with massive resistance and relentless attacks. We will find ourselves in the middle of a battle and a personal fight. We must engage in the conflict, or we will live in defeat.

In our day, one of the greatest weaknesses of the American church is failing to recognize we are at war and that Christ has called us to be spiritual warriors. In 2 Timothy 2:3-4, the Apostle Paul metaphorically refers to this calling when he writes, "You therefore must endure hardship as a good soldier of Jesus Christ. No one engaged in warfare entangles himself with the affairs of this life, that he may please him who enlisted him as a soldier."

Charles Pope has compared the mindset of churches to either a cruise ship or a battleship.[35] It is an appropriate metaphor. Christians with a cruise ship mentality focus on how they are being served, if their needs are being met, the quality of entertainment they are receiving, and how comfortable they are. In contrast, the crew on a battleship focuses on "a clear and noble mission" that requires commitment, sacrifice, and determination. On a battleship, it is all-hands-on-deck to defeat the enemy. Followers of Christ are not called to be on a pleasure cruise, but are at war against the world, the flesh, and the devil. We are warriors.

Besides 2 Timothy 2:3-4, Paul also describes followers of Christ as warring soldiers in Philippians 2:25 and Philemon 2. In 1 Timothy, Paul instructs young Timothy to wage a good warfare and to fight the good fight of faith (1 Tim. 1:18, 6:12). We are soldiers under our commander-in-chief, Jesus Christ. As warriors, Christ expects us to conduct warfare. As those who have been born of the Spirit, "fight" is part of our spiritual DNA.

The Apostle Paul explains the nature of this war in his second epistle to the Corinthians. He writes, "For though we walk in the flesh, we do not war according to the flesh. For the weapons of our warfare are not carnal but mighty in God for pulling down strongholds, casting down arguments and every high thing that exalts itself against the knowledge of God, bringing every thought into captivity to the obedience of Christ." (2 Cor. 10:3-5)

We live in a physical and material world. However, our battle is not material, but spiritual. The real conflict is a battle of thoughts, mindsets, and worldviews. A worldview is a prism by which we look at everything in our lives. The Barna Group recently completed a study that found the church in America is flunking the worldview test, as only 9% of professing Americans had a biblical worldview. Even among born-again Christians, only 19% had such an outlook on life.[36] This means that instead of using the Bible as a lens for thinking about the world, they have taken on the viewpoints and the mindset of the godless culture. Rather than operating according to godly wisdom, they operate according to what the Apostle James calls earthly wisdom that is sensual and demonic (James 3:15).

A stronghold over a person, a church, or a city is the predominant worldview and mindset that controls them. It is a citadel of lies, deceptions, and distortions that have formed how people think and how they live. In the personal warfare in which we are engaged, Paul tells us that our responsibility is to identify strongholds, pull them down, and bring every contrary thought captive.

In this book, our focus is on joining the cosmic spiritual battle between the kingdom of God and the forces of evil that oppose the expansion of God's kingdom. Paul gives us an overview of this war in the heavenlies and our responsibility to be battle-ready.

"Finally, my brethren, be strong in the Lord and in the power of His might. Put on the whole armor of God, that you may be able to stand against the wiles of the devil. For we do not wrestle against flesh and blood, but against principalities, against powers, against the rulers of the darkness of this age, against spiritual hosts of wickedness in the heavenly places. Therefore take up the whole armor of God, that you may be able to withstand in the evil day, and having done all, to stand. Stand therefore, having girded your waist with truth, having put on the breastplate of righteousness, and having shod your feet with the preparation of the gospel of peace; above all, taking the shield of faith with which you will be able to quench all the fiery darts of the wicked one. And take the helmet of salvation, and the sword of the Spirit, which is the word of God; praying always with all prayer and supplication in the Spirit, being watchful to this end with all perseverance and supplication for all the saints." (Eph. 6:10-18).

Our strength for battle is not found in our own stamina or prowess, but our strength is found in Christ. In the spiritual battle we are engaged in, our eyes must be fixed on Jesus, or we will become weary and discouraged in the fight (Heb. 12:3). Jesus Christ has already thoroughly defeated Satan and all His demonic forces (Col. 2:15), and we proceed out from His victory to enforce His rule.

THE ARMOR OF GOD

Infused with the Lord's strength, we are to put on our armor and take up our weapons. This armor and our spiritual weapons are necessary for battling our invisible foe. For though human beings may oppose us, our warfare is not against personalities but against principalities. There is an unseen maleficent adversary who has a strategic battle plan to bring about our destruction (John 10:10, 1 John 5:8). In response, the Lord has given us His armor that, when employed, will enable us to stand against the Evil One victoriously. Every piece of armor can be found in the person of Jesus and in the Word of God. The finished work of Jesus Christ on the cross and His Word are the two great keys to our victory. Let's briefly examine each piece of armor.

The **belt of truth** holds all the other armor together. This can be seen in 1 Peter 1:13 where Peter tells us, "Gird up the loins of your mind." In the ancient world, people wore long flowing robes. If you were planning to do physical activity, whether manual labor or fighting as a soldier, you would pull up your robe and cinch it tight with your belt. As we have seen, our thoughts can be dictated by circumstances, situations, emotions, and lies. We need the objective truth of God's Word to pull all our thoughts together and not allow them to trip us up. Jesus is the truth, and His word is truth (John 1:17, 14:6, 17:17). It is critical that God's Word becomes the highest authority in our life and we become firmly established in a biblical worldview. Even if everything else in our life seems to be falling apart, the belt of truth allows our armor to stay in place, enabling us to always be ready for battle.

The **breastplate of righteousness** protects us from the guilt, shame, condemnation, and sense of unworthiness that often sidelines believers. Our adversary will attack our identity and condemn us. In those times, we must know that though our own righteousness is insufficient (Is. 64:6), we have been made the righteousness of God in Christ (2 Cor 5:21). Jesus is our righteousness (1 Cor. 1:30, 2 Cor 5:21) and it is revealed to us in the Scripture (Rom. 1:17). Through God's Word, we develop humility, boldness, and confidence in being the righteousness of God in Christ.

The New International Version of Proverbs 4:23 says, "Above all else, guard your heart, for it is the wellspring of life." The breastplate of righteousness also provides that inner discernment of what is righteous and unrighteous and what we should refuse to allow in our minds and heart. This includes the movies we watch, the internet sites we visit, and even the music we listen to. We had a young woman in our congregation who had come to our church and been set free from suicidal thoughts and feelings of depression. She was taught to guard her heart and was very diligent about it. Sometime later, she moved to another city and fell into her old habits of not guarding her heart. This young lady stopped going to church and discontinued the habit of spending time in the Scripture. She laid down her breastplate of righteousness. She began listening to dark music again and started spiraling back into her former depression. Thankfully, she returned to Radiant for ministry, received godly counsel, and put back on her breastplate of righteousness once again, enabling her to regain her former freedom.

Our feet are to be shod with the **gospel of peace**. In this battle, we must know the war between God and us is over, and we now have both peace *with* God (Rom. 5:1) and the peace *of* God (Phil. 4:6). In addition, we are to have peace with our fellow Christian soldiers (1 Thess. 5:13). Jesus is our peace (Eph. 2:4) and we appropriate that peace through the gospel (Eph. 1:13, 6:15). The gospel is found in God's Word. In Colossians 3:15-16, Paul explains that when we let the Word of Christ dwell in us richly, the peace of God will rule in our hearts (Col. 3:15-16).

We are to take up the **shield of faith**, with which we can quench all the fiery darts of the wicked one. Biblical faith is not having faith in our faith, but it is faith in God's faithfulness. It is faith in our Lord Jesus Christ (Gal. 2:16) and that faith comes by hearing the Word of God (Rom. 10:17). The more we saturate our lives with God's Word, the more our faith in God grows.

On our heads, we put on the **helmet of salvation.** The word salvation is the Greek word *SOZO*, and it is pregnant with meaning. It includes the idea of salvation, deliverance, healing, and wholeness.[37] God's desire is for us to be free, healed, and whole. With the helmet of salvation on our head, this piece of armor particularly deals with the salvation of our mind, will, and emotions. The saving of our soul is accomplished through the work of Jesus (Acts 4:12) and occurs as we submit ourselves to God's Word (James 1:21). As we renew our mind to God's Word, we experience freedom, healing, and wholeness in our soul (Rom. 12:2).

Finally, Paul tells us that the **sword of the Spirit** we wield is the Word of God (Eph. 6:17). The Apostle John also makes it clear that Jesus is the Word (John 1:1, Rev. 19:13). God's Word is not only our protection and defense, but it also our offensive weapon. We have seen that in the wilderness, Jesus used the Scripture as an instrument of attack in defeating Satan (Matt. 4:1-11, Lk. 4:1-13). We are to counter every worldly and Satanic lie with the truth of God's Word.

The whole armor of God can be summed up in two ways: putting on Christ (Rom. 13:14), and abiding in His Word (Rom 13:14, John 8:31). Yet, it's not enough to just know the word; we also must live out the truth of Scripture in our lives. The Apostle James commands, "But be doers of the word, and not hearers only, deceiving yourselves" (James 1:22). This reminds me of a comment of our son Luke when he was just three years old. He had been disobedient, and Kelly warned him that if he persisted, she would have to discipline him with a spanking. Luke immediately grabbed his toy Captain America shield, placed it on his rear and said, "I have my shield of faith on my bottom, and I come against you with the Word of God." Kelly said, "Son, that will not work when you are being disobedient." It is not enough to put on our armor, we must also be obediently surrendered to Christ for our weaponry to be effective (James 4:7).

When we lived in Texas, I had a normal routine of getting up early, running on our treadmill, taking a shower, getting dressed, and spending time in prayer and the Scripture. One weekend, I had exercised and taken a shower and was getting ready for my day. All I had on so far was my underwear, when I experienced the need for a drink of water, so I slipped off for the kitchen to quench my thirst. What I didn't realize was that a friend of my wife's had stopped by our home to see her. At the same time, I was leaving the bedroom in my BVD underwear, and was headed for the kitchen, she was leaving the kitchen and moving toward the bathroom. We met in the hallway. When she saw me, she threw her hands up over her eyes, broke her glasses, screamed, and ran back to the kitchen. I also let out a scream and scampered to my bathroom. As she ran into the kitchen, she was crying out, "Aah, I saw my pastor naked, I saw my pastor naked, I saw my pastor naked." Kelly immediately ran into the bedroom and yelled, "Todd Hudnall, what were you doing running through the house naked?" I looked up at her pathetically, and said, "I had on my BVD's." Kelly burst out laughing. It kind of bothers me that when women think of me in my underwear, they either scream in terror or laugh hilariously. Ever since that day, I always leave the bedroom with more on than my BVD's.

Some followers of Christ leave the house in the morning with nothing on more than their spiritual BVD's. We fail to put on the armor of God by spending time in God's Word and in prayer. I have a feeling when the angels see us, they cry out to God, "Aah, I saw that Christian naked, I saw that Christian naked, I saw that Christian naked." We cannot afford to be without our armor because we are in a battle.

In the next verse of the passage, Paul tells us what the armor is for: "Praying always with all prayer and supplication in the Spirit, being watchful to this end with all perseverance and supplication for all the saints" (Eph. 6:18). We are armored up to engage in the spiritual arena of kingdom-advancing prayer.

PRAYER IS ESSENTIAL

Prayer is an essential part of the Christian's life. It has been said that for the follower of Christ, prayer should be as natural as breathing and as enjoyable as eating. A. J. Gordon rightly stated, "You can do more than pray after you have prayed, but you can never do more than pray until you have prayed." We have more to do than pray, but we must never neglect the importance and efficacy of prayer.

Jesus is the ultimate example. He saw prayer as of such supreme importance that He put it above other things. You would think the more sinless and perfect one became, the less prayer one would need. But Jesus, though He was the perfect Son of God, was also totally dependent on His Father. Jesus received His strength and direction from His Father in prayer, therefore He prayed more than anyone had ever prayed. Jesus came to minister to people, having already prayed. We should do the same.

In its most basic sense, prayer is talking with God. Prayer is seen in various forms throughout the scripture. Verse 18 of Ephesians 6 in the New International Version reads, "And pray in the Spirit on all occasions with all kinds of prayers and requests." We are armored up to employ all kinds of prayers. All kinds of prayer would include *worship* (Ps. 148:13), *praise* (Heb. 13:5), *thanksgiving* (Ps. 100:4), *confession* (Ps. 32:5), *consecration* (Matt. 26:26-27), *lament* (Ps. 88:1-7), *waiting* (Ps. 130:5, Hab. 2:10), *listening* (John 5:30), *petition* (Eph. 3:14-21), *declaration* (Is. 44:24-26), *reflection* (Ps. 139:23-24), and *intercession* (Col. 11:9-12 1 Tim. 2:1-4). They are all important.

Paul's command in verse 18 to pray in the Spirit is significant. In 1 Corinthians 14:14-15 Paul writes, "For if I pray in a tongue, my spirit prays, but my understanding is unfruitful. What is the conclusion, then? I will pray with the spirit, and I will also pray with the understanding. I will sing with the spirit, and I will also sing with the understanding." In these verses, Paul defines "praying in the Spirit" as praying in tongues. Rather than being a merit badge of spiritual attainment, speaking in tongues is a tool for spiritual refreshing (Is. 28:11-12), worship of God (Acts 2:11, 10:46), personal edification (1 Cor. 14:4, Jude 20), and a means of praying when you do not intellectually know how to pray (1 Cor. 14:2, Rom. 8:26).

One day, Kelly was vacuuming the carpets in our home when she suddenly was overwhelmed with a need to pray for her sister, Robyn. She tried calling her, but there was no answer. She did not know how to pray, but she knew she had to pray. Kelly got on her knees and began praying in other tongues. After a long season of prayer, she felt a release and went on about her activity. Later, she talked to Robyn, who told her a horrifying story. While driving on a lonely stretch of Kansas highway with her young son strapped in his car seat, an 18-wheel vehicle suddenly tried to pressure her off the road. This went on for some time. Robyn was terrified and did not know why this truck driver was driving is such a threatening way. Then suddenly, he stopped his wild antics and continued down the road ahead of her. Kelly asked when all of this happened, and it was the very time she had felt the burden to pray for her sister. Neither of them believes this was a coincidence and we believe Kelly's intercession in the Spirit is what changed the actions of the truck driver.

Praying in the Spirit undoubtedly includes praying in other tongues, but it has another dimension. Today's English Version translates Ephesians 6:18 as, "Pray on every occasion, as the Spirit leads." As we pray, if we will ask for the Holy Spirit to lead us in prayer, He will give us direction in our praying. If the Spirit is leading us, it will always be in alignment with the Scripture (John 16:13) and will probably include declaring God's Word over the situations we are praying for. As we do, prayer becomes an exciting adventure of praying God's will and purpose on earth as it is in Heaven.

KINGDOM ADVANCING PRAYER

We can see the power of the prayers of God's people throughout the Hebrew Scriptures. In prayer, Abraham bargained with God over the terms of the destruction of Sodom. Elijah prayed and called down fire from heaven and then ended a 3 ½ year drought. Regarding this event, James tells us the effectual, fervent prayer of a righteous person avails much (James 5:16). Hezekiah brought his enemies' threatening letter to the Lord and his prayer changed the history of Israel and Assyria (2 Kings 19). Having read the scrolls of the prophet Jeremiah that God's will was for Israel to return to their homeland after 70 years, Daniel prayed God's will would be accomplished, and it was (Daniel 10). God decided, but it seems His people on earth had to pray His will into existence.

We can conduct spiritual warfare in prayer. Speaking of having a wartime mentality in prayer, John Piper said, "The number one reason prayer doesn't work for saints is because we have taken a wartime walkie-talkie and turned it into a domestic intercom." As we cry out to God for the lost, a spiritual battle will ensue for the souls of lost men and women. As we call out to God for the persecuted church, angels will strengthen them, protect them, and give them supernatural grace to endure and to be a witness. As we plead with God for our nation and its leaders, God will raise up some and pull-down others. He will turn the tide of events and even block, or ensure passage of legislation that would have turned out differently had we not prayed. This kind of prayer demonstrates a Holy Rebel's rebellion against the status quo. It is declaring things are not the way God intends them to be and, through prayer, we will see them changed.

STRATEGIC FASTING

Fasting should be a regular habit of every believer's walk with God. In Matthew 6:16-17 Jesus said to His followers, "When you fast." Jesus had an expectation his disciples would fast. We are to fast as a regular spiritual discipline according to our personal convictions. Fasting in both the Old and New Testament had to do with setting aside food, and I would not want to minimize this strict definition of fasting. Yet, there are some who, because of health concerns, cannot abstain from food and others who miss out on the full spiritual benefits of fasting by missing the deeper purpose.

I've found a helpful definition of fasting is that a fast is setting aside other things to wholeheartedly pursue God. Many lack a hunger and a thirst for God because they are so full of other things that their desire for God has become satiated. Fasting is refusing to satiate our natural hunger for God with substitutes. We put aside those pursuits and distractions so that we can pursue God. We do not just fast—we replace whatever we are fasting with a pursuit of God through prayer, time in the Scripture, solitude, and other spiritual disciplines. So, a legitimate fast can include setting aside television, social media, or a myriad of other activities that dull our hunger for God. Nonetheless, there is unique spiritual value to fasting from food.

One of the great benefits of fasting food is its humbling effect on our hearts. In Psalm 35:13 David said, "I humbled myself with fasting." It is one reason fasting supercharges our prayer life—because pride is the number one hindrance to prayer. Both Peter and James tell us God resists the proud, but He gives grace to the humble. Fasting is God's appointed way to humble ourselves. You could call fasting a hunger strike against pride. Going without food does a work in our life to strip away our pride.

In 1 Kings 21:27-29 wicked King Ahab heard the words of a prophesy of judgment against him. In response, "...he tore his clothes and put sackcloth on his body, and fasted and lay in sackcloth, and went about mourning." God's word to Elijah concerning the King was, "See how Ahab has humbled himself before Me? Because he has humbled himself before Me, I will not bring the calamity in his days." To that point in Israel's history, Ahab was the most evil king the nation had known and his actions in the death of a man named Naboth were horrific. But God responded to him in compassion and mercy when he humbled himself with fasting. How much more will the Lord respond to the humility of His blood-bought church when we humble ourselves before Him?

In Matthew 17, the disciples of Jesus cannot cast a demon out of a child. But Jesus commands the Spirit to leave the boy and the young man is made whole. The befuddled disciples asked why they could not cast it out. Jesus said it was because of their unbelief. Then he added in Matthew 17:21 that, "This kind does not go out except by prayer and fasting." There are some strongholds that only come down, some bondages that are only broken, and some mountains that only moved when our prayer is accompanied by fasting. In his beautiful teaching on fasting in Isaiah 58, the prophet speaking for the Lord declares, "Is this not the fast that I have chosen: To loosen the bonds of wickedness, to undo the heavy burdens, to let the oppressed go free, and that you break every yoke?" (Is. 58:6).

We regularly fast as a spiritual discipline. Then there are strategic times of fasting, where you are not just fasting as a disciple, but you are fasting for a strategic purpose. Often in the Scripture, God's people fasted in times of spiritual necessity or intensity. There are things that will happen through prayer and fasting that will never happen through prayer alone. When the church in Antioch was at a critical juncture of shifting to be a missionary-sending church, they sought the Lord through prayer and fasting (Acts 13). When King Jehoshaphat and the nation of Judah were being invaded by enemy armies, the king called the nation to fast and seek the Lord (2 Chron. 20). The time that Queen Esther planned to risk her life by going before the king of Persia to persuade him to intervene for the Jewish people, she called for every Jew to hold a fast on her behalf (Esther 4:16). In desperate need of a revelation from God, Daniel fasted certain foods to pray and seek after God (Dan. 10). This setting aside of certain foods has been called a Daniel Fast, and many have found great value in it (Dan. 1). Mario Murillo jokingly told us, "A true Daniel fast is what the lions did when Daniel was in their den."

With the boldness of a general, our friend Lou Engle said, "We have taught a generation to feast and play but the times demand we fast and pray." Lou has seen multitudes of believers respond to his call to fasting and prayer. Explaining the value of fasting, he wrote, "Fasting is a God-given means to return to first love encounter with Jesus. Fasting softens the soul, that impertinent part of your being that demands the feeding of the flesh, that surly part that wants its own way that demands to be fed. The fleshly soul is a hard taskmaster. In fasting, we command the soul to obey the spirit. In fasting, the food lusts, sexual desires, and greed grasps are diminished and the spiritual desires inside us become strong."[38]

At Radiant Church, every winter and fall, we call on our congregation to participate in an extended time of prayer and fasting. We see these times as a spiritual surge, and have seen breakthroughs where sin has been exposed, critical prayers have been answered, and clear direction has been given. Personally, the greatest spiritual breakthrough in my life followed a 21-day juice fast. Shortly afterwards, I had an encounter with Jesus Christ that transformed the rest of my life. Kelly and my dramatic calling to Radiant Church came through a prophetic dream that occurred during a 40-day liquid fast. The biggest ministry breakthrough during our time at Radiant Church followed a church-wide 40-day Daniel Fast.

God has given us His armor to engage in spiritual warfare through prevailing prayer and strategic fasting. Every Holy Rebel is called to take up our supernatural weapons and enter the realm of the spirit world through faith. We can join together to demolish demonic strongholds, counter Satanic schemes, and overthrow the kingdom of darkness as we see God's kingdom come on earth as it is in heaven.

CHAPTER EIGHT

PRAISE FILLED WARRIORS

FRIDAYS ARE OUR sabbath day in the Hudnall home. This is the day each week that we honor the Lord through rest, worship, and spending time together. God commands us in Exodus 20 to keep a sabbath. This is one of the Ten Commandments, and He instructs us to honor Him by working six days and resting from our labor and work on the seventh. We are also told to teach our sons and daughters to honor the Lord by keeping a sabbath.

Our kids are teenagers now and this has been our family tradition since they were small. Admittedly, life can become so busy that it's difficult to keep a sabbath. Yet, God's way is still the only way that leads to life, blessing, and lasting fulfillment. One of the best things about a sabbath day is setting aside more time for family prayer, praise, and worship. Two important weapons for every Holy Rebel are our prophetic decrees and our shouts of praise. Occasionally, we will decree the names of God, and praise Him for who He is. Each member of the family takes turns leading in praise to God using one of His biblical names, for example, Jehovah Rohi: the Lord our Shepherd, Jehovah Shalom: the Lord our peace, Jehovah M'Kaddesh: the Lord our Sanctifier. One day, something unique happened when it was my turn to lead in praising God for being Jehovah Nissi: the Lord our Victor. It was as if the Holy Spirit hit a divine pause button and spoke these words into my spirit: "This is for you. This is for now. Do not miss this. I am Jehovah Nissi, the Lord your Victor". The tangible presence of God seemed to wrap around me as I decreed His name and praised Him for being the Lord our Victor.

AN UNUSUAL BATTLE

This experience compelled me to open the Bible to Exodus 17, where God is exalted as Jehovah Nissi. As I read these verses again, I could sense the Holy Spirit highlighting the holy text and bringing it to life. The whole time I was reading and digging deeper into the text, there was a sense of urgency and a whisper that seemed to be repeated over and over: this is for you, this is for now, don't miss this.

Exodus 17 gives us the account of when the Lord gave Moses and His people victory over the Amalekites. This was a very unusual battle in that Joshua was leading the army in the battle against the Amalekites, while Moses stood on the mountain with his arms lifted to God. As long as Moses' arms were lifted high in praise, reverence, and supplication to God, they prevailed against their enemies.

However, as the battle waged on, he became tired, weak and his arms began to fall. When his arms became too heavy and lowered, the Israelites would begin to be overcome by their enemies. Therefore, Aaron and Hur came alongside Moses to stand with him, support him, and hold up his arms. This act resulted in God giving Joshua and his men the victory over the Amalekites. Moses then built an altar to God to worship Him and praise Him for His victory. He named the altar Jehovah Nissi: the Lord is my banner, or the Lord is my Victor.

Throughout history, enemy forces have arisen to defeat and destroy God's people. These battles have been waging since Lucifer was cast out of heaven and the battle continues today. Enemy forces driven by the powers of darkness have conspired relentlessly to kill, steal, and destroy (John 10:10). Hatred, persecution, and the execution of the people of God continue to increase around the world (Ps. 2). Therefore, be sober, vigilant and on the alert because you have a real adversary and he has declared war.

We must remember that He is Jehovah Nissi, the Lord our Victor. When the forces of hell press in against you, lift your arms like Moses, fix your eyes on Jesus and decree His victory over your life, family, city, church, and nation. This is how we fight our battles. We destroy the enemy as we lift our hands in surrendered praise to the God who has already won the victory.

ALWAYS BATTLE READY

Recently, I was alone with our daughter when she became quiet and contemplative. The silence was broken when she spoke these words: "Mom, I have this funny feeling inside that even as bad as things seem in the world right now, we are in the still before the storm; and things are about to get a lot worse." When Faith spoke those words, I could feel God's presence with us again tangibly. As I pondered her statement, I heard these words in my spirit loud and clear: things are bad in the world right now and they're going to get worse. You must be prepared, and you must prepare your family and church to be battle-ready.

This is our present reality as Christians and as American Christians. We have never been this way before. We have entered a whole new battle and it will require a shift in the way we have thought, reacted, lived, and behaved. It will demand that we pay close attention to what God is saying to us now, in order to be battle-ready. Jehovah Nissi, the Lord our Victor, is with us, and He is calling us to prepare for battle now and remain steady in the days ahead.

The Lord, Jehovah Nissi, was with Moses and Joshua in Exodus 17. The same God is with us now and He is leading us in a similar way. God is calling us now to a very unusual war strategy in which we are commanded to put on garments of praise in place of the spirit of heaviness (Isaiah 61).

We are called to be praise-filled warriors who take up the weapons of the high praises of God in our mouths and a double-edged sword in our hands (Psalms 149:6). This is one of the most important messages to the church today. This strategy is very unusual by man's standards, and it makes little sense to the natural-thinking person. Human reasoning cannot grasp the concept of the "high praises of God" in our mouths being a credible war strategy against the enemy.

AN UNUSUAL STRATEGY

One of the greatest war stories in history is in 2 Chronicles 20. God's people were coming under attack by a multitude of enemies that had joined forces against them. Their situation looked hopeless as they faced the massive armies that were advancing to destroy. Their king, Jehoshaphat, humbly cried out to God with sincere desperation: "We don't know what to do but our eyes are on You" (v.12). God heard his cry and answered by giving them the most unusual war strategy. He did not tell them to sharpen their swords and take up physical arms. He did not tell them to fight in their own strength and power. Nor did He tell them to shrink back in cowardice and fear, or to go hide in the caves. He called them to take up the spiritual weapon of praise and go to war against the enemy as praise-filled warriors.

This made little sense in the natural realm, to the carnal mind or to human reasoning. That's not how men fight wars if they desire victory. Jehoshaphat was a man like us and we can be sure that he had a mental war in his own mind that had to be won first. The carnal mind always wars against the Spirit of God. There were certainly those among them who would have heard this unusual strategy and risen to oppose it vocally. Jehoshaphat would not only have to win the battle to overcome the doubts in his own mind but would also have to overcome the opposition of those within his own camp.

THE UNUSUAL WEAPONS OF PRAISE

2 Chronicles 20:1-4 explains what happened and how Jehoshaphat and the people of God responded: "It happened after this that the people of Moab with the people of Ammon, and others with them besides the Ammonites, came to battle against Jehoshaphat. Then some came and told Jehoshaphat, saying, 'A great multitude is coming against you from beyond the sea, from Syria; and they are in Hazazon Tamar' (which is En Gedi). And Jehoshaphat feared, and set himself to seek the Lord, and proclaimed a fast throughout all Judah. So, Judah gathered together to ask help from the Lord; and from all the cities of Judah they came to seek the Lord."

Jehoshaphat did what we all must do when hell is coming against us, our family, our health, or our nation, to destroy us. The report had come to him, and it was very distressing. Yet, his first response was the most important step towards victory. He set himself to seek the Lord. And second, all the cities of Judah came together to seek The Lord.

Jehoshaphat sought God first. He didn't seek the counsel of his officers first. Turning to other sources and seeking worldly wisdom on how to fight this battle was not his response. This is pertinent to us now because we are in a veritable war today. The battle has intensified; yet many are choosing to live in denial and go on with life as usual. Pretending that everything is as it always has been and ignoring the advancing enemies will only prove to be disastrous. Ignorance is not bliss when you are in a war against the powers of hell.

While it is vital that we engage in the battle today by taking a righteous, bold stand for freedom, life, morality, and truth, we must not put the cart before the horse. As biblical citizens, we must engage in what is happening in our nation. Anyone who tells you otherwise is not following biblical truth. Jesus calls us to be salt and light in the world. Christians are called to be influencers in business, government, culture, education, science, medicine, media, and entertainment. Jesus said, "you are the light of the world…" Light is not effective until it goes into the darkness, exposes, and overcomes the darkness. Yet, if we become passionately engaged in these various arenas without first seeking the Lord and following His strategy, we will be destroyed.

General George Washington knew this, and that's why he called upon the nation to seek the Lord in a time of crisis. President Abraham Lincoln called the nation to fast, pray, repent, and seek the Lord. Since the founding of this republic, much like Jehoshaphat, Americans and our leaders have humbly and corporately appealed to God in times of crisis. One constant in America's presidents (until recently) has been their acknowledgement of our desperate need to seek the God of the Bible. When we refuse to do this, we operate in the power of our flesh rather than the power of God. The arm of the flesh or the power of man is no match against the powers of hell and forces of evil. We must become one nation under God, once again, or we are through. The remnant of God's people today must recognize our desperate time of crisis, humble ourselves, seek His face, repent of our own sinfulness, turn from wickedness, and cry out to heaven for mercy and intervention (2 Chron. 7:14).

SEEK GOD IN COMMUNITY

Jehoshaphat led the way by example in seeking God first. Then, all the cities of Judah came together to seek the Lord. The power of unity exponentially increases when we come together to seek God's mercy, grace, and intervention. In Hebrews 10:24-25 (NIV), God emphasizes the necessity of corporate worship: "not giving up meeting together, as some are in the habit of doing, but encouraging one another and all the more as you see the Day approaching." There is a supernatural increase of divine power when God's people come together to worship, pray, and praise Him.

Closing churches during the COVID-19 pandemic led to a surge in on-line worship services and a major decline in church attendance. While on-line services are more convenient and widely accepted, joining in person to seek the Lord and worship Him corporately cannot be replaced. This aspect of the Christian life is so important to God that He instructs us to not forsake it and to gather even more often as the day of His return draws near. By all means, let us not forsake coming together with other believers for worship, praise, prayer, and seeking the Lord in biblical community.

PARENTAL GUIDANCE

2 Chronicles 20:13 highlights another important strategy for victory: "Now all Judah, with their little ones, their wives, and their children, stood before the Lord." They sought the Lord together as families, with their children. Clearly, part of God's strategy for victory is to make weekly church attendance a priority for you and your family.

Parents are in a serious battle today, and it is our kids who are in the enemy's crosshairs. We must lead our children well in this war. Parents and grandparents must lead first by example. Let them see you seeking God first. Live out the godly example before them of putting God first in everything. The greatest influence in your family is you. When they see and hear you praying, praising, seeking God first, making His Word highest priority, committed to His Kingdom, and His people, they will most likely follow your example. Throughout my life, I have heard the phrase that "it's more caught than taught." You must live it out before them and then also bring your family together to seek Him with you. This, of course, begins at home praying together, worshipping together and reading God's Word together. Victory in the battle begins with making God, His Word, and His mission the highest priority in your life and in your family.

The argument that it's too hard or that we are all too busy to come together to seek the Lord is a strategy of hell. God does not lie, and He has promised that His grace is sufficient for us. Determination, steadfastness, and a desire to win the war against the strategies of Satan are where it must begin. Pushing through our flesh, the carnal nature, natural reasonings, and the noise of the world is the next step. Remembering that we can do all things through Christ who strengthens us and relying on the power of the Holy Spirit brings the follow-through that leads to victory.

America was once a Christian nation and as long as the nation's families were centered on Christ, church, and biblical morality, we remained strong. We were the land of the free and the home of the brave. However, as the nation's families have turned away from God and church is no longer valued in America, we have become wicked, corrupt, weak, and compromised. The only hope for victory in this war is for God's people to humble themselves, turn from their worldly ways and seek His face again, both individually and in biblical community (2 Chron. 7:14). We must come together again with our families and worship God corporately with other believers. God moves in power when we come together in unity. However, there is one addendum that must be included with this strategic priority. Beware of and avoid compromising churches, pastors and leaders who are influenced by the world, embracing anti-biblical values and the "woke" agenda.

SEEK HIS FACE

"Seek the Lord and His strength; seek His face evermore!" (1 Chron. 16:11, Ps. 105:4) Praise-filled warriors seek God's face, rather than His hand, or His back, or just His blessings. Ponder this with me for a moment: what does it mean to seek someone's face? First, when you seek someone's face, you must draw near to them. You must be up close and personal in order to seek, study, and search their face. You draw near to gain insight, wisdom, and understanding about that individual. This is how we are counseled about coming to God. We must take the time necessary to draw near to Him, study Him, know Him, learn His ways, hear His voice, and live to please Him alone.

God speaks to the prophet in Jeremiah 1:7-8 and tells him: "You shall go to all to whom I send you, and whatever I command you, you shall speak. Do not be afraid of their faces, for I am with you to deliver you." Too often we start out seeking God's face and looking to Him for His counsel and guidance, and then we get sidetracked by the faces of people. We may begin in obedience to God's truth and counsel, but the disapproving faces of men, women, religion, culture, family, and friends often causes believers to shrink back in fear. Demonic forces of hell advance with intimidation, telling us to back down, back off, and be silent. One mega-church pastor justified his silence in the face of the cultural roar by stating that we don't need cultural warriors, we just need to love our neighbors. It grieves my heart to see Christian leaders choose to be silent when their voices are needed the most. Love for our neighbors is what compels us to speak up and confront evil. We must boldly oppose the forces that are destroying our fellow Americans precisely because we do love our neighbors.

God's sons and daughters have often been stripped of their power to influence people with God's truth because they have been afraid of the "faces" of culture, religion, and the radical leftist agenda that is powered by hell to enslave a nation and take it down. God is sounding the alarm now and saying to His praise-filled warriors, "do not be afraid of their faces." Seek His face and live to please only One. The Spirit of God is shouting this message to the church today: stop seeking the approval of man, culture, and the world. Seek God first and seek His face. This is vitally important because if you are looking to the faces of the world, you will become a modern-day golden calf worshipper.

Golden calf worshippers or idolaters are all around us, everywhere we go. Golden calf worship is more prevalent among God's people today than it was in Moses' and Aaron's day. Moses went to the mountain to seek God's face and to receive God's counsel and directives. But Aaron looked at the people and searched their faces to receive his orders and directives and it led to idolatry. The people didn't approve of the way Moses always sought God for His direction, and they complained. Aaron wanted to please the people, so he complied and out came the golden calf.

The truth is that you cannot be a people pleaser and a God pleaser at the same time. Yet many pastors, leaders, and people in the body of Christ today are just like Aaron and the Israelites. Here's how it works: people complain about the God of the Bible. They argue He is too harsh in the Old Testament, and they don't approve of His narrow ways. Therefore, pastors and leaders who are seeking the approval of man decide that they must avoid the portions of the Bible that people disapprove of. Many well-known pastors and leaders today have joined with this idolatrous message, saying that we need to unhitch from the portions of scripture that people don't like. While this may sound like a good idea, it is not a God idea. God is God. Man is not God. Any man, woman, or group that rises up to determine what is accepted and what is not accepted in the Word of God is an idolatrous golden calf worshiper. It matters not how popular they may be in the eyes of the world, the culture, and the church. This is a serious issue today and the idolatry in the church is leading many into darkness.

I know many people who identify as "Christian," yet they insist that God's standards are too high and must be lowered to appeal to the world and culture. Many "Christian" denominations have stopped seeking God's face, and they have given in to the world and are worshipping around their "golden calves." Determined that they know better than God, they have embraced what God has declared to be sin, calling good evil and evil good. This is a very prominent trend today and must be avoided at all costs by every true follower of Jesus Christ.

It will cost you something to follow the one true God of the Bible. Choosing to follow Jesus means we may lose followers on social media platforms who disapprove of biblical standards and truth. Following Jesus will almost always result in the loss of relationships, friendships, and even family ties when we are forced to choose whom we will worship. Loyal followers of Jesus must decide if they are going to worship the God of the Bible and seek His face, or seek the world's approval, creating a false god that the world, culture, religion, and our peers are more comfortable with.

This is "Idolatry 101." When people, culture, society, and religion don't like what God says, they edit out those things that make them uncomfortable. Rejection from culture, disapproval of society, along with rebukes of religious figures are all fueled by the evil one to force God's people into submission. Therefore, many turn away from seeking God's face and they turn to seek after the approving faces of man. Since culture and society do not approve of the God of the Bible, some religious authorities and leaders create a "god" in the image of man, and in the culture's likeness. Then they present their "god" to be worshipped, embraced, and celebrated, claiming they are worshipping the one true God. Yet, they are simply deceived and tricked by the enemy, just like Aaron was in his day. They claim the title of "Christian" while celebrating the sin that God condemns, in order to gain the approval and acceptance of the masses. Then they call it something that sounds impressive and righteous, so that many will grab hold of it in ignorance. They call it progressive Christianity and they work to marginalize, silence, and destroy those who still seek God's face like Moses did, and refuse to bow to their golden calves. Religion hates those who refuse to worship the golden calf and those who rise to demolish the modern-day idols in the church. Psalm 27:8 is the cry of God's true worshippers: "When You said, 'Seek My face,' My heart said to You, 'Your face, Lord, I will seek.'"

God's praise filled warriors cannot be moved by the faces of men, women, culture, and the world.

A CALL TO ACTION

"Let the high praises of God be in their mouth, and a two-edged sword in their hand" (Ps 149:6). Christian, this is your call to action in this battle. This call to action will not make sense to your carnal mind or to natural human reasoning. Your flesh and carnal nature will fight against the call to put on garments of praise and let the high praises of God be in your mouth. The powers of darkness will come against you with powerful forces of apathy, complacency, fear, intimidation, resistance, and pride. God calls us into the battle with the high praises of God in our mouths, just as He did in 2 Chronicles 20. Therefore, it is no surprise that the forces of hell are against us to subdue us and keep us from the high praises of God.

Satan's minions work to convince God's warriors that this is silly and that their high praises will not make a difference. Amazingly, we have had people tell us throughout the decades that taking part in high praise just isn't their thing. Yet, to be clear, God makes no exceptions, excuses, or exemptions for any of us. He does not call His people to go to war with the high praises of God in their mouths, while making a list of exemptions for those who claim that it just isn't "their thing." Interestingly, the same people who claim this is not something that they feel comfortable doing will jump, shout, yell, scream, dance, and cheer for their favorite sports teams.

Dear Holy Rebel warrior, it's time to crucify our flesh, our carnal nature, human reasonings, and go to war with the high praises of God in our mouths. God clearly explains that when we do this, we are taking up a massive double-edged sword in our hand against the powers of darkness. In this unusual battle, we are called to go to a whole new level of praise. I believe it is important for every follower of Jesus to seek His face and sincerely ask Him to show them what the "high praises of God in their mouth" sound like and look like. Personally, as I read and re-read the Bible, I am deeply moved and inspired by David and how he danced, sang, shouted, and praised God loudly, with total abandon. God records in scripture that David was a man after IIis own heart. When we ponder the victory of Jehoshaphat in 2 Chronicles, the enemy armies were thrown into confusion when they heard the high praises of God in the mouths of His people. Undoubtedly, they were singing and shouting loudly as they went into battle. Why? Because this was a war, and the shouted praises of God's people are a mighty weapon of war. While some may be uncomfortable with the high praises of God's people, it is imperative that we get over the inhibitions and strongholds of pride or religion that keep us from entering this next level of high praise. The walls of Jericho came down when the shouted praises of God's people went up (Judges 7:20). At midnight, Paul and Silas praised God so loudly in jail that all the prisoners could hear them. When the high praises of God went up from their mouths, the prison doors broke open, the shackles fell off them, and the jailer got saved.

God has called us to raise our weapons of praise to a whole new level in this battle. So, let's drop all the excuses and praise Him with all our heart, soul, mind, and strength. Praise Him with shouts of joy. Praise Him with dancing. Clap your hands, lift them high in praise to the Lord Jehovah Nissi. He is our victory in the battle.

Evangelist Mario Murillo spoke to me recently about what God is doing today and how it differs from the past. He described the Jesus movement in the 70's and how God inspired the intimate, deep worship songs that drew the masses in. Today God is moving again, but we are in a new era and God is moving in a new way. When Jesus came the first time, He came as the precious, spotless Lamb, to offer His life upon the cross for our sins. Now we are preparing for His return in these last days, and this time He's coming as the mighty, roaring Lion of Judah. The sound that He is releasing through His people in this hour is the roar of the Lion of Judah.

When you are in a war, you need bold generals who will lead you to victory. God's generals don't seek religion for their orders; they seek His face and His voice. God's generals don't seek the world and culture for their direction. God's true generals are listening to the rhythm of the Lion of the tribe of Judah. We are marching to His sound and, like Jehoshaphat in 2 Chronicles 20, it's a distinct sound. It is, in fact, the sound of the high praises of God in the mouths of His people. This sound is different, but if the church ignores the sound of the Lion of Judah in this time of war, we will be defeated.

God sounds the alarm, and He is calling us into the battle with His high praises in our mouths. If the church ignores this call and goes back to our old methods—church as usual and what is familiar—we will be destroyed. The new sound of high praise coming from God's warriors differs from what many are used to. Religion does not approve of the new sound of praise coming from His warriors. So don't look at their faces; instead, seek His face and advance with the high praises of God in your mouth and a double-edged sword against the powers of hell in your hand. The religious leaders did not like the sound of the Lamb of God when He came the first time. Assuredly, the religious leaders now will not approve of the sound of The Lion of Judah as He is coming this time. We have experienced this firsthand as lead pastors of Radiant.

One newcomer to Radiant was extremely excited about the amazing worship experience and the passionate praises of God coming out of the congregation. This person was deeply moved by the dynamic praises of God's people and His presence among us. She and her husband repeatedly expressed that they didn't know churches like this existed. But another first-time guest to the same service was not so enthusiastic about the high praises of God among His people. This person stated emphatically that they were uncomfortable with this kind of fervent praise. Two guests were thrilled by the sound of praise-filled warriors, while another was uncomfortable with it. The roar of the Lion of Judah through the praises of His people is thrilling to one and uncomfortable for another. I've learned that God is not interested in making us comfortable. He consistently calls us out of our places of comfort in order to advance His Kingdom and plunder hell's strategies.

So let the high praises, the loud praises, the exuberant shouts of praise, be in your mouth as a mighty holy weapon against the enemy's plans. This simple strategy will bring you victoriously through the battles that hell wages against you. So, take up your weapon of praise and go to war! Let the powers of darkness hear your Holy Rebel war cry. The high praises of God in your mouth are a double-edged sword against the enemy.

POSITION YOURSELVES

2 Chronicles 20:17-19 testifies how the people of Judah, under Jehoshaphat, positioned themselves as praise filled warriors. Verse 19 says they praised God with voices loud and high. The rest of this amazing war story is that they went out into the battle with the high praises of God in their mouths and the Lord destroyed their enemies before them. This was indeed an unusual battle. The battle was the Lord's, yet God's people played a significant role in securing the victory. This story would have ended differently if God's people had decided that God's call to action was silly or foolish. Jehoshaphat could have ignored God's call to go into the battle with

the high praises of God as their weapons of war. The Israelites could have done what was familiar and made more sense to them. They could have just done what all the other tribes and nations did in times of war. They could have done their own thing, gone the way of other kings and armies, and they would have been destroyed.

Now we must choose, as Jehoshaphat did in his day. We are in a serious battle for our families, our nation, and for future generations. The kingdom of darkness is real, and hell is advancing in fury to eradicate the family, the church, this nation, and this generation of young people. The church (the body of Christ) is in a very precarious position today. The choice to seek the faces of men for direction, wisdom, and approval will lead to utter devastation. In this critical hour, we must choose to seek the face of God and answer His call to action as praise filled warriors. Let go of the old wineskins of religion and move forward with the high praises of God in your mouth and a double-edged sword in your hand. This call to action will not make sense to the world or to the religious. God's ways are not our ways, and His thoughts are higher than ours. Today, He is calling you to action by telling you to position yourself as a praise filled warrior and advance with His high praises continually on your lips.

CHAPTER NINE

HOLY SPIRIT ADVANTAGE

A S HOLY REBEL warriors we are engaged in a cosmic battle, warring against the world, the flesh, and the devil. The powers arrayed against us are formidable, but we have the upper hand. Followers of Christ have been given the authority of Jesus through His shed blood and finished work on the cross. We have also been given the Holy Spirit advantage.

Volumes have been written concerning the Holy Spirit. The purpose of this book is not to do an in-depth study of the person and work of the Holy Spirit but to see you experience Him personally and to see Him work through you. The Holy Spirit isn't simply a force or power, but He is God, the third member of the Trinity. The Scripture clearly teaches that God is one in substance but three in person: Father, Son, and Holy Spirit. All that is essentially true of the Father is true of the Son and is true of the Spirit because the Holy Spirit is God. And just like the Father and the Son, the Holy Spirit is a person with all the attributes of a person. He has a mind, will, and emotions (1 Cor. 2:10-11, 1 Cor. 12:11, Eph. 4:30). The Scripture tells us the Holy Spirit loves (Rom. 15:30), He can communicate (Acts 13:2), and He can enjoy relationship (Phil. 2:1; 2 Cor. 13:14). Just like the Father, and the Son, the Holy Spirit longs to have a relationship with you.

We find the person of the Holy Spirit throughout the scriptural narrative from the beginning of Genesis to the end of the book of Revelation. The Bible begins with the Holy Spirit making everything out of nothing. The Psalmist reinforces the Genesis account, telling us, "God sent forth

His Spirit and everything was created." In Job 33:4, Elihu tells us, "The Spirit of God has made me, and the breath of the Almighty gives me life." To fulfill His will, we see the Spirit of God coming upon numerous followers of Yahweh under the Old Covenant.

Other than with King David, the Spirit would come upon individuals for a season, and for a purpose. When God's purpose was accomplished, the Spirit would be lifted. Isaiah told us that when the Promised Messiah, the Anointed One, came, God's Spirit would rest upon Him (Is. 11:1-2, 61:1-4). Ezekiel spoke of God's Spirit moving from the Holy of Holies, out of the temple and away from Jerusalem (Ezek. 10-12). Israel then experienced a lack of God's manifest presence and prophetic voice for 400 years until the Holy Spirit came upon a young virgin girl in Nazareth. Within Mary's womb was conceived the Anointed One, the God-man, Jesus Christ.

When John baptized Jesus in the Jordan River, Luke says the Holy Spirit descended on Him in bodily form like a dove (Lk. 3:22). The Spirit then led Jesus into the wilderness (Lk. 4:1), where He defeated Satan and returned from the wilderness in the power of the Spirit (Lk. 4:14). Immediately afterward, Jesus stood in the synagogue in Nazareth and quoted the Messianic prophecy of Isaiah 61:1-2, "The Spirit of the Lord GOD is upon Me, Because the Lord has anointed Me To preach good tidings to the poor; He has sent Me to heal the brokenhearted, To proclaim liberty to the captives, And the opening of the prison to those who are bound; To proclaim the acceptable year of the Lord."

Peter tells us in Acts 10:38 that God anointed Jesus of Nazareth with the Holy Spirit and power, which enabled Him to go about doing good and healing all who were oppressed by the darkness. And indeed, blind eyes saw, lame legs walked, deaf ears heard, and captives were set free. No one has ever operated in miraculous signs and wonders like Jesus did, as the Father gave Him the Holy Spirit without measure (John 3:34).

Can you imagine daily walking and talking with the physical Jesus and being able to observe His supernatural ministry firsthand? Not only were they living during the time of the Messiah, but they could also have a front-row seat to see His ministry and could even participate in it (Matt. 10:1). As God's Holy Rebel warrior, Jesus was devastating the kingdom of darkness. The disciples who followed Jesus were living the dream, and they could not imagine how it could get any better. But, in anticipation of His crucifixion and resurrection, Jesus said in John 16:7, "Nevertheless I tell you the truth. It is to your advantage that I go away; for if I do not go away, the

Helper will not come to you; but if I depart, I will send Him to you." Jesus spoke of His leaving and said it was to their advantage. It must have sounded like a cruel joke. That may be why Jesus reinforced his statement with, "I tell you the truth," because what He said is so utterly shocking and completely counterintuitive.

A modern-day sports example may be helpful. Let's pretend you are a passionate Green Bay Packers football fan, and it is the year 2007. Your star quarterback Brett Favre announces, "I tell you the truth. I am leaving the Green Bay Packers football team, but it is to your advantage that I go away." As a fan, you question how this could be. Favre has been your football Messiah. He has won three NFL Most Valuable Player Awards and taken your team to the Promised Land, a victory in the Super Bowl. It would sound impossible that his leaving could be to your team's advantage. What you could not have known was that Aaron Rodgers was prepared to take the helm as your new quarterback, and that he would win four NFL M.V.P. awards and take your team back to victory in the Super Bowl. Rodgers would successfully continue to lead your team for more than a decade after Favre retired.

In a far greater way, Jesus' leaving to make way for the era of the Holy Spirit was an advantage to the people of God, because the Holy Spirit would be to all followers of Christ what Jesus was to the disciples. While his physical body limited Jesus to one geographic location, the Holy Spirit is everywhere, and while Jesus only came alongside the disciples, the Holy Spirit miraculously comes inside and empowers believers to do what they could never do in their own ability.

If we are to be part of a holy rebellion against the world, the flesh, and the devil, we must know how to experience the Holy Spirit advantage. We do so by honoring the Holy Spirit, depending on Him, and making room for Him.

It is critical that we learn to honor the Holy Spirit. Unfortunately, too many followers of Christ do not even acknowledge the Spirit. For some believers, He has become the ignored member of the Trinity. Yet, in John 14:16-17, Jesus said, "And I will pray the Father, and He will give you another Helper, that He may abide with you forever--the Spirit of truth." For the word *another*, John could have used the Greek word *HETEROS*, which means "one of another kind," but the Greek word chosen in this verse is *ALLOS*, which means "another of exactly the same kind."[39] Jesus is saying, the Holy Spirit will be another, just like Me.

This again affirms that the Holy Spirit is a person and, as the disciples had a relationship with Jesus when He walked the earth, we now have a relationship with the Holy Spirit. You could say the Holy Spirit is Jesus in another form. Now, instead of God coming among us in human flesh, we have God coming among us in the Spirit. This means that much of what we know of Jesus, we can transfer to the Holy Spirit (John 16:14).

Through the New Birth, followers of Christ have come into a relationship with the Father and the Son, yet we have a special intimacy with the Holy Spirit. The Message Translation quotes Paul's benediction beautifully: "The amazing grace of the Master, Jesus Christ, the extravagant love of God, the intimate friendship of the Holy Spirit, be with all of you" (2 Cor. 13:14). We should be so thankful for the grace given us by Jesus Christ that allows us to receive everything God has provided for us (Eph. 2:8-9). It is wonderful to know that God loves us with an unconditional love that pursues us (John 3:16). We should also experience a close, personal relationship with the Holy Spirit (Eph. 4:30).

You can have an intimate friendship with the Holy Spirit. He is to you what Jesus was to His disciples. That is why it is important to be aware of, recognize, talk with, and go through life in a relationship with the Holy Spirit. You can see this lived out in the book of Acts. In Acts 8:29, Philip the Evangelist hears the Holy Spirit's voice telling him what to do. The reason Philip knew the voice of the Holy Spirit was because he had spent time with Him. I could be at a gathering with a dozen people who are conversing in such a way that their voices become indistinguishable. Yet, if my wife Kelly walks in the room and says something, I am immediately aware of her voice. I know her voice because I know her and have spent a great deal of time talking with and enjoying life with her.

In Acts 15, the church leaders are having a critical meeting about the future of the church. After much strong discussion, they come to a consensus. James, the leader of the church in Jerusalem, says of their decision, "For it seemed good to the Holy Spirit, and to us" (Acts 15:28). The Holy Spirit was their senior partner. He made known His will, and they were confident of it, because they walked closely with Him. As we continue on in this battle, we must learn to pause and wait for His Divine guidance and direction.

. . .

DEPEND ON THE HOLY SPIRIT

We should honor the Holy Spirit, but we should also learn to depend on Him. In John 14:16 we saw the Holy Spirit called "another Helper." The King James Version calls Him "another Comforter." We derive this Greek word *PARACLETE* from a Latin word that means "strengthener."[40] This title implies that the Holy Spirit should be our help, comfort, and strength. For help, strength, and comfort, people turn to all kinds of things. This includes people, entertainment, alcohol, narcotics, sex, and even food. In fact, there is a type of food that is called "comfort food" because people actually find psychological comfort from it. A good question for us is this: when you are in trouble, when you are hurting, when you are in need, where do you turn for help and comfort? We should foremost find our comfort, our help, and our strength in the Holy Spirit.

In the book of Acts, despite some persecution, the young church found its Jerusalem confines comfortable and familiar. Acts 2:41-47 describes this church as a utopian community. There was a possibility that in its comfort, the church would have stayed a sect within Judaism and never have fulfilled their Lord's commission to go and make disciples of all nations (Matt. 28:19-20). The early church in Jerusalem needed Saul of Tarsus to make things uncomfortable so they would step out of their comfort zone and learn to depend on the comfort, help, and strength of the Holy Spirit to fulfill their mission (Acts 8:3-4).

If you are experiencing discomfort in your life, this principle may explain the reason. The Lord may put you in a position of need so that you will pursue the comfort and the help of the Holy Spirit. I certainly believe it explains what has been happening in the church in America. For most of our history, it has been comfortable being a Christian in our nation. In fact, affiliating as a Christian often provided privilege and advantages. That day is past. Now you may be mocked, persecuted, fired, or cancelled by standing for biblical values. The secular elites have marginalized our Christian faith to the fringes of society. Candidates for public office have been made suspect and have been severely questioned for taking their faith seriously. It is no longer comfortable to be a true follower of Christ in America. Maybe God is saying it is time we find our comfort, help, and strength in Him, so that we can live as Holy Rebels, shining as lights amid this crooked and perverse generation (Phil. 2:15). We need the Holy Spirit's direction and His empowerment to fulfill our calling. Thankfully, He promised to provide what we need if we will depend on Him. The Holy Spirit will provide the advantage we need to be Holy Rebels against the powers of darkness, but we must learn to depend on Him and to make room for Him.

MAKE ROOM FOR THE HOLY SPIRIT

Jesus' disciples were witnesses to the extraordinary miracle of His walking on water. This event can be instructive in understanding our relationship with the Holy Spirit, as we find in the accounts in Matthew, Mark, and John.[41] Each of the Gospels gives us a different perspective on the life of Jesus. Their accounts are not contradictory but *complementary*, and each approaches the life of Jesus from a different angle.

After feeding the 5,000, we read, "Immediately Jesus made His disciples get into the boat and go before Him to the other side, while He sent the multitudes away" (Matt. 14:22). The word "made" is strong. It means to compel or force someone to act.[42] Jesus then sent the multitude away and found a solitary place where He could pray. By going across the Sea of Galilee, the disciples were obeying the command of Jesus. They sailed into a storm at sea, not knowing that there would be difficult times ahead. As with the disciples, sometimes Jesus will lead us into a challenging situation. God does not tempt us but will lead us into situations we cannot handle or overcome on our own (James 1:13, Luke 4:1-2).

While the disciples were traveling into the middle of the sea, they entered strong winds that tossed the boat. Jesus led the disciples into rough waters, where they would need Him. We all face opposition and challenges in life, and, for some of us, we do not realize how badly we need the Lord until we really need the Lord. But Jesus is always there in our time of need. Somewhere between 3 a.m. and 6 a.m., Jesus went out to them, walking on water (Matt. 14:24-25).[43] Matthew explains, "And when the disciples saw Him walking on the sea, they were troubled, saying, 'It is a ghost!' And they cried out for fear" (Matt. 14:26). They did not initially recognize the figure on the sea as Jesus. "But immediately Jesus spoke to them, saying, 'Be of good cheer! It is I; do not be afraid'" (Matt. 14:27).

I believe that is a picture of how we should approach the Holy Spirit. Remember, He is to us what Jesus was to his disciples. We recognize our need for help. The Holy Spirit wants to be a part of our life, but we are afraid. He tells us, "It's okay; it's Me; don't be afraid." It is essential to get over any fear you have about a relationship with the Holy Spirit. Do not be afraid of His presence, conviction, leadership, or power. Remember, He is our helper.

JESUS' LESSONS ON FAITH

Peter audaciously asks, "Lord, if it is You, command me to come to You on the water" (Matt. 14:48). Peter sees what Jesus, the Lord of all creation, is doing, and He asks Jesus if he can do it too. Some of us are the same way because we see how Jesus lived and ministered in the New Testament, and we would say, "If you enable me, I can do it too."

Jesus' answer to Peter is one simple word: "Come." When Peter stepped out of the boat, he walked on water to go to Jesus (Matt. 14:29). Like Peter, when Jesus tells us to come and be like Him, He will enable us to do it. Jesus said as much in John 14:12: "Most assuredly, I say to you, he who believes in Me, the works that I do he will also do and greater works than these he will do because I go to My Father."

By the power of the Holy Spirit, we can do what we could never do in our own ability. We can forgive those who wrong us, love our enemies, live a holy life, winsomely and boldly share our faith. We can have joy, peace, and patience and be faithful, gentle, teachable, and self-controlled. The Bible calls it walking in the Spirit (Gal. 5:16, 25). We can do the same miraculous works that Jesus did and even greater works, according to John 14:12. It requires getting out of the boat, taking steps of faith, and seeing the Holy Spirit enable us to do the impossible.

That is what Peter did; he walked on water for a time. He did what he could never do on his own. He was not walking on water as much as he was walking by faith in the words of Jesus. But Matthew tells us, "When he saw that the wind was boisterous, he was afraid; and beginning to sink he cried out, saying, 'Lord, save me!'" (Matt. 14:30). While Peter kept his eyes on Jesus, he could do the impossible, but he felt he was in over his head and began to sink when he looked at the conditions and circumstances.

We do the same. I have often stepped out in faith to obey Jesus and realized, "I'm in over my head." I look at the circumstances and situations and get my eyes off Jesus and His Word, but He is still there for me. "And immediately Jesus stretched out His hand and caught him, and said to him, 'O you of little faith, why did you doubt?'" (Matt. 14:31). Notice that even when we fail, stumble, and are sinking, Jesus is there for us.

Peter's problem was that he had doubts. Doubt comes from the word "duo" or "double." It is to be double-minded. The Apostle James explains that those who doubt are like a wave of the sea, blown and tossed by the wind. They become unstable in all their ways (James 1:6-8). Peter tried to look to Jesus but was distracted by the surrounding circumstances. We can only keep our minds fixed on one thing at a time. In the battles we face, we must always keep our eyes on Jesus (Heb. 12:2, Col. 3:2).

As the narrative continues, Peter and Jesus get into the boat (Matt. 14:32). Remember, the Holy Spirit is to us what Jesus was to the disciples. The Holy Spirit comes to help us, strengthen us, and enable us to do what we could never do in our own ability. As the disciples made room for Jesus, we must make room for the Holy Spirit.

The boat the disciples were in would have held about 15 people.[44] There were 12 disciples, and Jesus made 13. There also would have been other items they were carrying. So, there was enough room for Jesus, but there was not an abundance of room. For Jesus to get into the boat, they would have had to make room for Him. The disciples would have had to reposition themselves and their things so Jesus could come aboard. But they made room, and John tells us, "Then they willingly received Him into the boat" (John 6:21).

The same is true for us in our relationship with the Holy Spirit. If we want the Holy Spirit to be active in our lives, we must "willingly receive" Him into our lives and make room for Him. We may have to rearrange our schedules so there is enough margin to follow His promptings to help someone in need or share our faith with a neighbor. There will be a need to let Him interrupt our devotional times to speak to us and direct our Bible study and prayer time. We will have to make a margin in our finances so that we have the financial capacity to give money to a mission project, a person in need, or some other kingdom purpose when the Holy Spirit directs us. I've learned to carry extra cash in case the Spirit prompts me to give to someone in need. In church worship gatherings, room must be made in the service for the Holy Spirit to move and have His way. We have learned the necessity of making room for the Holy Spirit's guidance and leadership. Some of the worst mistakes I've made in life and ministry could have been avoided if I simply had stopped to listen to the Holy Spirit.

Years ago, I heard a church leader say that we should "pray first."

- Before you start your day, pray first.
- Before you eat a meal, pray first.
- Before you travel, pray first
- Before you go to work or school, pray first
- Before you go into a meeting, pray first
- Before you send a text or email, pray first
- Before you go to bed at night, pray first

Part of praying first is stopping to make room for the Holy Spirit, so we can listen for His voice, through His promptings, leadings, and whispers.

Matthew concludes his account by telling us, "Then those who were in the boat came and worshiped Him, saying, 'Truly You are the Son of God'" (Matt. 14:33). When we make room for the Holy Spirit and obey His voice, it will result in God being glorified, which is exactly what the Holy Spirit came to do (John 16:14). It is not primarily about us making it through the storm or even walking on water, but about Jesus being glorified.

THE MINISTRY OF THE HOLY SPIRIT

The Holy Spirit will minister in our lives to *convict* (John 16:8-11, James 2), *convert* (Rom 8:16), *teach* (John 14:26), *sanctify* (2 Thess. 2:13, 1 Thess. 5:23), *empower* and *guide* us to bring God glory (John 16:14). All these ministries are vital, but we will focus on His guiding and empowering works.

THE HOLY SPIRIT GUIDES

Jesus told His disciples, "When He, the Spirit of truth, has come, He will guide you into all truth" (John 16:13a). When first visiting a part of the world that is new to them, people will hire a guide to help them navigate this unfamiliar territory. Living as a Holy Rebel in this fallen world can seem like unfamiliar territory. We must let the Holy Spirit be our guide into the unknown. He will guide us with His promptings and leadings. The more we walk with Him, and the better we come to know Him, the easier it is to discern His guidance. We live in a time when it is essential that we learn to hear the voice of God and follow the leadership of the Holy Spirit.

Before the days of GPS, when I was driving in an unfamiliar area, I would ask someone if I could follow them to our destination. I am a person who can tend to be navigationally challenged. I would follow them closely because I knew I could be in serious trouble without someone leading me. That is true for navigating life. To do it effectively, it is imperative to stay close to the Holy Spirit and remain attentive to His leading. Paul warns us not to quench the Spirit by refusing to follow His leadership (1 Thessalonians 5:19).

People wonder how they can know if the guidance they are receiving is truly from the Holy Spirit. I have learned to ask these three helpful questions for confirmation.

First, "Does it line up with the Scripture?" Jesus said the Holy Spirit "will guide you into all truth" (John 16:13). The Spirit will always lead and guide us in line with the revealed truth of Scripture. There is much unbiblical nonsense that is too often attributed to the Holy Spirit.

Second, "Is it holy?" Remember, He is the *Holy* Spirit. He will always lead us on paths of righteousness and a highway of holiness. The Holy Spirit will never have us do anything sinful but will always take us to deeper levels of holiness.

Finally, "Does it glorify Jesus Christ?" The Holy Spirit did not come pointing to Himself; He came to point us to Jesus. When we enter a relationship with the Holy Spirit, He will bring us closer to Jesus and allow our lives to bring Christ more glory.

To be a holy rebel against the forces of darkness, we must experience a close, intimate relationship with the Holy Spirit. We need to allow the Holy Spirit to lead us, guide us, and empower us to do the works of Jesus. For this to happen, we must draw near to Him, follow His promptings, and expect His gifts to flow through us. When they do, captives will be set free, the lost will come into the kingdom, Satanic strongholds will be toppled, and Jesus Christ will be glorified.

EMPOWERS

Before His ascension to the Father, Jesus told His disciples, "But you shall receive power when the Holy Spirit has come upon you; and you shall be witnesses to Me in Jerusalem, and in all Judea and Samaria, and to the end of the earth" (Acts 1:8). Jesus told His small group of disciples to go out into a world where they have no influence, affluence, or political clout and be witnesses to His life-transforming Gospel. The Scripture narrative describes a group that was often foolish, quick-tempered, and cowardly. But they obeyed Jesus, went out from there, and saw their ministries transform the world. Only the empowerment of the Holy Spirit can explain the world-changing impact of their lives. The key was that Jesus did not just send out His disciples; He sent them out with the Holy Spirit. The Holy Spirit reshaped a cowardly band of disciples into a group that boldly proclaimed the Gospel and turned the world upside-down (Acts 17:6).

The Holy Spirit, who was *with* Jesus' followers before the cross (John 14:14), came *into* those original disciples after Jesus' resurrection (John 20:22), and then came *upon* them on the day of Pentecost (Acts 1:8, 2:1-4). God still works in the same way today. The Holy Spirit is *with* the unconverted before salvation, drawing them to Christ (John 6:44). He comes *into* believers at conversion, baptizing them into the body of Christ (1 Cor. 12:13; Rom. 8:9). After conversion, the Holy Spirit comes *upon* followers of Jesus to empower them for life and service (Acts 1:8, 2:38, Matt. 3:11).

The New Testament speaks of Holy Spirit baptism as *coming upon* (Acts 19:6), *enduing* (Luke 24:49), *baptizing* (Matt. 3:11), *filling* (Acts 2:4, Eph. 5:18), *pouring out* (Joel 2:28-29, Acts 10:45), and *falling upon* (Acts 10:44) believers. In the baptism of the Holy Spirit, followers of Christ have a life-changing encounter with God.

Consistently throughout the book of Acts, when believers received the baptism in the Holy Spirit, it was accompanied by speaking in tongues. Speaking in tongues is a supernatural language of the Spirit. Later, we will look at its value in the life of a follower of Christ. For now, I want you to see that the experience of speaking in tongues (when the Holy Spirit came upon believers) happened to the original 120 disciples on the day of Pentecost in Acts 2. It also happened with the Gentile believers at the house of Cornelius in Acts 10, and with the disciples in Ephesus in Acts 19. It also occurs in Acts 8 in the lives of the new converts in the revival at Samaria. All the Lord's first disciples and all the writers of the New Testament had this experience. It has become increasingly normative today, with about 644 million Pentecostal and Charismatic believers worldwide, and their number is rapidly growing.[45]

Throughout the New Testament, when believers are filled with the Spirit, besides speaking in tongues, they are praising and magnifying God (Acts 2:11, 10:46), speaking the Word of God with boldness (Acts 4:8, 31), making prophetic proclamations (Acts 13:9-10), prophesying (Acts 19:6), and speaking in psalms, hymns, and spiritual songs. In every case, being filled with the Spirit will empower the believer's speech. In a day when followers of Christ are being silenced and threatened, we desperately need bold, Spirit-empowered speech.

MOVING IN THE MIRACULOUS

Spiritual gifts are divinely entrusted to God's Holy Rebels to minister in the power of the Holy Spirit. The New Testament mentions various spiritual gifts, including *motivational gifts* (Rom. 12:6-8), *ministry offices* (Eph. 4:11-12, 1 Cor. 12:28-30), and *spiritual manifestations* (1 Cor. 12:8-10). Gifts of the Spirit are given to enable followers of Christ to serve others (1 Peter. 4:10). Each list of gifts operates uniquely from each other, according to their distinctiveness. All the gifts are important but too few believers operate in the spiritual manifestations of 1 Corinthians 12. Theologians have divided them into three categories: the *vocal gifts*—tongues, interpretation of tongues, and prophecy; the *revelation gifts* – word of knowledge, word of wisdom, and discerning of spirits; and the *power gifts*—gift of faith, gifts of healings, and working of miracles. Compared to the Gospels or the book of Acts, most Christians in the western world observe few genuine displays of these spiritual manifestations and of healing miracles. Thus, many conclude miracles no longer occur. Yet, these gifts are available to us, as the Spirit chooses to operate them through us (1 Cor. 12:11).

Though the gifts of the Spirit operate as the Spirit wills, there are ways to cultivate the gifts. We can study how the gifts of the Spirit worked in the Scripture and do a study on the healing miracles of Jesus (Rom. 10:17). We can also demonstrate a desire to be used in the gifts of the Spirit to glorify God and help people in need (1 Cor. 12:31). In faith, we must ask the Lord to use us in the gifts of the Spirit, moving out with an expectation that when the Lord chooses, the gifts will operate (Mark 11:22-24). This includes having a hunger for God and His miraculous power to be displayed.

The gifts of the Spirit are not about us, but about meeting the needs of hurting humanity. In 1 Cor. 12:31, Paul tells us that even a greater catalyst for the gifts of the Spirit than desire is love. Often, the Gospels records that before Jesus performed miraculous signs and wonders, He was moved by compassion.

John G. Lake frequently operated in the gifts of healings. He tells of a bedridden woman dying of terminal cancer. He had prayed for her multiple times and attempted to build her faith to receive healing by teaching her what the Scripture said concerning the subject. The doctors had concluded that there was no more they could do for her other than give her pain relievers to lessen her misery. Yet, she continued to trust Christ as her healer. "This woman was in such pain," Lake said, "that one minister of the church and I stayed at her bedside around the clock, praying. As we prayed, she would get relief." One morning, after praying all night, Lake went home just long enough to bathe and shave. On his return to the house, he reports, "I came within two blocks of the house, and I heard the woman screaming in pain.

Somehow, at the sound of those screams, I seemed to enter into a divine compassion. I ran those last two blocks without even thinking about what I was doing. Without thinking, I rushed into the room, sat down on the edge of the bed, picked up that emaciated body in my arms like a baby, and began to weep. While I was weeping, she was perfectly healed."[46]

If we are to be used by Christ in the gifts of Spirit, we must develop Christ's compassion for the hurting.

The Bible is a book of miracles, beginning with the book of Genesis all the way through to the book of Revelation. God's Word gives no support to the notion that miraculous gifts of the Spirit will suddenly end prior to Christ's return. Of course, they will end after Christ's Second Coming and the establishment of His eternal Kingdom (1 Corinthians 13:8-10). At that point, miraculous gifts are unnecessary, but until then, they are essential.

From a historical standpoint, signs, wonders, and miracles of God have never ceased from the days of Jesus until now. They are certainly prevalent throughout the New Testament period and the first few hundred years of the church. Though there were more healings and supernatural manifestations of God in some periods than others, there has never been a time when God withdrew these gifts. It would be more accurate to state the church did not appropriate them. John Wesley wrote, "The grand reason why the miraculous gifts were so soon withdrawn, was not only that faith and holiness were well-nigh lost, but that dry, formal, orthodox men began even then to ridicule whatever gifts they had not themselves, and to decry them all as either madness or imposture."[47]

Signs, wonders, divine healing, and the operation of miraculous gifts are still prevalent today. New Testament scholar Craig Keener says, "In 2000, experts estimate that 50% of all conversions in the Chinese evangelistic movement were because of faith healings." And in Nepal, 80% of converts become believers because of healings and exorcisms. Scholar J. P. Moreland approximates that up to 70% of the growth in evangelicalism worldwide over the past few decades is through signs, wonders, and miracles.[48]

You would expect a continuation of miraculous signs and wonders in the church based on Jesus telling us in John 14:12, "... he who believes in Me, the works that I do he will do also; and greater works than these he will do because I go to My Father." The writer of Hebrews boldly explained, "Jesus Christ is the same yesterday, today, and forever" (Heb. 13:8). Based on the Bible and church history, we should expect the continuation of supernatural gifts.

Throughout the New Testament, we see examples of how signs, wonders, and miracles resulted in the conversation of the lost. In Romans 15:18-19, Paul writes, "For I will not dare to speak of those things which Christ has not accomplished through me, in word and deed, to make the Gentiles obedient — in mighty signs and wonders, by the power of the Spirit of God, so that from Jerusalem and round about to Illyricum I have fully preached the gospel of Christ." To Paul, fully preaching the Gospel of Christ includes presenting it with mighty signs, wonders, and miracles. Throughout the third world, signs, wonders, and miracles commonly accompany the preaching of the Gospel. You can see this chronicled in the ministries of men like the late T. L. Osborn and Reinhard Bonnke, and many others.

When I began in ministry, the statement, "The Bible says," had significant credibility, even with unbelievers. Over the years, that has increasingly declined. I have debated the Scripture with atheists, agnostics, and those of other religions and cults with minimal effectiveness. Over time, I built a relationship with a young fitness trainer who worked at the athletic club where I was a member. I had shared the Gospel with him, but he expressed little interest, and he even mentioned he was "having too much fun to want to change his life." One day he shared with me issues he was having with his shoulder. The pain was keeping him from doing his regular workouts. I asked if I could pray with him. He gladly welcomed the prayer, and at the end, I asked him to try moving his arm in a way that previously caused pain. He did, and in wide-eyed amazement he shouted, "There's no pain. My shoulder feels great!" This got the attention of both him and others in the club and his pain never reoccurred. Though I did not personally lead him to Christ, from that point on, he showed much more respect and attention to my attempts to share God's Word with him.

In July of 2022, we partnered with Mario Murillo to conduct a four-night Living Proof tent crusade in Colorado Springs. Nightly, the 3,000-

seat tent was filled, with over 1,000 people standing (often in the rain) outside the tent. Each night, we saw undeniable signs, wonders, and miracles. People we personally knew were miraculously healed of long-term sicknesses and infirmities. Some of these healings were confirmed by follow-up visits with doctors. Also, each night of the Crusade, hundreds came forward in response to Mario's public invitation, with approximately 3,600 documented responses during the four nights.

Kelly shares the testimony of Donna Wilcox, one of many healed at the crusade. "Our friend, Donna, had lived with chronic pain for nine years due to severe physical disabilities that limited her greatly and forced her dependence upon a cane, as well as the help and assistance of others. Donna could not bend over. She struggled to walk even with a cane. She would fall often, causing additional pain and injuries. In her own words, she had lived 'not a second without pain for the past nine years.' We had been praying for Donna to be healed, and I had even questioned the Lord about why He hadn't healed her yet. The night she came to the tent, I believed God was going to heal her. She sat right behind Todd and me on the second night of the crusade. Mario did not know Donna; we had not told him anything about Donna. When the Holy Spirit gave him a word of knowledge about her, he pointed to her, described the pain in her body, and he called her to come forward to receive her healing. He said to her, 'The Lord is healing you now...', and as Mario spoke, we watched God's power in demonstration and our dear friend was completely and miraculously healed! She threw down her cane, and she began to run, jump, dance, bend, twist and shout out praises to God for this amazing miracle in her body. She went home to be a witness to the healing power of Christ to her clients, friends, and to skeptics. Over 26,000 people have watched her miraculous testimony on video."

Now, more than any period I have witnessed, it is important that we present the Gospel not only in word but also in power. The Gospel is powerful, but in the life of Jesus the Gospel included signs, wonders, and miracles. He desires the same for us today. Though the gifts of the Spirit are to operate as the church gathers, I believe it is more important that these supernatural gifts operate through the church as God's Spirit empowered Holy Rebels to go out and impact their world for Christ.

CHAPTER TEN

EXTREME EVANGELISM

> He said to them, "The harvest is bigger than you can imagine, but there are few workers. Therefore, plead with the Lord of the harvest to send out workers for his harvest" Luke 10:2 (CEB).

EXTREME TIMES NECESSITATE fervent prayer, fasting and seeking God's clear direction. As we entered the beginning of another new year, the Lord spoke clearly and unmistakably to me (Kelly), "This is a season of extreme evangelism." That year was the beginning of 2022, and I knew that those words were spoken to take us into a whole new level of evangelism that would lead us into the greatest harvest of souls we have ever seen.

Pondering and praying through this clear mandate from our Lord, I was reminded of the message He had given us over a decade before concerning the urgency of the hour we are living in. Todd and I were praying together late into the night. Our prayers were focused on souls and on the soul of our nation. We put our kids to bed and then plunged into a season of deep intercession and travailing prayer over the desperate condition of our country. Miraculously, our young children slept through the sound of our weeping, wailing and loud travailing for God's mercy and intervention.

Psalm 126:4-6 is a defining passage for this holy rebellion, "Bring back our captivity, O Lord, as the streams in the South.⁵ Those who sow in tears shall reap in joy. He who continually goes forth weeping, bearing seed for sowing, shall doubtless come again with rejoicing, bringing his sheaves with him." We must first sow in tears of intercession for the lost and for the soul of a nation before we will see and bring in the harvest. This is not a quick, casual prayer that we conveniently include in our prayer lists. This kind of passionate, deep, pressing prayer precedes a move of God that leads to a great harvest. Those who rebel against hell's agenda and whose mission is to see the captives set free must make room for times of deep, heart-rending prayer. This kind of prayer is similar to Jesus' prayer in Gethsemane when He pleaded with the disciples to stay awake and pray with Him for one hour. This was not a casual, convenient, or comfortable prayer; it was agonizing. Our current condition and season necessitate this kind of travailing prayer.

Jesus continues to petition His disciples today to join Him in times of deep intercession for the lost. This is where extreme evangelism begins. There is a great harvest of souls to be gained and the harvest begins with fervent, passionate prayers that are fueled by the Holy Spirit. God moves miraculously and mysteriously through the effectual, fervent prayers of righteous men and women who will give themselves completely to sacrificial prayer.

UNDERSTANDING THE SEASON

Seasons are important to understand and live in harmony with. The sons of Issachar in 1 Chronicles 12:32 understood the times and the season they were in and therefore they knew what to do. The Lord of the harvest is sounding the alarm. Awaken oh sleeper. Awaken from your slumber and realize the urgency of the hour we are now in. The harvest is greater than we can imagine, and we dare not continue with life as usual, business as usual, or ministry as usual during harvest time.

"It's not a time to back up, back off, or back down...it's time to press in!" Our dear friend Ron McIntosh spoke those words and they exploded inside of me. Growing up on a farm in Kansas, I understand harvest time. When the harvest is ripe, it cannot wait. You cannot put off bringing in the harvest until it's more convenient, when you feel like it, or when you don't have anything else to do. When the fields are white and ready for harvest, everything else goes on hold, and everyone works together to bring in the harvest. In John 4:35, Jesus said, "Don't you say, 'Four more months, and then comes the harvest'? Look, I tell you, lift up your eyes and look at the fields! They are white and ready for harvest." Jesus is telling us now, "lift up your eyes and look at the fields! They are ready for harvest." The harvest is ready, and the harvest is now. The Lord of the harvest is sending His laborers into the fields. And harvest time is extreme.

Remembering well from my youth, harvest time was "all hands-on deck." No one stayed at home, lying on the couch, eating cookies, and staring at a screen. We all had an important job to do and an essential role to play in bringing in the harvest. Many of us were sent out into the fields from morning till evening, working hard to bring in the crop. Others drove the trucks back and forth from the fields, gathering the grain and hauling it to the co-op -- while others prepared the meals, fed the workers, cleaned up the mess, and began preparing all over again. We didn't all have the same job, but we all had an important part to play, and we had to work together with unity and focus.

There was no time for pride, selfishness, apathy, complacency, jealousy, strife, or division. We had a mission to accomplish, and it required unity, selflessness, and commitment. The hours were long, and the workload was great, but we knew it would be worth it, and it couldn't wait. That is precisely where we are right now. God is moving and revival fire is falling. Another great awakening has begun and those who are watching and listening, like the sons of Issachar, know and understand the season we are in.

Rescuing souls from hell and bringing in the lost (the harvest) is the holy rebel's most important mission. Yet most Christians never realize or fulfill this calling. Satan's strategy is working when 95% of believers in Jesus never lead anyone to Christ.[49] The church must awaken and rebel against hell's agenda to capture, enslave, and destroy the souls of men and women in hell. We need a fresh revelation of hell and the reality that many are going there. Jesus, the first Holy Rebel, rebelled against hell's mission against mankind. Luke tells us in Luke 19:10, "the Son of Man has come to seek and to save that which was lost." This was His holy mission and as His followers, this must be our holy mission.

FAMOUS LAST WORDS

Our church's youth group will periodically do something called, "Famous Last Words". They invite a passionate follower of Jesus to share their own "famous last words" with the students. The idea is that if these were your last moments on earth, what is the most important message that you would convey to the church? This is exactly what Jesus did just before His ascension in Matthew 28:18-20, and the message is unmistakably simple and clear: Wherever you go, make disciples. Jesus said, "All authority in heaven and on earth has been given to me. So wherever you go, make disciples of all nations: Baptize them in the name of the Father, and of the Son, and of the Holy Spirit. Teach them to do everything I have commanded you" (Matthew 28:18-20 GWT).

These famous last words of Jesus before His ascension are what we know as the Great Commission. God has called us, authorized us, and empowered us to fulfill this mission. So why are there so few laborers fulfilling this charge?

This is the most important mandate given to each of us (His disciples). To be clear, it is not the great possibility, or the great suggestion, or the great idea. This Great Commission is a holy mandate to the body of Christ, from Jesus Himself, and it is not optional. It is mandatory. Satan has cleverly and subtly infiltrated the body of Christ with his lies, intimidation, and deception, turning the Great Commission into the great omission.

Satan has deceived the church and convinced 95% of the body of Christ that evangelism is someone else's responsibility. The agenda of hell is to keep us consumed with us: our life, our plans, our agenda, our career, our ministry, and our family. We become so caught up with me, myself, and mine that we become completely blind to the harvest all around us. The last thing the devil wants you to do is to pray for the lost and lead them to Jesus.

NO GREATER JOY

There is no greater joy than leading someone to Christ. It does not matter how old, how young, how bold, how quiet, how outgoing, or how introverted you may or may not be. He has called all of us to make disciples everywhere we go. Jesus said, "come follow Me and I will make you fishers of men" Matthew 4:19. Should anyone tell you that this does not apply to those who are quiet or shy, you must know that is a lie from the enemy. There are no introvert clauses. There are no exemptions for those who feel uncomfortable, uneasy, unqualified, scared, or intimidated.

When I was young and before I surrendered my life to Christ, I was very shy and introverted. I was the quiet one who hung back in the shadows and was afraid to speak up. My dad had to push me out of my comfort zone, and I am so glad that he did. He didn't make excuses for me and pat me on the head, telling me that I was shy and timid so I should remain silent, and in the shadows. Interestingly, our daughter Faith is naturally quieter and more introverted. She would have remained unseen, unheard, and unnoticed if we had not gently pushed her out of her comfort zone. Today she is a powerful, anointed, passionate worship leader. Satan would have loved to shut her up and shut her down because her voice and her passion for God terrifies hell.

Christian, it is time to rebel against hell's strategy to shut you up, keep you hidden, silent and held back. God has given you a voice, a purpose, a divine holy calling in this hour. Do not be silent. Proverbs 28:1 declares this about every child of God: "...the righteous are bold as a lion." Now is the time for every son and daughter of the King to come out of the shadows and run into the roars of hell's fury because the roar of the Lion of Judah is with you, behind you, in you and ready to be released through you. Do not hold back any longer.

At the age of 20, I became a passionate follower of Jesus and was baptized in the Holy Spirit and fire (Matthew 3:11). That is when Proverbs 28:1 became a reality for me.

I no longer shrunk back in fear or intimidation. It wasn't easy and it felt safer to just keep quiet and stay in the shadows, but I knew that I couldn't. Playing it safe and staying comfortable is not biblical. This kind of thinking is satanically inspired to keep us from being the Holy Rebels our Lord has called us to be. When I am silent, hell rejoices. When I lift up my eyes, open my mouth, and go after the lost, hell trembles. My Lord Jesus did not shrink back from the cross for me. Therefore, I certainly will not shrink back from telling others about Him.

As a new, young disciple of Jesus, I began to pray, "Lord, Your Word says that the righteous are as bold as a lion. So, I will step out in faith and trust in Your power to move through me to reach others." Years later, I still pray this prayer, because my flesh still wants to shrink back in fear and intimidation. The kingdom of hell fights me constantly to keep me quiet. This is why we must rebel against hell's agenda with our weapons of love and truth that will set the captives free.

One of the greatest joys you will ever know this side of heaven is reaching others and seeing them come to faith in Jesus. Just think about it; when you reach out to someone and invite them to church, to youth group, or invite them to receive Christ, a person's eternal destiny can be changed. A person who had been on his or her way to hell is now going to heaven. A person who was empty, lonely, and without hope is now filled and complete—all because you took the time to pray for them, reach out to them, share the gospel message with them, or invite them.

EVERYWHERE YOU GO MAKE DISCIPLES

The words of our Lord ring loudly throughout the scripture: "Lift up your eyes and see the harvest. The harvest is bigger than you can imagine. Everywhere you go, make disciples. Follow Me and I will make you fishers of men" (Luke 10:2, CEB). Hell's agenda is to force us to turn a blind eye to the souls around us, every day, everywhere we go. Therefore, we must choose to rebel against hell and go out looking for those who need Jesus. We are called to rescue souls from the traps and snares of the enemy and lead them to freedom in Christ.

Everywhere you go, make disciples. Allow those words of our Lord go down deep into the good soil of your heart to transform you into a fisher of men. No more excuses. God does not accept excuses. Gideon told God he was too weak; Jeremiah was afraid of their faces; Timothy thought he was too young; Moses insisted that he couldn't speak well, and God was never impressed or moved by any excuse. Actually, the less qualified we feel we are the more powerfully God can move through us. With less of us, there is more of Him. Therefore, when you feel weak, incapable, intimidated or unqualified, you are the best candidate for a divine appointment.

Out of hundreds of stories of transformed lives, perhaps the greatest lesson learned for me came through a young woman named Britta. Todd and I were involved in the wedding of a church member. Admittedly, it had been a long, hard week and my flesh did not want to go to a wedding rehearsal. I wanted to retreat, stay home, go to bed, and sleep off the exhaustion. Lesson number one: when I am weak, He is strong. Even when I feel that I am emotionally, physically and even spiritually drained, God is greater, stronger and bigger.

Following the wedding rehearsal was the dinner party and nothing in me wanted to be there. Selfishly, I prayed that God would work out the seating so that I could sit with someone I knew well. Lesson number two: God does not answer selfish prayers. Todd and I were seated across from a couple we had never met before and immediately, I sensed that this was orchestrated by Holy Spirit. The message of our Lord seemed to be woven into that evening: "Wherever you go, make disciples".

During the next couple of hours, I learned a lot about Britta and the fact that she did not know Jesus. Toward the end of the dinner, I invited her to come to the Bible study that I led. The following Tuesday, she showed up with a big smile and a sincere excitement to be there. She continued to come for several weeks, asking many questions, and she also began coming to church. That simple invitation to come to my Bible study group resulted in her decision to become a passionate follower of Jesus Christ. There is no greater joy than partnering with Heaven in seeing another soul set free and brought into God's family. Lesson number three: this is a divine partnership. We partner with the Godhead in seeing people delivered from the power of hell and translated into God's kingdom of light. This is the Holy Rebel's most important mission.

THE REST OF THE STORY

Several months passed and I was called to go to the hospital because Britta had just received a terminal medical diagnosis. After bone marrow transplants, radiation, and chemotherapy she was sent home and told there was nothing more that the medical team could do for her. She was in her early twenties, with a death sentence and hospice was the next step. However, she had just received Jesus as her Lord and Savior, and she was about to receive another miracle from Him.

She had lost her hair, and her body was emaciated and ravaged by the cancer and the treatments. She came to church in a very weakened state. Interrupting the church service, the Holy Spirit gave Todd a word of knowledge that day. Todd called Britta out of the congregation, and she came forward. Todd spoke these words, "Britta Gray, you need to come forward because the Lord is going to heal you today." God showed Todd that He wanted to do a miracle in Britta, and that is exactly what He did.

I and a few others gathered around her, laying hands upon her, as Todd led in prayer. The power of God fell upon her, and she collapsed to the floor. Those of us close to her could feel the tangible power of the Lord. Britta described the sensation as that of a supernatural heat that seemed to run throughout her body as we prayed. She got up declaring, "I'm healed!" We all cheered wildly because we knew we had witnessed a miracle.

She returned to MD Anderson, where they ran multiple tests, and they all came back completely clear. The miracle of Jesus in her body was medically confirmed. When the medical teams and treatments failed, God's power prevailed.

Britta came to me one day several months after her healing and said, "The Lord told me to come and tell you something." There was a holy solemnity in her tone and if the Lord told her to tell me something, I wanted to hear every word of it. She sat down and then continued, "if you had not invited me to your Bible study, I would be in hell right now." Stunned by the words she had shared, I sat in silence, feeling the full impact of this revelation. Britta began to cry as she continued to admonish me with the message God had sent her to deliver.

That message is not for me alone. God's message sent through Britta that day is for you right now. There are people all around you, everywhere you go, who are like Britta. They do not even realize what they are missing. Unaware of their own lost condition, they are dead in their trespasses and sins. The enemy of their soul has blinded their eyes to the truth. You are the Holy Rebel warrior that God has placed in their path, to lead them to the Way, the Truth, and the Life. The Lord of the harvest is calling you into the fields that are ripe all around you -- because if you do not reach out and invite them, they may end up in hell. Remember the words of Britta, "if you had not invited me...I would be in hell right now."

Today's Americanized Christianity falls very short of true, biblical Christianity. This statement is not to shame or condemn, but rather to awaken and repent. Unfortunately, we have been conditioned to believe that Christianity is all about me and what makes me feel good and comfortable. The real truth is that God made His church the way He *wanted* it, and He is calling His church to come back to the way He *made* it. When Christians are satisfied with not leading people to Jesus, hell's deception has crept into the church and taken us off course. Course correction is essential in this time of harvest. Everyone has a vital role to play in bringing in the harvest and no one is exempt.

STRATEGICALLY PLACED

Remember Jesus' words: "Wherever you go, make disciples." God places us strategically in certain places, schools, and neighborhoods with people He wants to reach through us. Be aware, awake and alert because God has placed you strategically in your city, state, and community with the people He wants you to reach.

Several years ago, two members of our intercessory prayer team expressed that they both felt compelled to pray that our family would move to a certain area of town. Personally, I did not feel any divine compulsion to be in that neighborhood but these two men both shared their sense. Amazingly, at one point, a door opened, and it seemed as though God was moving miraculously to get us into a home in that very neighborhood. These two intercessors both continued to express that they felt it was God's plan because we were to reach people in that neighborhood.

We moved into our new home and began praying for our neighbors. One day we were outside talking to the woman, and I invited her and her family to come to church. That one simple invitation led to a radical transformation in her life and family. She rededicated her life to the Lord, was baptized in the Holy Spirit and filled with a holy passionate fire for God. Her personal testimony is that up until that time she was a nominal, lukewarm Christian, someone who believed in Jesus but was not living as His disciple. However, she accepted the invitation, came to an Easter service, and encountered Jesus. That one invitation completely changed her life and it led to her mom and her sister also committing their lives fully to Christ.

I could tell you story after story like this. I could tell you about a lady named Jean who had never stepped foot inside of a church until we invited her. She came, experienced the power of God's presence and His truth that led to her salvation. Jean committed her life to Christ, became a child of God, and two weeks later she died unexpectedly.

Many times, I have reflected on the fact that if we had not invited her, she would likely be in hell today. We partnered with Heaven and rebelled against hell's agenda for Jean's soul. We invited her to come to Christ, she accepted, and Heaven won. A simple invitation was all it took to change her eternal destiny from hell to heaven. Remember the words of Jesus: *Wherever you go, make disciples.*

BEER CANS, BEARDS, AND BEER BELLIES

Another of my favorite evangelism stories was when I went door to door with our church evangelism team. The lady I partnered with that day was a petite, little, firebrand for Jesus. We stepped over several empty beer cans and garbage to get to the door of one house. Pushing through the strong feelings of fear and intimidation, we knocked on the door and waited for an answer. Nothing could have prepared me for the big, hairy dude that stood in the doorway, weighing about 275lbs with a bushy beard, beer belly and no shirt. It took my breath away and everything in me wanted to bolt. But I remembered the words of scripture, "the righteous are as bold as a lion."

He actually looked pretty shocked himself when he opened the door and saw the two of us standing there staring at him. I'm pretty sure we were trembling as we began to tell him that God had sent us to his door that day to tell him that Jesus loved him. The big, strong man began to tremble himself, and tears welled up in his eyes as we told him that Jesus loved him so much that He died for him and that through the finished work of Jesus he could be forgiven of all his sins and receive eternal life. We asked him if he would like to make Jesus his Lord. Through his tears and quivering voice, he said, "yes." We led him in a prayer right there and he asked Jesus to save him and be his Lord. There truly is no greater joy than the miracle of a soul turning from darkness to light and surrendering their life to Jesus Christ. Rebelling against hell's agenda for the souls of men, women and children is what every son and daughter of the King is called to.

Wherever you go, make disciples. This is your Holy Rebel calling. If every child of God will take this calling seriously, we will indeed bring in a great harvest of souls. Through the years, people have come to me and thanked me for inviting them to church. Excitedly, they share how their lives have been transformed through Christ and many times I didn't even remember inviting them. Jesus said wherever you go, make disciples. When you go to the store, post office, salon, park, school, hospital, restaurant, and coffee shops, invite them to encounter Jesus. Wherever you go, look up and see the people all around you and in front of you. Everywhere you go, pray for God to direct you to people. Talk to people, pray with people, share the love of Jesus and invite them to come and encounter Him. You do your part and God will do His. This is a divine partnership. Some of them will come, give their lives to Christ, and thank you for inviting them. You will experience the greatest joy you can imagine. There truly is no greater miracle than when a person runs to Jesus and becomes a passionate follower of Christ.

Through the years I have invited countless people to come to Christ, or to come to church and encounter Jesus. Many of them rejected my invitation but some of them came and surrendered their hearts and lives to Him. A few people even verbally attacked me for talking to them about Jesus, inviting them to church or simply asking them if I could pray for them. The hateful remarks and rejections are never fun, but they will not stop God's Holy Rebel warriors from plundering hell and going after souls. This is our most important mission. Proverbs 11:30 states, "he who wins souls is wise."

ANGELA WATSON: MESSENGER OF THE LORD

God often speaks to me through prophetic dreams and on May 13th, 2022, I was visited by a messenger of the Lord in a dream. In the dream I was at our church's Central Campus, and I was leading a spontaneous song of praise at a Fusion service. Fusion is where all of our campuses come together for a Holy Spirit-led service of prayer, intercession, praise and worship.

There were beautiful banners trimmed in gold hanging toward the front of the worship center. I didn't know where they had come from, so I began asking questions about them. One of our staff members told me that a woman named Angela Watson had recently started coming to the church. She pointed her out to me and told me that she brought the banners.

I went to introduce myself to her and ask her about the banners. She confirmed that she was the one who brought them, but she had something else that she wanted to address. She very quickly and emphatically began to point to empty seats in our auditorium and she said, "Look at all these empty seats. It's time to hit the streets and fill these seats."

I woke up and immediately began to process the dream and ask the Holy Spirit for His revelation. First, I do not know anyone by the name of Angela Watson. Clearly, the fact that I met a stranger, and her name was unmistakably articulated to me was significant. The name of this person was Angela, which literally means "angel" or "messenger of God." This was the first revelation, and it took my breath away as I considered the fact that an angel of the Lord had just visited me in this dream. Tears filled my eyes, making it difficult to see as I searched for the meaning of the name "Watson." When I read the meaning of the name Watson, I was completely floored. Her last name was Watson, which means "ruler of the army." God's presence seemed to completely envelop me as I took this all in and waited for more. Without a doubt, this was indeed another prophetic dream from God.

I had been visited by an angel, a messenger of God, in this dream. This angel was a "ruler of the army" or a general in the army of angels sent to fight in this holy rebellion with us against the forces of hell. God sent the angel to confirm and compel us to understand the season we are in and act accordingly. God's messenger emphatically pointed out the empty seats, stressing that they needed to be filled, and implying that it was up to us to get them filled.

The only thing I could compare this to would be a mother going to her son or daughter and pointing out the mess in their room that was not okay. Responsible parents don't go and clean up their mess for them and let them just go on about their business of playing video games, watching TV, or doing whatever they feel like. No, a good parent points out the problem and then instructs them to change their ways and get it cleaned up. Angela Watson had come to address what was wrong with our room and the matter at hand was that there were empty seats that needed to be filled.

The dream took place during a Fusion service which is where we passionately worship, praise and enter into deep intercession. God's messenger had brought beautiful banners with our names embossed into the gorgeous fabrics. The Lord had them delivered and placed on the platform to commend us for leading the way in Spirit-led worship and fire-baptized prayer and intercession. Just as He did with the churches in the book of Revelation, He first commended us on what we were doing right and well. However, He quickly had the angel of His army address what we were doing wrong.

We had done well in the area of prayer, intercession, praise and worship; but we were lacking in the next step of bringing in the harvest. Her words continue to echo in my heart, "Look at all these empty seats! It's time to hit the streets and fill these seats." This was indeed a general in God's army who had been sent to wake us up to what we were lacking. The harvest is now, and the laborers are few. We must come to attention and hit the streets to get His church filled up.

THE GREATEST HARVEST OF SOULS WE HAVE EVER WITNESSED

The greatest harvest of souls we have ever witnessed personally was this year (July 2022) when Mario Murillo held a Living Proof Tent Crusade on our North Campus property. We heeded the message of the angel in the dream, and we hit the streets. Mario's Inner-City Action Team came from California, and we partnered with them going door to door, inviting people to come to the tent. Everywhere we went, we invited people to come and encounter Jesus.

The Living Proof tent was overflowing night after night, with thousands of people in attendance. Over 3,600 people committed their lives to Christ during the four nights of the tent meetings. The salvation response night after night was comparable to a Billy Graham Crusade. Mario would give the invitation to surrender to Christ and every night, the front of the tent was packed full of men, women, teens, and youth. Amazement, awe, and wonder filled our hearts as they rushed to the front of the tent in response to the call to follow Jesus. The massive area in front was filled, with all the aisles jammed and people backed up even outside the tent. Night after night we witnessed firsthand the greatest harvest of souls we had ever seen. Yet we know God is just getting started.

Many miracles took place every night as the Holy Spirit demonstrated His power through words of knowledge and many miraculous healings. Mario stated repeatedly that the greatest miracle of all is the miracle of salvation. This is why we must rebel against hell's agenda for souls, and partner with Heaven in rescuing the lost. This is our most important mission. The fact will always remain that salvation is the greatest miracle of all.

The greatest harvest of souls we have ever witnessed with over 3,600 commitments to follow Jesus was not the result of just scheduling a week of meetings on the calendar, raising a tent, and then telling people to come. This began with several months of intense prayer, fasting, intercession, waiting on God, listening to His orders, following His instructions, partnering with other believers, and hitting the streets to fill the tent. We held prayer meetings every night for a month leading up to the tent crusade. Believers from all over the city and from other churches came together to pray and cry out to God for souls and for revival in our city. These gatherings of God's sons and daughters, worshipping and praying in one accord, were essential for bringing in the harvest. When the crusade took place, hundreds of volunteers from all over the nation came to serve. In all, over 1,500 volunteers helped reap this bountiful harvest.

ANGELS SENT BEFORE US

Throughout the past 35 years of passionately following Jesus, I have had numerous people come and tell me they saw angels around me or a massive angel behind me. People have told me they have seen angels in our worship centers from time to time. Yet, I had never had an angelic encounter until recently. Over the past year, I have been visited by four different angels in my dreams. These angels bring urgent, prophetic messages to me concerning the harvest. Their primary message is clear: "The harvest is bigger than you can imagine, and the workers are few" and, "It's time to hit the streets and fill these seats."

Evangelist Scott Hinkle listened to me share the angelic messages I had received over the past few months. Solemnly, he responded with a question that pierced my soul with conviction: "Isn't it sad that God has to send angels to us to tell us to do what He has already told us to do?" These angelic messengers have undoubtedly been sent to awaken and activate us to go out and bring in the harvest.

We must all shift our focus to the fields that are white and ready for harvest. An angel in another dream emphatically stressed that this shift is not optional, it is mandatory. He admonished us to shift our focus to bringing in the harvest. We dare not wait and hope the harvest will make its way into the church. Heaven's mandate is now, and it is to go out, find them, reach them, and bring them in.

Please join me in this prayer: "Lord, from this moment forward, I pray You will give me a burden and concern for people who do not yet know You. Help me see them as You do. Help me care enough to share Your Gospel with them. Give me a burden for the lost like You have. Lord, I admit that at times I am afraid to step out. Please give me a new boldness to do that. In Jesus' name I pray, Amen."

CHAPTER ELEVEN

SPIRIT OF ELIJAH

"Behold, I will send you Elijah the prophet before the coming of the great and dreadful day of the LORD. And he will turn the hearts of the fathers to the children, and the hearts of the children to their fathers, lest I come and strike the earth with a curse"(Mal. 4:5-6).

ELIJAH IS ONE of the most significant figures in the Hebrew Scriptures. He is also mentioned 30 times in the New Testament. At every Seder meal, the Jews set an extra cup of wine on the table and open the door, hoping Elijah will enter, for he was to usher in the Messiah.⁵⁰ John the Baptist came in the Spirit of Elijah to prepare the way for Christ (Mark 1:1-9). We also know Elijah will return to earth during the Tribulation preceding Christ's Second Advent (Rev. 11:1-6). The spirit of Elijah ushers in a move of God and calls people to repentance.

We need Elijahs today, as we strive to resist the evil forces that dominate our culture, our government, and other major institutions in our nation. To learn how to operate in the spirit of Elijah, we will look at the life, times, and ministry of this man.

In 874 B.C., Ahab came to the throne of Israel in Samaria. Israel was a divided nation. Under Rehoboam, the son of Solomon, the nation of Israel had been split between Samaria (also referred to as Israel) in the north and Judah in the south. Disregarding God's command not to intermarry with pagan peoples, Ahab's father, King Omri, had arranged a marriage between Ahab and Jezebel, the princess of Sidon (Deut. 7:3-4), whose name is now associated with perversion and evil. The northern kingdom's first six kings were ungodly leaders, but "Ahab did more to provoke the Lord God of Israel to anger than all the kings of Israel who were before him" (1 Kings 16:33).

King Ahab was a self-centered, ungodly man, but his greatest sin was allowing his nation to be controlled by his wife. Jezebel, the daughter of Sidonian King Ithobaal, was a high priestess of the religion of Baal.[51] She was fanatical about turning Israel from the worship of Yahweh to the worship of her demonic god. What you permit, you promote, and what you tolerate you deserve, and thus it was Ahab and his permissive weakness that was most responsible for the nation's apostasy.

When Ahab became its king, Israel was already a backslidden nation. The people had lost their dynamic relationship with God, and their religion had become more cultural and social than real. You could say that even before Jezebel arrived, Israel was living in a post-Yahweh nation. The country was moving from the monotheistic worship of the one true God and obedience to His truth, to polytheism, syncretism, and relativism. When Jezebel established residence in the palace, one of the first things she did was provoke Ahab to set up a Temple to Baal Melqart in Samaria (1 Kings 16:32). In addition, the queen brought with her from Sidon 450 priests and 400 priestesses of the Baal religion.

THE SEDUCTION OF ISRAEL

Baal means "lord, master, owner, or possessor" and his worship had various manifestations throughout the Near East. In the New Testament, he is called Beelzebub (2 Kings 1:2, Mark 3:22). In Sidon, they worshiped Baal Melqart, who had a cohort named Asherah. Baal was the storm god, the bringer of rain, a fertility deity, and a god of power. If you wanted power and control over others, you worshiped Baal Melqart. Asherah was a goddess of lust and sensuality. Her deluded worshipers believed her blessing would cause their crops to thrive—which was desperately desired in an agrarian culture.

The worship of Baal and Asherah was disgusting and barbaric (1 Kings 14:23-24). Every winter they thought Baal fell asleep and to wake him up every spring, the male population was called on to have sex with temple prostitutes. There were both male and female priestly prostitutes,[52] many of whom were sex slaves who had been captured during military conquest.

Baalism also involved the worship of Molech (the Ammonite counterpart to Baal), which required child sacrifice (Jer. 19:5). Worshipers carrying their children—many the offspring of their ritual sex—approached a brass statue of Molech, which was a furnace with a fire in its belly. They placed their children on the burning hands of the idol, while drums beat loudly to drown out the screams of the burning child. If the parents cried or winced, their offering would not be received.[53] Sidon was a violent nation devoted to Baal and living for power, greed, and sexuality. The nation was rotten to the core.

GOD'S REPRESENTATIVE

When God has a will and purpose to achieve on the earth, he seeks a person through whom he can accomplish it. When God wanted to deliver Israel out of Egypt, he needed a man. Moses was that man, and he became the founder of the nation of Israel. God declared through Ezekiel, "So I sought for a man among them who would make a wall and stand in the gap before Me on behalf of the land, that I should not destroy it; but I found no one" (Ezek. 22:30). God found the man He needed in Elijah, who was called to lead a revival and bring reformation to the nation of Israel.

The name Elijah means, "Yahweh is God." In a time when it appeared the whole nation had departed from Yahweh to worship Baal, his name was a profound statement. In reality, there were 7,000 believers who had not bowed their knee to Baal (1 Kings 19:18), including 100 prophets of Yahweh (1 Kings 18:13). God could have used any of them. But they were all hiding in caves in fear of Jezebel. In today's terms, Jezebel had cancelled the opposition. Those in hiding were probably discussing how bad everything in the nation was, how Ahab and Jezebel were taking the nation in the wrong direction, and how Israel was desperately in need of revival. Elijah was the only one willing to stand up and confront the culture and take on King Ahab and the priests of Baal. Elijah was a holy rebel.

BAAL AMERICAN STYLE

In our day, our nation has been given over to a spirit like the demonic god

Baal and his high priestess Jezebel. The spirit of Baal wants to control others, and we certainly see it operating through many politicians, educators, corporate leaders, and entertainment moguls. Jezebel had taken control and influence over the life and culture in Israel. In the same way, in our nation, cultural Marxists operating in the spirit of Jezebel have taken over the political, media, entertainment, and educational institutions in the United States. They have also infiltrated and influenced religious organizations and the family.

Like Israel under Baal's influence, America is given over to greed, and materialism. A symbol of Baal was a bronze bull, reminiscent of the bronze charging bull located in the Financial District of New York City.[54] Like apostate Israel, the worship of Baal has resulted in violence, the occult, and sexual perversion throughout America. As with God's covenant people of Old Testament, the spirit of Jezebel has turned the heart of our nation away from God and His truth. We even offer our unwanted children as a sacrifice on the altars of Planned Parenthood and the abortion industry. At the time of this writing, in the United States, since 1973, over 63 million babies have been aborted.[55]

Over the years, I have known women and men who have wept and grieved over the decision they made to take the life of their unborn child through abortion. Their choice to take a life left deep emotional scars and painful regret. Thankfully, they could find cleansing, freedom, and hope through the forgiveness God offers in Christ.

Much has changed since 1992 when presidential candidate Bill Clinton spoke of the need for abortion to be "safe, legal, and rare." Safe depends on your definition. It is certainly not safe for the baby nor for the emotional health of many of the women. Rare, it is not. In fact, the Democratic party has dropped the word *rare* from its platform. Amelia Bonow, a co-founder of the pro-abortion-rights group "Shout Your Abortion" said, "I cannot think of a less compelling way to advocate for something than saying that it should be rare. And anyone who uses that phrase is operating from the assumption that abortion is a bad thing."[56] Statistics also tell us abortion is far from rare. The Guttmacher Institute, World Health Organization, and United Nations puts the average annual number of abortions in the U.S. around 886,000.[57] Clearly, abortions are not rare.

Certainly, the most gruesome abortion is the late-term, or partial-birth, abortion. Brenda Pratt Shafer, a registered nurse from Dayton, Ohio, testified before the House Judiciary Committee on March 21, 1996, about a partial-birth abortion she witnessed on a pre-born baby boy at six months' gestation. Shafer testified, "The doctor delivered the baby's body and the arms—everything but the head. The doctor kept the baby's head just inside the uterus. The baby's little fingers were clasping and unclasping, and his feet were kicking. Then the doctor stuck the scissors through the back of his head, and the baby's arms jerked out in a flinch, a startled reaction, like a baby does when he thinks he might fall. The doctor opened up the scissors, stuck a high-powered suction tube into the opening, and sucked the baby's brains out. Now the baby was completely limp. He then delivered the baby's head. He cut the umbilical cord and delivered the placenta. He threw that baby in a pan, along with the placenta and the instruments he'd used. I saw the baby move in the pan. I asked another nurse, and she said it was just 'reflexes.' I have been a nurse for a long time, and I have seen a lot of death—people maimed in auto accidents, gunshot wounds, you name it. I have seen surgical procedures of every sort. But in all my professional years, I had never witnessed anything like this."[58]

Instead of being horrified by such barbaric acts, many in our country applaud and celebrate it. In 2019, when the state of New York passed its pro-abortion law, which allowed abortions up to the very moment before delivery, the legislators cheered, and One World Trade Center was lit up in pink.[59] Each year in New York City there are more black babies aborted than are born.[60]

The overturning of Roe v. Wade was an historic victory for life, and it will most certainly save the lives of millions of children in the years ahead. But it will not end abortion. In fact, it will only strengthen the determination of those who are committed to the non-existent "right" to terminate the life of unborn children. As valuable as court rulings and legislation that uphold biblical values are, we desperately need a moral and spiritual awakening that changes the human heart.

If a child in America survives the womb, the spirit of Baal and of Jezebel work to rob them of their innocence and wreck their lives through sexual sin, perversion, and confusion. The Internet has become a primary pathway for endless corrupting forms of pornography. It has also enabled the widespread practice of "sexting"—sending, and getting people to send, sexually explicit photos of themselves, leading to horrific examples of bullying, sexual extortion, and countless suicides among young people.

Schools across America have indoctrinated kids as young as pre-K with the idea that their gender identity is fluid. It is not something they were born with, but something they choose based on how they feel. They can decide to be a boy, a girl, or something else entirely. For example, schools are urging students to read books about trans-identified children as part of a new annual campaign to "support transgender and non-binary youth."[61] Some of our public schools take this even a step further, encouraging, and even assisting kids with gender confusion to begin the "transition" to a different sex, often without the knowledge or consent of their parents.

LGBTQ indoctrination now extends to virtually every American institution: businesses, non-profits, colleges and universities, the entertainment industry, the media, the military, and even health care. Often it is carried out under coercion and mandate. In Psalm 94:20 the Psalmist writes, "Shall the throne of iniquity, which devises evil by law, have fellowship with You?". Holy rebels cannot align with this agenda but must resist and oppose it.

The normalization, celebration, and massive indoctrination of the homosexual agenda are winning converts on an impressive scale. A 2022 Gallup poll showed that 7.1 percent of Americans now identify as LGBTQ, double what it was 10 years earlier.[62] What was most significant in the Gallup poll was the dramatic increase in the number of younger Americans identifying as LGBTQ. Roughly 21 percent of Generation Z Americans who have reached adulthood—those born between 1997 and 2003—identify as LGBTQ. That is nearly double the proportion of millennials who do so. Being gay or transgender is now wildly celebrated and considered "Supercool."

The rush to embrace transgenderism has also caused some parents to make reckless decisions involving their children. Sadly, today when children express some type of gender confusion, which is usually something that kids experience and then grow out of, we will often see parents rushing to dress them in clothes of the opposite sex and even seek medical practitioners to help them complete their child's transition to a different gender.

And a growing segment of the medical profession is mobilizing to assist. For example, the American Academy of Pediatrics now actively promotes what it calls "gender-affirming health care" for children and teens who express a desire to "transition" to a different gender. This includes everything from puberty blockers and hormone treatments to permanent, life altering surgeries.

One particularly tragic case involved a girl who publicly identified as a boy when she was 15. She started taking testosterone and had her breasts surgically removed. Now she realizes what an awful mistake she made, but that most of the damage cannot be undone. Recently, she said this: "I can't stop thinking about how different my life could have been. I've got the voice of a man. I used to love singing... now I can't finish a song without crying." This young woman has an Adam's apple, a beard, and heavy body hair. And two big scars on her chest. She now says, "I wonder what would have happened if I hadn't changed my name and identity. I just don't see how it can get better from here." That's the dark side of transgenderism we do not hear about.

The transgender movement not only defies the Bible and common sense, but it also contradicts basic biological science. Human sexual identity is determined entirely by a "Y" chromosome. Humans with an X and a Y chromosome are male, and those with two X chromosomes are female. The DNA you received at birth is immutable. People may undertake a gender transition that makes them look or sound like someone of the opposite sex, but if they die in an accident, the autopsy will identify them as the gender they were born with, either male or female.

This ungodly agenda does not stop with the five letters LGBTQ. Having achieved the normalization of this long list of what for thousands of years was considered deviant sexual behaviors, it is now moving into a whole new phase: the normalization and acceptance of pedophilia—sex between adults and children—something that has always been considered not just immoral but criminal. Some LGBTQ+ activists and academics have now started pushing for the sympathetic acceptance of adults who desire to have sex with children. They refer to the individuals as "minor attracted persons"—or MAP for short.[63]

So where is the LGBTQ+ movement going next? We can only guess. Here is what we know: when Satan leads a person or a society into sin, there is no bottom in terms of where he will take them. We see that with Baal and Jezebel in the times of Elijah, and we see it today.

CENSORING THE PROPHETS

When prophets revolted against evil in the times of Elijah, Jezebel had the prophets of the Lord killed (1 Kings 18:13). The terror of Jezebel caused those she could not kill to go into hiding. The whole land was paralyzed in fear, unable to stand up to the wicked queen of Israel.

In America today, we have a cancel culture. If we stand for biblical values, then instead of having a free expression of ideas, the leftist culture will exert an all-out effort to cancel us. They do it by removing us from social media platforms, censoring our speech, forcing our firing or expulsion, and attacking our assumed motives. They will shame us into submission or silence us. What they are primarily trying to cancel are biblical values and scriptural truth. We see the adage lived out, "The further a society will drift from the truth, the more it will hate those who speak it." A study conducted on the silencing of Christians concluded the church has allowed itself to be self-censored. Christian leaders have freedom to express themselves, but they rarely take advantage of it.[64] Holy Rebels refuse to be intimidated into silence, but boldly proclaim God's truth.

Personally, as I have encouraged pastors and followers of Christ to be bold and take a stand for truth and against evil, I have been surprised by the extreme resistance. This resistance comes in various forms and through numerous arguments. Some seem very sincere yet misguided. Others appear to be cowards who hide their cowardice in terms that sound more palatable and soothe their consciences. Still others act oblivious to the desperate state of our nation or are ambivalent concerning it.

One of the strongest pushbacks I've received is that Christians should avoid involvement in politics. I am thankful abolitionists like politician William Wilberforce in England, evangelist Charles Finney, and others in America did not take that stand when it came to the "political issue" of slavery. Instead, they recognized slavery's violation of biblical values, and they strived to eliminate it. I am grateful that Martin Luther King Jr. and other preachers did not take that position when they decried the "political issue" of segregation by quoting Old Testament prophets. We now honor Christian leaders like Dietrich Bonhoeffer who were willing to take a stand against the holocaust and the Nazi agenda at the price of their ministry and their lives. These were not just political issues; they were biblical issues. In his *Lectures on Revival*, Charles Finney said, "Christians must do their duty to God... God will bless or curse this nation according to the course Christians take in politics."[65]

REFUSING TO BE SILENT

I am convinced the Bible speaks to a wide range of "political issues," and followers of Christ should know what the Bible says about these subjects and must vote and speak up accordingly. If we are biblical Christians, we are going to face subjects that are perceived as political. And these issues matter. They mattered to the millions of Eastern Europeans who lived under Soviet-imposed communism but were freed because of good American political policy.

The reason for supporting biblical values and making a stand for truth is not to gain power or control or to create an American theocracy. Rather, it is because we love people and, as followers of Christ, we believe God's Word lays out what is His best for individuals and for the flourishing of a nation. It is not that we hate our neighbor when we stand for biblical values, but that we love them and want the best for them (Matt. 22:38). Remaining silent and uninvolved in the face of evil is not love (Luke 10:25-37).

As followers of Christ, our primary allegiance is to God, and our true citizenship is in heaven (Phil. 3:20). That should make us the best citizens of any nation in which we live. We are to strive for the peace and prosperity of our nation (Jer. 29:7), and in America, we have a wonderful opportunity to affect the health, goodness, and prosperity of our country.

In the garden of Eden, man was given dominion and the responsibility of being a good steward (Gen. 1:28, 2:15. 1 Cor. 4:2). In the same way, we are called to be good stewards of our American citizenship, making a positive difference for Christ and for people. We are to stand against moral decay and lawlessness, to preserve freedom, justice, and social flourishing. Christ has called us to bring the light of God into the darkness (Matt. 5:13-16). We are to pray and work toward seeing God's Kingdom come and His will be done in America (Matt. 6:10). This is not Christian Nationalism but biblical stewardship and fulfilling Christ's command to love our neighbor.

I was taught and once espoused an idea that has been called "The Third Way." The concept was that instead of being a Republican, or Democrat, a conservative or liberal, we as Christians should walk in a middle ground between the two. I have since recognized this as a fallacy—primarily because our calling as Christians is not to be conservative, liberal, or something in between, but to be biblical. This view may have had some credence in the past—for on some issues, the Bible is too conservative for traditional progressives, and too progressive for traditional conservatives. Yet, in recent years, the progressive left has become so radically anti-God, and their policies so contrary to biblical truth that the "middle ground" has become a position totally contrary to God and His Word.

In fact, some of today's political policies and positions arouse the anger of God and should enrage us as well. Over 400 times in the Scripture, God expresses anger. When God came in the flesh in the person of Jesus, he displayed anger (John 2:13-17, Mark 3:1-5). Yet, it was a holy anger because it was for the sake of others, and it was under control. There is a holy anger that every follower of Christ should feel when he or she sees the demonically inspired policies that are devastating the lives of people. Church Father John Chrysostom said, "He that is angry without cause sins. He that is not angry when there is a cause sins. For unreasonable patience is the hotbed of many vices."[66] We need to be angry, but with a righteous and holy anger that causes us to act on behalf of those being mistreated and abused.

All of this requires remembering that though our enemy uses people to accomplish his purposes, our battle is not with people, but with demonic forces of evil. We can be ruthless against the darkness, while being kind, understanding, and gracious with people. It is critical that we honor others, present our arguments in a winsome manner, and avoid falling into the rancor and snarkiness that is so often evident in today's public discourse (1 Pet. 3:15-16).

Yet, we must be engaged in elections and in the national conversation. Should we choose not to vote, we will have abdicated an opportunity to elect candidates who are most aligned to biblical values. But what about when you must decide between the lesser of two evils? Unless Jesus Christ is running for office, we will always be voting for the lesser of two evils. We must realize that if Christians remain out of politics and public discourse, we allow anti-biblical dogmas, philosophies, and worldviews to control our society. If we avoid political discussion, biblical views and values will not be represented. As followers of Christ, we are to identify the problems in our world and offer biblical solutions.

I also have heard pastors say they are "called to preach the Gospel, not to be involved in politics." In the words of noted Christian author and commentator Eric Metaxas, "What dead, thin, useless Gospel are you preaching that is unwilling to stand up to evil?"[67] We must speak the truth in love and be willing to confront evil (Eph. 4:15). Every pastor is called to teach the whole counsel of God (Acts 20:27). If we do, we will teach the truth of Scripture on subjects like abortion, human sexuality, racism, and other controversial biblical issues. We must speak out against evil that is destroying people's lives. If we are concerned about the spread of the Gospel, we will stand against the tyranny that would rob us of our freedom to preach the Gospel.

Then there are the pastors I have talked to who will admit that they do not boldly speak the truth on controversial issues because they are afraid of losing people in their congregation. Others sounding more noble have told me they are concerned that if the church speaks out on biblical issues that are unpopular, we cannot reach the next generation. Of course, the commission of Jesus is that we reach the lost, but that should not be at the price of fidelity to the scripture or biblical clarity on the major issues of our day.

I have also talked with Christian fatalists, who believe the escalation of evil and increasing totalitarianism in our nation is inevitable, as part of end times events or the process of the Lord refining His church through suffering. Ultimately, there will be a world ruler the Bible refers to in various ways, including the title of Antichrist (1 John 2:18). As John says in his first and second epistles, the spirit of Antichrist is already at work in our world. Yet, John's response to this spirit is not to roll over and let him take control. Rather, in 1 John 4:4, he declares, "You are of God, little children, and have overcome them, because He who is in you is greater than he who is in the world." We are to be overcomers in the face of the antichrist spirit, opposing evil in every age, and occupying until Christ returns (Luke 19:13, KJV). Certainly, anyone unwilling to stand up to and speak out against the evil in our day will most certainly not have what it takes to stand up or speak out then.

In his powerful book *Live Not by Lies*, Rob Dreher writes of those suffering under totalitarian regimes saying, "They stood up for truth and justice not out of an expectation of achievable victory in their lifetimes, but because it was the right thing to do."[68] Regardless of what the future holds, today we are to do the right thing by opposing evil. This may indeed mean suffering for our faith. But it does not mean we should sit silently by and allow totalitarianism and Christian persecutors to take over our nation, so that we might be purified through suffering. That would neither be noble nor biblical. We do not stand up for biblical truth and justice simply for ourselves, but for our children and future generations who may never hear the Gospel or live out the Gospel freely if the enemies of the cross prevail. We have seen these liberties stripped from entire populations following Marxist revolutions and communist takeovers. In the words of Nehemiah, "Do not be afraid of them. Remember the Lord, great and awesome, and fight for your brethren, your sons, your daughters, your wives, and your houses" (Neh. 4:14).

Finally, I had a pastor tell me he was not speaking on these issues because the consequences of bad policies would catch up with our nation, and those supporting them would be voted out in the next election. Yet, what is happening in America is so much bigger than an election or a new set of political leaders.

The words of Mordecai to his niece Esther resound in my soul. When the Jewish nation was on the brink of destruction, and Queen Esther was reluctant to make a stand, Mordecai declared in Esther 4:14, "If you remain completely silent at this time, relief and deliverance will arise for the Jews from another place, but you and your father's house will perish. Yet who knows whether you have come to the kingdom for such a time as this?" We are part of God's kingdom for such a time as this. If we want to save our nation, we must not remain silent.

I have been a pastor almost all my adult life. I love pastors, understand the challenges of pastoral ministry, and recognize we all have different focuses in our callings. However, every pastor is mandated not to compromise on biblical truth, and we are all called to stand against evil. It is time for pastors throughout our nation to choose to be counter-cultural prophetic voices of biblical truth rather than diplomatic appeasers who sanitize truth and remain silent to avoid offending a lost and confused culture. The masses in America have been seduced, deceived, and lied to by the spirit of this world, and they desperately need men and women of God who will boldly and winsomely proclaim the un-sanitized truth of God's Word. As Christians, we are to be a restraining force against evil.

Those in America who oppose biblical truth, despise godly values, suppress God-given liberty, and are propagating evil are aware of the potential of the church. They tremble at the realization that if every pastor who professes to believe the Bible boldly opposed their lies with the truth of Scripture, and if every Bible believing Christian would live out what they believe in their daily lives, these anti-Christian overlords would be displaced from their stranglehold on America. Nearly 2,400 years ago, Athenian philosopher Plato said, "The price good men pay for indifference in public affairs is to be ruled by evil men."[69] We must not abdicate our role, and in the face of evil we must not be silent. Yet, as it was in the days of Elijah, that prophetic, biblical voice will be strongly and forcefully opposed.

DECLARING THE WORD OF THE LORD

In some of the darkest days in Israel's history, Elijah suddenly and dramatically appeared on the scene. By stepping forward, Elijah made himself a target. He could do it because he was not afraid of King Ahab. In Proverbs 29:25, we are told, "The fear of man brings a snare." Yet Elijah feared God and not Ahab. This enabled him to proclaim God's Word boldly and unashamedly. In 1 Kings 17:1 we read, "And Elijah the Tishbite, of the inhabitants of Gilead, said to Ahab, 'As the Lord God of Israel lives, before whom I stand, there shall not be dew nor rain these years, except at my word.'" Elijah did not come declaring his credentials, education, or experience. He did not come with a resume, but with the Word of God. God does not require educational degrees, financial influence, or political clout. Elijah did not appear to have any of those things. But He had a word from God.

God's Word is powerful. Jeremiah 23:29 reads, "Is not My word like a fire?" says the Lord, "And like a hammer that breaks the rock in pieces?" The writer of Hebrews declares, "For the word of God is living and powerful, and sharper than any two-edged sword..." (Heb. 4:12). Elijah proclaims God's Word, not knowing how the King would respond. Yet that was not his concern. Rather, his concern was simply to be obedient. We have a word from God today in His written Word. It is an answer to the confusion and insanity going on in our broken culture. It is not popular, but we must not be silent.

When Elijah said, "before whom I stand," he was speaking of being a servant of God, standing in the presence of God, listening for His command to obey His Word. He was a person of God's presence. That is what people are seeking today. Elijah speaks God's Word, but he does not do it in a vacuum. In James 5:17, James tells us that before Elijah said it would not rain, he had earnestly prayed that it would not. I believe Elijah knew what Deuteronomy 11 and 28 warned: that if the nation rebelled against God, the heavens would become brass. He prayed and sought the Lord concerning these Scriptures and out of "*the* Word" Elijah was given "*a* word" for Ahab. We need time in the prayer closet to hear from God. But then there is a time to leave the prayer closet and speak His Word publicly.

Elijah announces to Ahab that there will be a drought in the land. Baal was a nature deity who was supposed to control the weather, including rain. This was a direct attack on Baal. The book of James tells us the drought lasted 3½ years. They had already had the spring rains, so there would have been an expectation of drought for a season, but the drought just kept going. In that agrarian culture, "no rain" meant an economic shutdown.

THE HIDDEN YEARS

Elijah confronted King Ahab, took a bold stand, made a prophetic pronouncement, and then went into hiding (v2-3), which is what other believers in Israel were already doing. But while others were hiding in fear, Elijah was to hide in faith. God was going to do a work *in* Elijah before He did a work *through* Elijah.

First, Elijah spent a season at the Brook Cherith, where he was miraculously supplied by a raven who brought him bread and meat daily (v4-6). This may have been supplied by the bird taking food from King Ahab's table at their home in Jezreel.[70] When the brook dried up because of the drought, Elijah was led to Zarephath (v7). There he was sustained by the generosity of a widow, who experienced supernatural daily multiplication of her meager provisions (v8-16). Later, the woman's son became fatally ill, and God used Elijah to resuscitate the boy from the dead (v17-24).

Through all this, God was preparing Elijah for his historic encounter with the prophets of Baal on Mount Carmel. Elijah's faith and confidence in God was being tested, and the Lord was continually proven faithful. Similarly, God uses all the challenges and difficulties we face in life to prepare us for a Divine purpose. Much like David, who before facing Goliath killed a lion and a bear as a shepherd protecting his sheep (1 Sam. 17:36-37), we must experience the trying of our faith before being used by God to do something equivalent to calling down fire on Carmel.

THE TRUE TROUBLER

After three-and-a-half years, Elijah was ready and prepared to confront Ahab, the demon-god Baal, and the nation. King Ahab had left Jerusalem with his trusted servant Obadiah to look for grass to feed his horses and mules. Obadiah was an undercover believer. He feared the Lord and secretly had hidden the one hundred fugitive prophets in two caves, making sure they were fed. Jezebel had a warrant on the prophets' lives. Like Elijah, Obadiah was risking his life, but in a non-confrontational way. Obadiah is an example of the rare times when God wants a person to be silent and undercover with their faith. God had him in a strategic position where he could not be bold in his witness. His influence was critical, but he would lose it if he spoke out. This is the exception, and we need wisdom to know why God has placed us in that kind of situation. The question is, are we doing it out of fear, convenience, and self-benefit, or are we going under the direction of the Holy Spirit?

While Obadiah was out seeking food for Ahab's horses, Elijah suddenly stands in front of him. Elijah tells Obadiah to summon King Ahab to meet with him. The "most-wanted" fugitive prophet has summoned the king, and the king obeys. The pompous apostate king stands before the camel hair-covered prophet of God.

"Then it happened, when Ahab saw Elijah, that Ahab said to him, 'Is that you, O troubler of Israel?'" (v17). Ahab still does not see the drought as the hand of God. He did not see it as a consequence of abandoning Yahweh. Instead, Ahab is trying to blame Israel's problems on Elijah. Yet, he was blaming the one who is offering the solution.

The prophet Isaiah declared, "Woe to those who call evil good, and good evil; who put darkness for light, and light for darkness; who put bitter for sweet, and sweet for bitter!" (Is. 5:20). That sounds like today. We have national leaders who fail to recognize that most of the problems we face in our nation can be traced back to jettisoning biblical values and rejecting the God of the Bible. In fact, the ungodly will often call out and blame those with biblical values for the troubles in the world but refuse to acknowledge the obvious consequences of sin.

Undaunted, Elijah answered Ahab, saying. "I have not troubled Israel, but you and your father's house have, in that you have forsaken the commandments of the Lord and have followed the Baals." (v18). Then Elijah directed Ahab to call the nation to meet on Mount Carmel, along with the prophets of Baal and Asherah. When Ahab told Jezebel the news about the gathering at Carmel, she must have been horribly upset. I can just imagine her yelling at the king for not arresting and executing Elijah on the spot. But it is too late. There is going to be a major confrontation between God and Jezebel's gods.

Mount Carmel is not a single mountain but a range of hills nearly 2,000 feet above sea level and covered with many trees. Baal worshipers preferred the high places and the mountain groves, so it had become a center for Baal worship. Elijah was going to confront Baal on his home turf.

Ahab arrived that morning in all his royal finery, with a huge entourage of escorts, probably including some of the military, 450 priests of Baal, and thousands of people who came to see the contest. On the other side there was ... Elijah. It appeared unfair, but God did not need an army, he only needed one willing to stand with Him on His covenant.

A TIME TO DECIDE

Alone with God on Mount Carmel, Elijah called the people to decide. He "came to all the people, and said, 'How long will you falter between two opinions? If the Lord *is* God, follow Him; but if Baal, follow him.' But the people answered him not a word" (v21). The word falter has the implication of limping.[71] He is telling them that their indecision had made them crippled as a nation. Israel had not yet fallen into total apostasy. They still believed in Yahweh but were not sure Yahweh was enough. The nation was becoming polytheistic and was involved in religious syncretism. They wanted to experience the advantages of Yahweh and Baal at the same time.

This way of thinking sounds attractive in our culture. We have seen the bumper stickers that say "co-exist." There are different faiths, and in a pluralist country like America, we need to respect each other and work toward cooperation. But multiple religions and multiple gods absolutely cannot co-exist in an individual's life.

Today only 9% of self-identified Christians and just 37% of pastors hold to a Biblical worldview.[72] Instead, like Israel in that day, they have embraced syncretism. They blend new spirituality, postmodernism, Marxist theories, secular humanism, and other non-biblical doctrines together as their religion.[73] It does not work to pick and choose what you like best from each religion. We cannot believe in the God of the Bible and embrace an anti-Biblical secular mindset. We also cannot remain undecided. It never works.

Suppose a man is dating three different women. He likes each of them and cannot decide whom to commit to. So, he says to one, "I'd like to marry you, but can I still date the other two women?" This, of course, will not work. In this scenario, they will never experience the commitment and intimacy that a good marriage requires. Yet, that is what many Americans who claim to be Christians try to do.

Jesus said this same thing about spiritual allegiances. In Matthew 6:24 He said, "No one can serve two masters; for either he will hate the one and love the other, or else he will be loyal to the one and despise the other. You cannot serve God and mammon." He also could have just as easily said, "You can't serve God and a culture contrary to God." If you try, you will never experience the abundant life Jesus promises.

In the battle we are facing now, there is no spiritual neutrality. If we attempt to be neutral, we will end up being silent, because we do not want to offend anybody. If God is not our master, then something else is. We will be spiritually crippled if we are not fully committed to Christ. Elijah told Israel, and he is telling us: quit wavering. If Yahweh is God, passionately follow Him. Now, if Baal or some other idol is God, go all in for it. The people of Israel were not making a choice. They were sitting on the fence. We cannot do the same. Elijah is telling us, "Get off the fence and fully devote yourselves to God." In our day he could say, stop being compromising, carnal, casual, cultural Christians. Instead, be passionate followers of Jesus Christ.

FIRE

"Then Elijah said to the people, 'I alone am left a prophet of the LORD; but Baal's prophets are four hundred and fifty men'" (v22). Elijah knew of the 100 prophets in hiding. He must have meant that he was the only prophet of the Lord left to challenge Baal openly. He then laid down the guidelines for a power encounter -- to determine which deity was worthy of worship. They would both cut up a bull, and, using no trickery or illusion, call on their god to send fire to the sacrifice (v23-24).

There on Mount Carmel, in view of King Ahab, was an altar to the worship of Baal Melqart. "So they took the bull which was given them, and they prepared it, and called on the name of Baal from morning even till noon, saying, 'O Baal, hear us!' There was no response; no one answered. Then they leaped about the altar which they had made" (v26). What the cultic priests would do has been documented. The priests of Baal come in white linen with white bonnets on their heads. They would have begun with howling. Then there was a hop dance they performed for their god. Next, they would rush around wildly in confusion. The worshipers would bow their heads to the ground—whirling them in circles and dragging their hair through dust and mire. Then they would bite themselves and finally cut themselves with knives.[74] It was a very strenuous, challenging, and difficult ritual. It is like all man-made religions. In religion, you must perform for your god.

God delights in praise-filled, passionate worshipers. This is illustrated throughout the Psalms and in the Biblical narrative. In the Old Testament Scripture, the various Hebrew words for worship include the activities of shouting, raving over, celebrating, lifting hands, kneeling, bowing, singing, making music, and dancing. As followers of Christ, we do not extravagantly worship God to get Him to act. We passionately worship God because of who He is, what He has done, and because He is worthy of worship. Yet as we extravagantly worship, God inhabits the praises of His people, and we often see extraordinary things we would see no other way (Ps. 22:3, 2 Chron. 20:22-24). Instead, the followers of Baal worshiped as they did out of a frantic striving to get Baal to act.

"And so it was at noon, that Elijah mocked them and said, 'Cry aloud, for he is a god; either he is meditating, or he is busy, or he is on a journey, or perhaps he is sleeping and must be awakened.'" (v27). Elijah went beyond boldness to taunt them sarcastically. It was apparently Elijah's personality. He taunted the priests. Maybe Baal was deep in meditation, so he did not hear you. Maybe he was away traveling, so not available. Perhaps he was sleeping because Baal was thought to fall asleep every winter. Elijah also says, "Maybe he's busy." Literally in the Hebrew, he is saying, "Maybe Baal can't be bothered because he's on the toilet."[75] He laughed at them— "That's your idea of a god." I am certain Elijah's comments would be banned on Twitter and he would have been placed in Facebook jail had he said these things today.

With the rest of God's prophets and outspoken believers in hiding, Elijah's boldness must have seemed incredible. It also would have been refreshing. I would have to say that today some antics of those who oppose biblical truth are so ridiculous it is difficult not to laugh at them and be sarcastic. There is a lunacy that goes with opposing God and His truth. As an example, have you not seen the pregnant man emoji that iPhone now offers?

"So, they cried aloud, and cut themselves, as was their custom, with knives and lances, until the blood gushed out on them" (v28). Sometimes the prophets of Baal entered such a frenzy they would bite themselves, thrash themselves with ropes, and then cut themselves with knives and swords. This is what idolatry does to you. There is an epidemic of cutting and self-harm in our society today. We also have a crisis of people mutilating their bodies in surgeries to appease the idols of our society.

"And when midday was past, they prophesied until the time of the offering of the evening sacrifice. But there was no voice; no one answered, no one paid attention" (v29). This is always how idols respond when you need them most. A piece of wood, a piece of clay, a piece of stone, a delusional ideology, can never respond.

Near the altar to Baal is a broken-down altar of Yahweh. The people were told to rebuild it (v30-31). The altar was built, a trench was dug around it, wood was stacked, and the sacrificial bull was cut in pieces and laid on it (v32-33). Finally, three times they took four large pots of water, and drenched the sacrifice (v34-35). There was no trickery; either it would be a total miracle of God, or nothing would occur. The people could feel the certitude of Elijah. There would be no dancing, no shouting, no cutting. It is not 450 priests, just a solitary man, fully confident in the God of Israel._

Elijah's prayer was a covenant-based prayer that included no travailing (though there is a place for travailing), no crying out (though God tells us there are times to cry out), no confessing or declaring that it would happen. It was just a simple, bold prayer of faith (v36-37). Elijah already had been praying in secret. He had heard from God, and he was filled with faith, enabling him to pray with great confidence.

This was a prayer of faith reminiscent of the ministry of Jesus when He rebuked demons and spoke to diseased bodies. Jesus said, "... the Son can do nothing of Himself, but what He sees the Father do; for whatever He does, the Son also does in like manner" (John 5:19). In verse 36, Elijah prayed, "I have done all these things at Your word." There was authority in Elijah's prayer because he had heard from God and was obeying the word God had given him. We sometimes see men and women of God who—like Elijah—do great exploits, and it seems so effortless. Yet we do not see the hours they spent before the Lord in the Secret Place. There is always a spiritual price to pay before a Mount Carmel.

"Then the fire of the Lord fell and consumed the burnt sacrifice, and the wood and the stones and the dust, and it licked up the water that was in the trench" (v38). Thousands of people witnessed the miracle. It is one of the great events in Israel's history. Many scholars believe the fire came by a lightning bolt—which was a symbol for Baal—but it is now evident that it is Yahweh who controls lightning.

"Now when all the people saw it, they fell on their faces; and they said, 'The Lord, He is God! The Lord, He is God!'" (v39). Today, America needs to experience God's fire. In Exodus, fire speaks of God's divine presence (Ex.3:2-6, 19:18, 24:17). John the Baptist foretold of Jesus baptizing with the Holy Spirit and fire (Matt. 3:11, Lk. 3:16). On the day of Pentecost, the believers were filled with the Holy Spirit, and "tongues of fire" rested over each of them (Acts 2:3-4). Fire is a sign of God's presence in a person's life.

The gifted French mathematician and physicist Blaise Pascal described his November 23, 1654, conversion experience with the one word, "fire." He explained it resulted in "total submission" to Jesus Christ, accompanied by "certitude, certainty, heartfelt, joy, and peace."[76] The great preacher and Christian leader John Wesley said of his conversion experience, as sensing "my heart strangely warmed. I felt I did trust in Christ, Christ alone for salvation; and an assurance was given me that He had taken away my sins, even mine, and saved me from the law of sin and death."[77] Though not initially as dramatic as Pascal, there was a new fire in the heart of Wesley. Every true follower of Christ can say they have experienced this divine flame.

Many people who are concerned about the death spiral in America are attempting to lead legislative reform in our country. They want to "drain the swamp" and see wise and effective leaders elected to office. This is commendable and needed. Others are focused on curtailing abortion. Every follower of Christ should support these efforts. Yet others desire to restore biblical principles in our laws and government. Their work is necessary and should be encouraged. Yet, all of this is still not enough.

Though you can legislate moral standards, you cannot legislate spirituality or lasting moral change. We must have the fire of God. We must have a heaven-sent awakening and a Holy Spirit outpouring, and we cannot settle for less. At the same time, without governmental and legislative action and God-honoring leaders, there will not be lasting change in our nation. The two go hand in hand. For lasting impact, there must be both.

ELIMINATING THE CORRUPTION

"And Elijah said to them, 'Seize the prophets of Baal! Do not let one of them escape!' So, they seized them; and Elijah brought them down to the Brook Kishon and executed them there" (v40). Elijah ordered the massacre of the priests of Baal. The killing of the pagan priests is difficult for modern westerners to accept, and they may even see this as moral justification to reject the God of the Bible. Yet, we need to know the background. Elijah was acting on Deuteronomy 13. This was a necessary surgery. The prophets were at the center of the spiritual and physical corruption of the nation. They were deeply involved in human sacrifice and sex trafficking. If they were not destroyed, they would have continued to be a horrible corrupting influence on the nation and the world, and they had to be executed.

Obviously, the Bible is not suggesting we do physical harm to others (Lk. 6:27, 35). Yet, it is teaching an important principle and is challenging us to be spiritually violent (Matt. 11:12). The Apostle Paul tells us in Romans 12:9, "Let love be without hypocrisy. Abhor what is evil. Cling to what is good." Not only are we to cling to what is good, but we are to hate evil. We must hate sin and corruption. That begins with the sin and corruption in our own lives, and we must be brutal in dealing with it. In the Sermon on the Mount, Jesus told His followers, "If your right eye causes you to sin, pluck it out" and "if your right hand causes you to sin cut it off" (Matt. 5:29-30). As Holy Rebels, we must remove anything from our lives that dishonors the Lord and can cause others to stumble (1 Cor. 8:9, 13).

After challenging the compromising nation to decide, calling fire down from heaven, and eliminating corruptive and destructive national influences, it still was not enough. Israel was dry and thirty and needed rain. The fire had to come first. Now it is time to birth an outpouring. Spiritually, we need the same in our day. We will examine how we can realize it in the next chapter.

———— CHAPTER TWELVE ————

BIRTHING AN AWAKENING

W E HAVE BEEN examining the ministry of Elijah to the nation of Israel in 1 Kings 16-19. The fire of God has fallen on Mount Carmel, the people of Israel have returned to the Lord, and the priests of Baal, who defiled and corrupted the land, were executed at the Brook Kidron (1 Kings 18:40). Now it is time for the 3½ year drought to end and the rain to come. While in the narrative this is a physical rain, in the Scripture rain is a picture of God visiting His people in revival (Ps. 72:6, Is. 44:3, Ezek. 34:26, Hos. 6:1-3). The Lord awakening the hearts of his people is essential, but after the awakening what is needed is spiritual outpouring (Acts 2:17-18).

Elijah knew it was time for an outpouring because he heard "the sound of abundance of rain" (v41). It was not thunder Elijah heard, but the sound of the Spirit of God. We hear things we cannot yet see, but God can tell us things yet to come (John 16:13). He can alert us to the season we are in and what He desires to do (1 Chron. 12:32). The Psalmist writes, "Blessed are the people who know the joyful sound!" (Ps. 89:15). This is beautiful, poetic language but the meaning may surprise you. In Hebrew, the phrase "the joyful sound" means "a shout, a shofar call to war, or a war cry."[78] It is a battle cry. God went to war for the hearts of His people. He sent a drought to arrest their attention. He sent fire to capture their hearts. And now He will pour out His rain.

Elijah knew what time it was on God's timetable, and we must as well. This is not a time of peace, but a time of spiritual warfare. Like Elijah, we must fight and contend for revival and spiritual outpouring. Elijah heard God say it was time for rain, but he still had to go to war and contend for it.

After this awe-inspiring miracle and the fatal defeat of Baal's priests, we read, "So Ahab went up to eat and drink" (v42a). He lazily expected a rainstorm instead of God's visitation. Like many believers today, Ahab did not know what time it was. In Ecclesiastes 3, Solomon tells us, "To everything there is a season . . . A time of war and a time of peace." In 1 Kings 18, it was a time of war to contend against the darkness that had taken over Israel. Ahab did not recognize this, because he had been seduced by Jezebel and by the expectation of the drought ending. Ahab was so deceived and deluded that he could neither perceive nor understand God's timing and plan.

Unlike Ahab, Elijah understood it was a time for war. So, while Ahab went up to eat and drink, Elijah "went up to the top of Carmel" (v42b). Elijah realized it was time to press into God — to pursue Him with all his heart, mind, soul, and strength. It was a time to go to war for the heart and soul of the nation, a time to birth revival through prayer.

Most American Christians, and too many pastors, fail to see what time it is. After the COVID-19 pandemic, they rushed to return to business as usual. There was no urgency to call their congregations to prayer. So many pastors simply returned to their Christian "TED Talks" and performance-oriented worship. But it was and continues to be a time for a prophetic word from the Scripture and a season for their congregations to press into God as praise-and-prayer-filled warriors. We need more pastors with the spirit of Elijah, who hear the trumpet and will go to war and battle for the heart of a nation and the souls of its people.

PRAYING FOR SPIRITUAL OUTPOURING

In Zechariah 10:1 the prophet says, "Ask the Lord for rain in the time of the latter rain. The Lord will make flashing clouds; He will give them showers of rain..." Zechariah is saying, it is Yahweh who brings rain, not Baal, and in the time of rain, ask Him for it. Elijah heard from God that it was the time for rain. Then he prayed for rain. The Apostle James writes, "The effective, fervent prayer of a righteous man avails much. Elijah was a man with a nature like ours, and he prayed earnestly that it would not rain; and it did not rain on the land for three years and six months. And he prayed again, and the heaven gave rain, and the earth produced its fruit" (James

5:16). Elijah's prayers brought the will of God into existence. Likewise, our prayers can bring down the rain of the Holy Spirit and provide a supernatural breakthrough in our lives.

At the end of verse 42 we read, "Then he bowed down on the ground, and put his face between his knees." In the Bible, there are many postures people took in prayer. People prayed on their knees, standing up, sitting down, looking up, bowing down, pounding their chest, walking across a room, facing the temple, and lifting their hands. You could say a posture in prayer is a body language to express what your heart is feeling.

Elijah assumed a unique prayer position. His head was between his knees — a birthing position. He was going to give spiritual birth. We live in a weird and perverted time. There are people in our society who with a straight face spout nonsense, contrary to basic biology and clear reality. They say men can have babies. For the record—for the entire history of humanity, until this moment, everyone knew men could not physically give birth. The Bible and biology tell us it is women who give birth physically. Yet, the Bible also tells us both men and women can give birth spiritually. Either men or women can birth spiritual results. Paul writes in Galatians 4:19, "My little children, for whom I labor in birth again until Christ is formed in you." In Isaiah 66:8 was told, "For as soon as Zion was in labor, she gave birth to her children."

When a woman gives birth, she does not continue in labor only until she gets weary of it. She does not labor only for a prescribed period. She is going to take all the time required to bring forth a new life. That is what prevailing prayer is like. You persist until God's will, plan, and purpose are birthed.

At this point Elijah, "Said to his servant, 'Go up now, look toward the sea.' So, he went up and looked, and said, 'There is nothing.' And seven times he said, "Go again" (v43). We saw in the showdown with the priests of Baal that sometimes prayer is answered after praying a brief prayer of faith. Yet, other times we are called on to persistently pray, and pray and pray, until the answer comes.

Elijah prayed, and his servant kept returning, saying he saw nothing. Yet the servant's observation did not stop the prophet from believing and pressing in. The servant had information, but Elijah had a *revelation*. And he knew revelation was far greater than information.

We must not let circumstances and evil reports stop us from believing and pressing in to receive what we know God has told us. We must avoid focusing on what we *see*, and instead depend on what we have *heard*. God gave Abraham a promise that the Lord would give him a miracle child, but after years of waiting, the child had not come. Romans 4 tells us that Abraham did not focus on his and his wife's aging bodies. Instead, he called those things that did not exist as though they were.

In Romans 4:20-21, we read that Abraham "did not waver at the promise of God through unbelief, but was strengthened in faith, giving glory to God, and being fully convinced that what He had promised He could also perform." Like Abraham, we must keep our eyes on the promise. Like Elijah, we should not focus on the cloudless sky, but keep our mind set on what we have heard. In Romans 4:17 we are told Abraham, "called those things which did not exist as though they did."

We must ask ourselves whether we will call those things which do not exist as though they did. Are we willing to call our friend saved when he is lost? Can we call our son or daughter restored when he or she is a prodigal? Are we able to call the church revived when so many in the church are asleep? Do we have the bold faith to call America saved and awakened when she is teetering on collapse? By faith, we must call those things which are not as though they were, and we must persist until we see a breakthrough.

In John 16:21, Jesus said, "A woman giving birth to a child has pain because her time has come; but when her baby is born, she forgets the anguish because of her joy that the child is born into the world." Persisting in enduring and prevailing prayer is hard work. Believing God's Word contrary to what we see can appear ludicrous, but the rewards for those giving birth to a miracle are a thousand times worth it. And when the breakthrough comes, you forget about the agony.

Just as a woman in labor is told to push, we must push in our travail. Push past the lies of darkness. Push past our flesh. Push past our insecurities. It is like the woman in Mark 5 with the issue of blood who pushed through the crowd to touch the hem of Jesus' garment to be healed. She pushed past her doubts, past her fears, past her pride. She pushed past offenses and what people had told her. She pushed past the traditions of her religion. And she broke through. Jesus commended her faith. We must do the same if we are to see spiritual outpouring and supernatural breakthrough.

AN ILLUSTRATION OF SPIRITUAL BIRTHING
(A PERSONAL ACCOUNT BY KELLY)

Our dear friend and prominent Christian leader Ron McIntosh was with us at Radiant. God had given him a message for the church, and it began with Isaiah 37:3. Interestingly, the week before Ron's arrival, the Holy Spirit spoke to me also, concerning Isaiah 37:3 (CSB), "... Today is a day of distress, rebuke, and disgrace. It is as if children have come to the point of birth, and there is no strength to deliver them." That is a very sad and distressing picture: to come to the point of giving birth, but to lack the power and the strength to deliver. The Lord warned me concerning the church in this hour with these words from Isaiah. Ron followed up with a confirming warning and this message: **There is a revival in the birth canal of the bride of Christ.** This move of God is huge, and the church must stay engaged and continue to push through all apathy, complacency, and every hindrance that would stop what God is birthing through His Church.

During this same time, God had opened my eyes to see the strategy of the evil one to stop the move of God. The Lord often shows me things in the spirit realm that are occurring, so that I can engage in prayer, warn the church, and activate His people to action. What the Lord revealed to me through a prophetic dream and the interpretation of that dream was troubling.

The body of Christ was pregnant with the next great move of God, yet most were completely unaware that they were expecting. They continued with a "business as usual" mentality. They sat motionless, inactive, watching others who were engaged, but were oblivious to the reality that they were pregnant and needed to engage in giving birth. The Lord unveiled the enemy's strategy of replacing God's holy mantle from His church and replacing it with an unholy mantle of apathy, complacency, and weakness. This initiated a sense of intense grief and anguish in my spirit. The words of Isaiah 37:3 sounded loudly in my head, "It is as if children have come to the point of birth, and there is no strength to deliver them."

The Spirit of God revealed a picture to me of where we are, and that the scheme of the enemy had been deployed. Now, we have to sound the alarm, awaken the church, and compel her to push through to the victory. This is not a time to back off, back down, back away, or back up. The Bride of Christ must rise up now and throw off the unholy mantle of apathy, complacency, and inactivity. It is time to push.

Just two days later, one of our staff shared a real-life illustration of the effort required to give birth. Krystal Clark, who heads our crisis pregnancy ministry, had just been in the delivery room with a woman as she was giving birth. What Krystal shared was dramatic. She said that after hours of hard labor, the mother was exhausted and becoming weaker. Then one of the nurses jumped on top of her, got in her face and began shouting at her: "You've got to push! You can't give up! This baby is huge! You must push now! Now! Now!"

As Krystal described this to me, it was as if the Holy Spirit had jumped on top of me and started shouting, "Kelly Hudnall, this is your calling now! You must awaken My bride. Awaken My church. Sound the alarm to My people. Awaken them now. You must jump on them, get in their faces and shout that it's time to push!" No doubt, this move of God is huge. We must throw off every weight and hindrance. It is time to push through in prayer and intercession like we have never pushed before. It is time to push through in praise and worship like we have never pushed before. God is sounding the alarm, and He is shouting to each of His sons and daughters to push through like a woman in labor and to give birth to the next great move of God.

PERSISTENT PRAYER
(TODD RESUMES)

Charles Finney is known as the father of American revivalism and was the leading evangelist of the Second Great Awakening. Perhaps his greatest campaign occurred in Rochester, New York, in 1830-1831.[79] Charles P. Bush, a native of Rochester who converted during the revival, later remarked: "The whole community was stirred. Religion was the topic of conversation in the house, in the shop, in the office and on the street...Grog shops were closed, the Sabbath was honored, the sanctuaries were thronged with happy worshippers...There was a wonderful falling off of crime. The courts had little to do, and the jail was nearly empty for years afterward." Of the Rochester revival historians say, "The place was shaken to its foundations."[80] There were many other cities similarly shaken by the ministry of Charles Finney, as a terrifying conviction of the Holy Spirit would fall on his audiences.

A key to Finney's extraordinary results was prevailing prayer. Not only was Finney a man of prayer, but he partnered in ministry with a great intercessor named Daniel Nash. Father Nash would arrive in a city 3 or 4 weeks ahead of Finney to prepare it for revival. He would find a few other intercessors to join in continuous, fervent, prevailing prayer for the community. His intense and effectual prayers were often accompanied by tears, groaning, and travail for the lost. Not coincidently, Finney left his ministry as a revivalist within a few months of Nash's death.[81]

This kind of prevailing prayer refuses to give up until the answer comes. Jesus spoke of this kind of prayer in His parables. In Luke 18:1-7, He tells of a persistent widow who would not give up in pestering an unjust judge until he gave her justice. The judge eventually ruled in her favor, not simply because her cause was just, but because she continually pushed for justice and constantly cried out for it.

In Luke 11:5-8, Jesus gives the example of a man who goes to a friend for bread to feed a hungry traveler. The neighbor finds it too inconvenient to help, so refuses to oblige his friend, until the man's relentless asking forces him to respond. Jesus points out that the man is given bread, not simply because of his friendship with his neighbor, but because of his persistent pushing for an answer. In these two stories, we learn the Lord does not respond to our prayers just because our cause is just or because He is our friend. Jesus is our friend (John 15:15), and when our cause is just, He delights in answering our prayers. Yet sometimes our requests to Him also require a tenacious faith that will not give up but keeps pushing for an answer. In fact, Jesus finishes the parable in Luke 18:8 by asking, "When the Son of Man comes, will He really find faith on the earth?" God is seeking for a faith that will not give up until the answer comes. In Isaiah 62:1-7 God challenges His people to give themselves no rest and to give Him no rest until His purpose in the earth is accomplished. This is the faith-filled prayer that will bring fire from heaven and provide great spiritual outpouring.

A few years ago, I had a dream that drove this truth home to me. In my dream, there was great turmoil. We desperately needed God's intervention, and prayer was required. At that point in my dream, I was told by a wise mentor, "It's not enough to spend a day and a night in the deep." Immediately, I awoke from my dream, and I heard an audible voice say, "For deep calls out to deep." This is a quote from Psalm 42:7. I had never experienced hearing the audible voice of God, but that morning I might have. I believe He was telling me that the deep things of God only occur through deep, fervent, persistent prayer.

Elijah had this kind of persistence. Verse 44 explains, "Then it came to pass the seventh time, that he said, 'There is a cloud, as small as a man's hand, rising out of the sea!' So he said, 'Go up, say to Ahab, 'Prepare your chariot, and go down before the rain stops you.'" Elijah has gone from nothing to something. But it does not seem like much. Sometimes, as much as we pray, the cloud looks so small. It may start small and disappointing, but it is going to grow and its rain will become a downpour.

We read in verse 45, "Now it happened in the meantime that the sky became black with clouds and wind, and there was a heavy rain." After Elijah's season of prevailing prayer, the answer comes suddenly. I love the "suddenlys" of God. Israel had been waiting for their Messiah for thousands of years, and then in Luke 2:13 we read, "Suddenly a great company of the heavenly host appeared with the angel" to announce to the shepherds the birth of Jesus, the long-awaited Messiah. Jesus told his disciples to wait in Jerusalem for the Promise of the Father. They had been waiting for ten days when in Acts 2:2 we read, "Suddenly a sound like the blowing of a violent wind came from heaven" and the church was birthed in Holy Spirit power — suddenly.

Israel had not seen rain for three and a half years. Elijah's servant had run to the top of the mountain six times but returned with nothing to report. Then suddenly, after the seventh time, everything changed, and the rain came. Within seconds the land went from dry to drenched. Now that the rains had come, it was time for Elijah to take advantage of it.

RUN INTO THE ROAR

In Chapter Four (The Theater of War), we discussed running toward the roar of a lion as an analogy for avoiding Satan's deceptive schemes by running toward the challenges we face. In verse 46, we find Ahab running toward the roar: "Then the hand of the Lord came upon Elijah; and he girded up his loins and ran ahead of Ahab to the entrance of Jezreel." There are a couple of possibilities in interpreting this passage. Maybe the heavy rains made for muddy conditions that hindered travel for Ahab's horses and chariot. Perhaps the hand of God that came upon Elijah was so empowering it impacted his physical capabilities. Regardless, he ran so fast he raced past Ahab's chariot and horses to Jezreel. I can imagine Elijah waving to Ahab as he speeds by.

Before Elijah ran, "he girded up his loins." He had to pull his robe up and cinch it so it would not trip him up. This incident echoes Peter's statement in 1 Peter 1:13, where he tells us to "gird up the loins of your mind." We must get our thoughts focused and not get distracted while on our mission. Elijah's mind was girded, and his spirit was determined.

Elijah ran to Jezreel, the capital of Israel. It was the headquarters of Ahab and Jezebel. He charged into the capital to bring the Word of God to the stronghold of the enemy, and he went into the belly of the beast to bring revival to the nation. However, as he ran into the roar, he suddenly was stopped in his tracks.

THE SPIRIT OF JEZEBEL

It appeared Elijah was going to lead a spiritual reformation in the nation. After the fire on Carmel and the outpouring of rain, it seemed the people who passionately declared "The Lord, He is God" would rally behind him, led by the 7,000 who had never bowed their knee to Baal. The 100 prophets would come out of hiding, and Obadiah would publicly announce his allegiance to Yahweh. None of that has time to happen. Instead, we read in 1 Kings 19:2, "Then Jezebel sent a messenger to Elijah, saying, 'So let the gods do to me, and more also, if I do not make your life as the life of one of them by tomorrow about this time.'"

Satan does not take an assault on his kingdom without retaliating. Even as God uses people to accomplish His purposes, so does the Evil One. Jezebel was a willing subject. We have seen that Jezebel was a high priestess of the demon-god Baal. She was also involved in witchcraft and the occult (2 Kings 9:22). Demonic powers were at work through Jezebel.

I've had multiple experiences where I've seen Satanic forces retaliate after a kingdom victory. Mario Murillo shared with us a key understanding of spiritual warfare. He told us that often in battle, an army will appear to have won in combat, but instead of continuing to rout the enemy, they pause to celebrate and enjoy their apparent conquest. While celebrating, their enemy regroups and launches a counter-offensive. What should have been great victory can be turned into a humiliating defeat.

When we are enforcing Christ's victory in the spiritual battle, and we have the enemy on their heels, it is not a time to celebrate. It is a time to complete our assignment and continue to drive out the darkness with God's truth, power, and light. We cannot let up, but we must remain vigilant before, during, and after a kingdom victory. Elijah fails to press forward to seal the victory and instead becomes neutralized by Jezebel's re-taliation.

After this demonic retaliation, almost instantly Elijah went from his finest hour to his most humiliating moment. The bold prophet arose and ran in fear for his life (v3). Clearly, Jezebel was bluffing, or she would have sent an assassin rather than a note. But Elijah fell for her ruse and aban-doned the most incredible opportunity of his life and ministry. From there, the prophet fell into deep discouragement and depression. We must ask, why? Obviously, physical, and psychological factors were involved but the primary explanation for Elijah collapse is spiritual retaliation. The reason is that Jezebel carried more spiritual power than a typical queen. Jezebel was empowered by demonic forces of evil, fear, and intimidation — forces that are still alive and active in our world today.

The same demonic spirits that empowered and operated through Je-zebel continued long after her death. In Revelation 2:20-22 Jesus, speaking to the church in Thyatira, addresses a woman named Jezebel. Undoubted-ly, this was not her actual name. She was referred to by this name because the same spiritual entities that worked through the queen of Ahab were at work through this woman nearly 1,000 years later. In Thyatira, Jezebel was a self-proclaimed prophetess and false teacher, who enticed people in the church into idolatry and sexual immorality.

The issue with Jezebel of Thyatira is not that she was a woman. Proph-etesses are mentioned throughout the Scripture (Judges 4-5, 2 Chronicles 34:14-33, Luke 2:36 and Acts 21:9) and Paul encourages women to prophesy (1 Cor. 11:5). Also, women like Phoebe, Junia, and Priscilla were deaconess-es, apostles, pastors, and teachers in the New Testament. So, the problem is not that Jezebel was teaching, but it is *what* she was teaching and what she was being allowed to do. Men can operate under the power of these spiritual influences. In fact, in my own life, I have witnessed this Jezebel type of activity in men as often as in women.

Ahab's greatest sin was allowing Jezebel to control him and the nation. The church in Thyatira's sin was allowing Jezebel to operate unhindered. Jezebel causes the most damage in an organization with a weak leader. I do not have a micromanaging bone in my body. I like to find capable lead-ers and allow them the freedom to grow and develop their ministries. As a leader, this has been one of my primary strengths and one of my greatest weaknesses. That is because I have used it as an excuse to tolerate a spirit of Jezebel. For what you permit, you promote and what you tolerate; you deserve.

Adam allowed Satan to deceive Eve in the garden when he should have driven the serpent out (Genesis 3). Eli tolerated his sons' reprehensible behaviors when they should have been confronted and disciplined (1 Sam. 2:12-36). Parents are accountable for the atmosphere in their homes, and employers are responsible for the culture in their workplaces. Followers of Christ are responsible for the moral and spiritual atmosphere of our nation. We must confront darkness and not allow it to continue unhindered.

Based on these passages, we learn that when Jezebel is allowed to have her way, there will be rampant idolatry, sexual immorality, occult activity, devaluing of human life, false teaching, the silencing of opposing voices, and the murder of innocent lives. It sounds eerily like 21st Century America. Some symptoms of being assaulted by Jezebel include fear, intimidation, weariness, discouragement, and depression — which describe many in the American church today. Like Old Testament Israel, clearly Jezebel has infiltrated our land and saturated us with her influence.

RESPONDING TO DEMONIC ATTACK

The greatest results in the ministry of the Apostle Paul occurred in the seaport city of Ephesus in modern-day Turkey. This center for idolatry and the occult experienced an extraordinary spiritual awakening that powerfully impacted the entire region for Christ (Acts 19). Like Elijah, Paul's highwater mark in ministry was met with demonic opposition. Of his time in Ephesus, the apostle writes, "For we do not want you to be ignorant, brethren, of our trouble which came to us in Asia: that we were burdened beyond measure, above strength, so that we despaired even of life. Yes, we had the sentence of death in ourselves, that we should not trust in ourselves but in God who raises the dead" (2 Cor. 1:8-9). A deep sense of discouragement, despair, and depression is not unusual for those under Satanic attack. Paul experienced it in Ephesus, and Elijah lived through it after Carmel, so do not be surprised if it assaults your life.

Wandering through the desert for forty days, ruminating on his situation, Elijah eventually ended up in the cave of Horeb, the very cave where Moses experienced the glory of God (Ex. 33:18-33). In his cave of discouragement, depression, and self-pity, the Lord ministered deeply and powerfully to Elijah. God was gracious with Elijah. The prophet wanted to end his ministry, and he asked that God take his life, but instead, God renewed Elijah and gave him significant tasks to accomplish (1 Kings 19:15-18). Elijah had felt as if he were the only follower of Yahweh left, but God reminded him there were seven thousand others still devoted to Him.

Paul was given a similar admonition when he arrived in Corinth in Acts 18:9-10. We read, "Now the Lord spoke to Paul in the night by a vision, 'Do not be afraid, but speak, and do not keep silent; I am with you, and no one will attack you to hurt you; for I have many people in this city.'" Undoubtedly, the reason the Lord told Paul not to be afraid was because he had fallen into fear. Jesus told him to not keep silent, because he was tempted to not speak up. The same spiritual opposition that affected Elijah in his day, and followers of Christ in our day, intimidated Paul in Corinth.

To strengthen Paul, Jesus gave him a three-fold promise. First, He promised His **presence**, "I am with you." In the immoral, idolatrous city of Corinth, Paul may have questioned if God was truly with him in his ministry there. I can relate to that feeling. I have often said to the Lord something like Moses' words in Exodus 33:15, "If Your Presence does not go with us, do not bring us up from here." Next, the Lord promised Paul His **protection**, "No one will hurt you." This is a unique promise that isn't always guaranteed when we step out in faith to obey Jesus — though often the threats we receive from opponents of truth are only intimidation tactics. Finally, Jesus encouraged Paul with His **perspective**, "For I have many people in this city." The Apostle apparently felt all alone as he entered Corinth. In reality, there were more people who were supportive of the mission of God in Corinth than Paul ever could have realized. The same is true for us today. Sometimes it feels like we are the only one standing for God's truth. Yet, when we bravely make a stand for the Lord and His truth, we may be surprised at how much support we will receive and how many other followers of Christ will stand with us.

PULLING DOWN JEZEBEL

If we want to defeat Jezebel in our lives and in our nation, we cannot be intimidated into silence. Rather, we must resist her evil influence and speak God's truth to confront her lies and deception. Years after the incident at Horeb, Elijah pronounced a prophetic word of judgment on Jezebel that came to pass just as the prophet predicted (1 Kings 21:23-24). Her end came at the hands of a strong, bold, and reckless leader named Jehu. We read about it in 2 Kings 9:30-33: "Now when Jehu had come to Jezreel, Jezebel heard of it; and she put paint on her eyes and adorned her head, and looked through a window. Then, as Jehu entered at the gate, she said, 'Is it peace, Zimri, murderer of your master?' And he looked up at the window, and said, 'Who is on my side? Who?' So two or three eunuchs looked out at him. Then he said, 'Throw her down.' So they threw her down, and some of her blood spattered on the wall and on the horses; and he trampled her underfoot."

In his excellent book, "Jezebel's War with America," Dr. Michael Brown writes extensively about the spirit of Jezebel and its influence on America.[82] We are not going as in-depth on the subject in this book, but I will share some similar observations on dealing with the Jezebel spirit.

While the death of Jezebel is a literal and historic account in the Hebrew Scriptures, it is not a call to physical violence. Remember, the physical battles of the Old Testament depict the spiritual battles we experience (Eph. 6:12). However, this narrative is instructive on how to deal with the Jezebel-like spiritual forces we battle as individuals and as a nation. While we forgive human opposition and bless those who curse us (Matt. 5:43-48, Rom. 12:14), we are forceful and merciless in dealing with demonic adversaries (2 Cor. 10:3-6, Matt. 11:12).

Jehu could bring down Jezebel because he did not fear her, he would not be intimidated or seduced by her, and he would not tolerate her. Jezebel's primary weapons are fear and intimidation. Her victims are unwilling to oppose her because they fear the price they will pay for doing so. Individuals operating under the influence of Jezebel can be extremely intimidating to confront.

When Jezebel calls Jehu by the name Zimri, she is speaking of a man who wrongly seized the throne and was shortly afterward killed. It is both a taunt and a weak threat that does not intimate Jehu. When we fear something, we are holding it in the highest regard, honoring and reverencing it. Jehu considered himself greater and more powerful than Jezebel, so he was not intimidated by her. As followers of Christ, we are strong in the Lord and we fear God alone. When we fear Him, we need to fear nothing or no one else. Like the Psalmist, we can say, "In God I have put my trust; I will not be afraid. What can man do to me?" (Ps. 56:11). We have courage to overcome intimidation and confront Jezebel, knowing the Lord is on our side.

To prepare for Jehu, Jezebel puts paint on her eyes and adorned her head, hoping to seduce her adversary. Yet Jehu had no interest in her attempts at seduction. We have seen that the spirit of Jezebel seduces people into sexual immorality (Rev. 2:20-21). America is a society that has yielded to the sexual seduction of Jezebel through all forms of sexual imagery, fantasy, and engagement. To overcome Jezebel, we must choose purity over perversion, holiness over pornography, and self-control over seduction. God created sex to be enjoyed inside His boundary of covenant marriage. Throwing off God's way has led to a whirlwind of societal disease and destruction. Only a decision to live for something greater than sexual pleasure can overcome Jezebel's seduction. It is time for a generation of followers of Christ to become Holy Rebels, who are the people of purity and holy passion that God has created us to be.

Jehu would not tolerate or compromise with Jezebel. The wicked queen would not repent, and the only alternative was to pull her down. When dealing with individuals operating in this controlling spirit, if they will not repent, you must cut off ties with them. Without repentance, there is no way to walk in agreement. Obviously, I am not talking about someone in a marriage situation, which is a topic outside of this book.

On a national level, those operating under the influence of Jezebel are devastating our nation and people. I pray daily for a national awakening where those influenced by Jezebel are swept into the kingdom, repenting of their sin and wickedness. If they refuse to repent, then the Bible and secular history show us that, like Ahab's bride and Jezebel of Thyatira, they will be pulled down from their places of power and influence. I pray they will be (Ps. 75:7).

It is interesting that eunuchs ultimately cast down Jezebel and her rule. She was overthrown by the men she had emasculated. In America, Jezebel has been emasculating men. Pornography renders men impotent. The tragedy of fatherless homes has probably done more damage to children and young men than anything else. Today, strong men are shamed and attacked for what is described as toxic masculinity. Lead male actors, particularly fathers, are most often portrayed in television shows and movies as childish, sexually unrestrained, helpless, bumbling idiots. The #MeToo Movement exposed the disturbing problem of sexual assault, domestic violence, and male bullying, and I am thankful these issues were brought into the light and confronted. However, most men do not engage in that despicable conduct. Most men in my life are godly, honorable men of integrity who love their families, come to the help of those in need, and are not ashamed of being men.

We need a holy rebellion of men of God to arise, countering the stereotypes and lies of the culture, serving their families, and leading our nation in a moral and spiritual awakening. This hour requires men with godly masculinity and women with godly femininity, who will rebel against the spirit of Jezebel to cast her down from her evil reign of demonic intimidation, immorality, witchcraft, and deception. It is time for Holy Rebel warriors who are bold truth-tellers, who will not be silent, to lead a kingdom revolution that shakes our nation with the power, truth, and love of God.

CHAPTER THIRTEEN

REVIVAL AND REFORMATION

O N AUGUST 17 of 2020, Kelly, I and twenty-four other pastors traveled to the four corners of Colorado Springs, Colorado to decree God's Word over our city. At each location, we buried a box containing a Bible, and we each took our turn driving a stake into the ground. Each stake had 2 Chronicles 7:14 embossed on it. The group prayed together, repented for the sins of our city, and proclaimed blessings from God's Word over the city, decreeing revival in the churches, awakening of the hearts of its people, and a Kingdom of God revolution throughout the region.

Several months later, Kelly was leading a prayer meeting. They prayed specifically for revival, awakening, and God's will to be done in our city. As these fervent intercessors cried out in one accord, Kelly saw a vision from the Lord. She said that it was as if she was back at the site of one of the four corners of the city. She saw us driving the stakes into the hard ground, and as the hammer struck each stake, sparks flew in every direction. Then she heard these words in her spirit: "The sparks of revival in this city began on that day." We are convinced the move of God has begun, and that He is just getting started. This passion, unity, and desire for revival will carry this move of God forward.

REVIVAL HISTORY

Having read of the great spiritual awakenings and revivals of the past, our hearts have always longed to see it again. One of our life verses is found in Habakkuk 3:2 (NIV) where the prophet prays, "Lord, I have heard of your fame; I stand in awe of your deeds, Lord. Repeat them in our day, in our time make them known; in wrath remember mercy."

In the early part of 1995, Kelly and I were in Springfield, Missouri for a conference on revival. Between sessions, I sensed the Lord saying, "I have called you to bring revival to East Texas." It surprised and excited me. Immediately I went home and fasted and prayed for revival to come to our city in East Texas. I was seasoned at fasting, but this fast gave me headaches and made me nauseous. Out of it, however, I realized the Lord was saying, "This is not up to you; follow Me." The primary contribution I was to make was my deep, gnawing hunger for a move of the Holy Spirit.

A few months later, I was asked to receive an offering at a large gathering of pastors in Austin, Texas. During prayer over the offering, the Spirit of God fell on me. I began weeping. Overcome by the Spirit, I collapsed on the floor. My wife and our youth pastor and his wife were in the audience. They were shocked to see me weep and fall to the floor. Their perspective changed when the Holy Spirit began moving across the auditorium. Soon hundreds of pastors were on their knees or on their faces, weeping and crying out to the Lord in repentance or thanksgiving.

Over the next few months, we saw the Lord manifest His presence uniquely, but sporadically, in our worship services. Yet we knew there was much more, and we continued to cry out for a visitation of God. Having heard God was pouring out His Spirit in Toronto, we attended a conference in Dallas, where members of the Toronto team ministered. The Holy Spirit clearly was at work through their ministry, but the ministry did not resonate with us. Next, I was told of a visitation of God at Brownsville Assemblies of God in Pensacola, Florida. Kelly and I, and two members of our staff, packed up and headed to Florida.

The church we were leading in East Texas was experiencing its fifth consecutive year of growth, and we were building a new worship center to accommodate the growth. Yet, I was not satisfied with what we were seeing. Driving the 8 hours to Pensacola, spiritual hunger and divine desperation consumed me. I was tired of church growth strategies and leadership models. I knew the Lord wanted to do more than what we were experiencing, and I longed for the supernatural move of the Holy Spirit.

By the time we arrived at the church, I had a terrible migraine headache. I was exhausted and just wanted to take a couple of Excedrin and lie down, but I did not dare miss the service. The people of the church were gracious, and there was an excited buzz in the room. However, running through my mind was the thought that I would be disappointed again. I was concerned the reports I had heard about God's activity were hype and exaggeration.

Worship pastor Lindell Cooley started leading the congregation into the first song, when suddenly the Holy Spirit fell upon me. His presence overwhelmed me, and, once again, all I could do was weep. Not normally a person given to public tears, I could not stop crying. The Holy Spirit swept over my soul, cleansing, healing, renewing, and refreshing me. I assumed everyone in the auditorium was having the same experienced and I was surprised to later learn no one else in our party was affected in this way. Evangelist Steve Hill shared a powerful message of repentance and over 200 people ran to the altars to give their lives to Christ. At that moment, I knew I had found what I had longed for. The next three nights I was at the altar each evening crying out to the Lord to do in our East Texas church what we experienced at Brownsville.

Sunday morning, I stood before those gathered at our 8:30 service to share with the congregation our experience at Brownsville Assembly. I told them the impact it had made on my life and the lives we had seen transformed by the Gospel delivered in the power of the Spirit. I explained that we must see the same spiritual outpouring in our city. I notified the church that we were cancelling all regular activities to meet at our church building every evening to pray until we saw the Lord pour out His Spirit. When I was done, I gave a non-traditional public invitation. I stood at the base of the platform and said, "Who is with me?" No one moved or demonstrated any emotion. It did not deter me from the mission, but in my mind, I was thinking, "This is going to be harder than I expected." Just as that thought entered my mind, a member of the church stepped out from the second row, with a tear running down his cheek. He did not say a word, but simply embraced me. At that moment, the Holy Spirit fell on our 260-seat worship center, much the way He did at the meeting in Austin. Congregants fell to their knees and on their faces, crying out to God in repentance, overwhelmed by the manifest presence of the Lord.

We held special services nightly. In our part of the country, any series of evangelistic meetings were referred to as revival services. But these truly were revival services. God manifested His presence in unusual, overwhelming, and awe-inspiring ways. Four nights a week we gathered to experience the power and presence of the Holy Spirit. As we worshiped and sat under the teaching of God's Word, we were revived in our spiritual lives. It was a taste of heaven.

These nightly meetings continued for a few weeks. Though some hungry believers from other congregations joined us, the meetings were primarily members of our congregation coming back each evening for another touch of the Holy Spirit. At one meeting I prayed, "Lord, unless this move of the Spirit reaches the lost and impacts our city, I'm going to end the meetings and we'll return to our regular schedule." The next Sunday morning, I gave a public invitation for people to come forward to receive Christ, and 20 people rushed to the altars of the church. That became our new normal, as people flooded to our church from all over the area. Some converts told us they were sitting in a bar getting drunk when they suddenly had a strange urge to leave and come to our church. They arrived and were gloriously saved. The most notorious drug dealer in the city came to Christ and his life was redirected. Prodigal teens were saved and restored to their families. Miraculous healings were reported. Our entire city felt the effects of the outpouring of God's Spirit. Soon, nearby pastors visited. They returned home to see unusual visitations of God in their congregations.

The residual impact of the revival continued beyond the initial outpouring. Our church, which had been recording about 100 conversions annually through our ministry, saw over 3,000 converts in a two-year period. In a town of 32,000, we became one of the 100 fastest growing churches in America for two consecutive years. It was not due to slick services, technology, or the latest church growth techniques. It was solely because of God's Spirit moving among us.

One insight that is significant to realize is that while the move of God's Spirit was the reason for the renewal and harvest, we had to cooperate with the Lord to retain the harvest. For us, revival was not a silver bullet. Nor did we abandon or suspend our church ministries for the revival. Rather, we allowed the revival to empower and enable what we were already doing. We continued and expanded our discipleship process. The church continued to raise up leaders and bring people into small groups. Pastoral ministry to the body never ceased, nor did our regular outreach ministries into the community. The ministry of Christ through His church continued, but with fresh power, anointing, and effectiveness.

Revival and spiritual outpouring converted the ancient sickle of our ministry programs into a modern harvesting combine. The revival and the outreach that resulted prompted the city manager to recognize our church as the primary reason for a reduction of crime and violence in our city. Today, we desperately need this empowerment of God's Spirit and this ministry of the supernatural.

There is a great cry in the heart of every Holy Rebel for revival. We believe revival in America has already begun. Certainly, many individual lives and numerous churches have experienced renewal, and they burn with a passion for Christ and His mission. I fervently pray it continues to spread. But I also know revival alone is not enough.

The church must be revived to go out and spark the fires of awakening. That awakening will result in a harvest of prodigals coming home and the lost coming into the kingdom of God. This awakening must be so grand that it impacts the ethos of the nation. Yet, even more than awakening, America needs a *reformation* that pulls down the demonic strongholds entrenched in places of power and influence – that drives out the forces of darkness and reforms systems and people who are enmeshed in Satanic strongholds of deception. There is a critical stream of revival that is flowing, but we need more than just revival.

TWO PROPHETIC STREAMS

One night, the Holy Spirit gave Kelly a powerful and detailed prophetic dream that has impacted our thinking about the solution to the severe issues our nation faces. In the dream, she saw a gathering of God's people praying, worshiping, praising God, and decreeing God's Word. She was then transported to another location where she saw two magnificent streams moving together, swerving around massive trees. An angel told her, "These are oaks of righteousness, the planting of the Lord to display His splendor" (Is. 61:3). Defying gravity and opposing the pull of the natural world, the two streams ascended toward heaven, cutting into the terrain. The angel then told her, "This move of God will be carried on prophetic streams. You shall decree a thing and it shall be established" (Job 22:28).

The trees in this dream represent a remnant of God's Holy Rebels. These mighty oaks of righteousness are planted by the Lord Himself in all areas of life, culture, and society. Wherever they are planted, they must display His splendor by intercession, shouting His praises, and decreeing

His power and purpose on earth. They are the very force that moves the pure, white waters up those streams.

Throughout the Bible, we read of decrees made by kings. They would make a decree and it would be carried out. Many kings issued evil decrees that were aimed at the destruction of God's people, but God's decrees always overruled the evil pronouncements. As God's royal priests today, we have the authority He has given to us, in His Name and according to His Word to overrule Satanic declarations. His Word is higher than every other word and decree in heaven and on earth.

The two streams represent two movements that are initiated by God and carried by His people. We believe these two movements are revival and reformation. This is a Divine partnership between God and His people to carry this move of the Spirit to its fullness. This visitation of God will only continue as God's holy remnant persists in united prayer, praise, and prophetic declaration. If we stop, the waters will stop, and the streams that carry this movement will stop.

To accomplish the purpose of God in America, we must have both revival and reformation — a moral and spiritual transformation in the hearts of people, but also the element of restoring Biblical values and principles into the fabric of American life. Only God's Word will reform broken and ineffective systems of society. This is not about establishing a theocracy, but about moving people to a proven path that leads to life, justice, abundance, and wholeness, rather than a path of confusion, devastation, division, and destruction. We need a Kingdom of God Revolution.

KINGDOM OF GOD REVOLUTION

The organizer of the four-corners event here in Colorado Springs was our friend Steve Holt, Senior Pastor of The Road @ Chapel Hill. Steve defines a Kingdom of God Revolution as "The ongoing move of God, administered through local churches, who are equipping the saints, the citizens of the Kingdom, to influence different cultural spheres in a local city, county, and state that brings kingdom transformation."

Christian churches and parachurch organizations have always been a source of extraordinary compassion and givers of hope to the hopeless. Philosopher Mark Nelson writes: "I would suggest that wherever you have an institution of self-giving for the lonely, schools, hospitals, hospices, orphanages for those who can never repay, this probably has its roots in the movement of Jesus."[83] I am extraordinarily thankful for what Christ's church is doing in feeding the hungry, creating clean water sources for the those who do not have any, visiting those sick and in prisons, rescuing those trapped in human trafficking, and providing educational opportunities and medical services to those without them. It is an honor to have participated over the years in these efforts. Yet, the church's impact on the world must be much more than providing compassion and care. America needs a kingdom transformation.

Jesus told His church to be the salt of the earth and the light of the world. We are to be a preserving influence against corruption and decay. As followers of Christ, we are called to bring the light of God's truth and love into the Satanic darkness that keeps multitudes enmeshed in spiritual blindness. For nearly 2,000 years, the church of Jesus Christ has impacted the world for good. Jesus and His church have lifted the dignity of all of humanity, promoted civil society and self-government, raised the level of justice, and contributed to science and the arts. They have brought a holy rebellion against hell and a kingdom revolution to culture.

BLACK ROBE REGIMENT

Today, the terminology of American secularists is that they will honor the church's freedom of worship. Which is code for, "You stay inside your buildings and do whatever you do, just don't you dare let it impact the culture and society. That's our job." Yet, as followers of Christ, we do not and cannot compartmentalize our faith. It must influence every part of our lives, including our citizenship. Our nation's foundations and history have been shaped by the truth and principles of the Bible and Christian thought. Historian David Barton writes, "America's elective governments, her educational system, and many other positive aspects of American life and culture were the product of biblical-thinking Christian clergy and leaders."[84]

David Barton references an interview Hezekiah Niles had with the second President of the United States, John Adams, in 1816. Niles asked Adams who the people were that were most responsible for what we enjoy as Americans. The names Adams gave were not names like Washington, Jefferson, and Franklin. Rather, they were the Reverend Samuel Cooper, Reverend Jonathan Mayhew, Reverend George Whitefield, and Reverend

Charles Chauncy.[85] According to Adams, pastors, preachers, and churches were the greatest influencers in the founding and flourishing of America.

The American clergy were so significant to the founding era (1750-1776), Barton explains, that the British named these courageous pastors "The Black Robed Regiment."[86] This moniker was given because in that day all ministers wore black robes in their pulpits. These pastors were the Holy Rebels of their time, whom the British blamed for fomenting American independence among the colonies' citizens. These American preachers opposed British tyranny and abuses of power that were encroaching on the colonists' civil and religious liberties. John Adams rejoiced in the ways these pastors "thundered from their pulpits." They not only declared the truth of God's Word concerning the events of their day, but they embodied them through their actions.

KINGDOM IMPACT

In 1 Chronicles 12:32 we read of the tribe of Issachar, who understood the times and knew what Israel should do. We need a generation of Holy Rebel pastors who, like the tribe of Issachar, understand the times in which we live and know how to respond. These Holy Spirit- driven leaders will stand against tyranny and stand up for Biblical truth, morality, and ethics. They are not political churches, but *biblical* churches, which prioritize worship, community, discipleship, servanthood, and evangelism, and which refuse to remain silent, back down, or cower in the face of tyranny, injustice, and evil.

Pastor Mark Cowart, founder of Church for All Nations (CFAN) in Colorado Springs, is such a pastor. He is one leader we have linked arms with to work together toward the transformation of our city and nation. Not only does Mark speak the truth of God's Word without compromise, but he is one of the church leaders leading a kingdom revolution through engaging his congregation in transforming society. In the summer of 2008, Mark had an encounter with the Lord that both shocked him and left him weeping uncontrollably. He had a strong sense our country was headed into an intense period of spiritual warfare that would result in transforming it into something far from God's heart and intent. This encounter led Mark into a season of studying our American Christian heritage. By 2012, Mark says the Holy Spirit's conviction became overwhelming. He knew he could no longer be silent about the issues of our day. He had decided that it was time to be courageous and boldly speak the truth no matter who it may upset, and it upset many. As he spoke on what the Scripture says concerning political issues, he had couples and families get up and walk out in the middle of his message. Mark was accused of being too political. He was also charged with being homophobic, racist, a hater, and other unmentionable names. Knowing Mark personally, I can tell you, he is the opposite of these things. He is a loving man of God who cares deeply for people, which is why he will speak the truth even in the face of severe opposition.

Out of deep conviction, Pastor Cowart started a Cultural Impact Team (CIT). The idea was conceived by the Family Research Council. Mark believes it is one of the most important ministries of his church. CIT rallies his congregation and members of the community around critical issues in our society and culture where the redeeming influence of the kingdom of God needs to be brought to bear. Mark discovered a vast majority of his church members were gravely concerned about the direction of our nation. Like most Americans, they felt the country was headed in the wrong direction and CIT showed them how to get involved in moving our nation towards biblical values. Cultural Impact Teams mobilize people who want to see the nation come back to its founding principles and values. They are committed to mobilizing Christians to vote, to become poll watchers, and to help secure integrity in our elections.

Mark sees school boards as an area where there is intense spiritual warfare. He explains, "Parents who are concerned about their children's education and what they are being taught have been labeled 'domestic terrorists' by the FBI. Parents have had their microphones turned off when attending school board meetings for inquiring or expressing concerns about their children's education. Parents have been ushered out of these meetings and even arrested. All of this would have been considered virtually impossible just a few years ago." Cultural Impact Teams act to keep parents and congregations informed as to what is going on behind the scenes. In conjunction with CIT, Mark has launched the Benjamin Rush Alliance for Liberty & Education (BRALE). It encourages, educates, and equips Christian and conservative school board members to be more effective. Following Pastor Mark's lead, Radiant Church launched its own Cultural Impact Team that is engaging our members in being educated, equipped, and empowered to make a difference in the political realm for Christ.

Steve Holt, Senior Pastor of the Road, believes the early church depicted in Acts 4 is a prophetic picture of how today's church in America should respond to the challenges of our day. These new believers responded to persecution by first going into a prayer meeting and then coming out to act in the power of the Holy Spirit (Acts 4:23-33). The great signs and wonders included impacting the culture with the truth and values of the Kingdom of God. It was the two streams of revival and reformation.

When COVID-19 mandates shut down churches in Colorado, Steve was vexed in spirit. He believed it was a test from God, whether the church was willing to stand against principalities and powers. Steve helped mobilize pastors in Colorado Springs to reopen their churches. Over 50 churches responded. Twenty-eight of us signed an op-ed in the Colorado Springs *Gazette* that disagreed with the shutdown. Steve says, "It would have been easy for the state to come against one church, but when we united, they weren't willing to take on all of us."

Steve followed up on this by inviting our church to join with them in hosting an outdoor worship concert with Sean Feucht at Memorial Park in Colorado Springs. It was against the law, but 6,000 people attended. The Colorado Springs Police Department was so impressed by the event, they put a ring of protection around the gathering against threats from Antifa. Steve also spearheaded a County Commissioner's declaration at a packed-out Centennial Hall, proclaiming El Paso County (the largest county in Colorado) a liberty and freedom county. The declaration received twelve standing ovations.

During the pandemic, The Road launched the Radical Resilience Ministry, which provided supplement kits that strengthened people's immune systems to fight off COVID. Three thousand people received the protocol kits. No one who started the kit within 4 days of contracting COVID had to be hospitalized. They also mobilized a Church Voter guide for the 2021 school board elections. Over 6,000 people received the guides, and another 4,000 accessed it online. Working with other churches, the 2021 school board election had a 45% increase in turnout and turned 5 out of 6 seats from progressives to conservatives. Conservatives gained a majority in three of our largest school districts, including two suburban districts and a Colorado Springs center-city district.

There is a critical need for Holy Rebel pastors to partner with other like-minded pastors and churches to see a Kingdom Revolution in our nation. When we do, we are able to share resources and expertise. Each church adds its unique DNA to produce a Holy Spirit synergy that enables us to do far more together than we could ever do on our own.

THE SHIFT

Every Holy Rebel church I know has made prayer and intercession a priority. At Radiant Church, Kelly and I know we have a mandate to be a house of prayer that is engaged in birthing revival and awakening in America. Having experienced true revival, we know we dare not settle for less. This move of God will not look identical to what we have seen in the past, but however it manifests, we long to see the church revived, society awakened, and God glorified. We cannot accomplish it through savvy leadership or human ingenuity. We must experience a heaven-sent revival. We prioritize humility, repentance, warfare worship, fasting, and fervent prayer. Yet, we also know revival is not enough. We must have a reformation in how followers of Christ see their role in society.

We have made a shift in our ministry to have a greater influence for Christ in the culture. The people of God need more than an understanding of Biblical truth that applies to their own lives. They need to be equipped to be salt and light in the world around them. A steady diet of "how to" messages focused on how to live our best lives now is an old wine skin that will not bring the societal transformation that is needed.

From the Radiant pulpit, we explain the Bible and apply Scripture to the times in which we live. In teaching the Bible, we have addressed the sanctity of life, the sanctity of marriage, sexuality, gender confusion, racism, bioethics, lawlessness, government tyranny, and other hot-button issues in our society. On each subject, we have unapologetically presented God's perspective from the biblical text. We have been criticized and had people leave our church because of our bold stand on God's Word, but we have refused to compromise the truth.

The modern American educational system has in large part failed to teach basic civics and what it means to be a good citizen of our nation. Radiant Church is, therefore, equipping believers to be Biblical citizens. We have drawn on the resources of organizations like Patriot Academy, Wall Builders, the Truth & Liberty Coalition, Well Versed, Turning Point USA, and others to educate and empower members of our congregation in this calling. They are taught how to defend the Biblical values of marriage, family, ethics, and morality, along with the principles of liberty. We are not training "Christian nationalists," but Christians with a Biblical worldview who are empowered to be salt and light in our nation.

In recent years, I have seen some silliness and absurdity that gives Christians who are patriotic a bad name. However, almost every follower of Christ I know who also cares about the well-being of our nation is not in this category. They love God and are committed to Christ and His Kingdom first. Their second allegiance is to their family, and thereafter their nation, and its citizens. The term Christian Nationalist seems primarily designed to shut believers up and keep them from making a positive difference for Christ in our nation. The dark powers know that if the body of Christ in America would commit to a Biblical worldview, stop being silent, and act to defend truth and liberty, their plans to destroy the American church and bring destruction to our nation would be over.

CALL TO ACTION

Not only can churches educate and empower their members for ministry in the culture, but they should provide opportunities for their members to be engaged. It is easy for smaller churches to be intimidated by what mega-churches can accomplish, but every church can do something. Radiant Church is determined to make a kingdom impact for Christ. Rather than re-inventing what is already working, we have partnered with churches like The Road and CFAN in what they are doing to make a bigger difference. The national crisis is daunting, but we have seen together that we can make a significant impact locally. Throughout his presidency, Ronald Reagan kept a sign on his desk that read, "It's amazing how much you can get done if you don't care who gets the credit." This is certainly true with this move of God. Beyond our regular ministries, Radiant has also found unique ways we can influence the culture with truth and compassion.

God's Word is unapologetically pro-life, and Biblical Christians should be as well. One accusation hurled at those who believe in the sanctity of life is that we only care about unborn children and do nothing to help them or their mothers after the babies are born. Radiant is working to demonstrate the fallacy of this claim. Radiant Church's Krystal Clark and her husband, Pastor Rashad Clark, lead the Embrace Grace Ministry at our church. Through this ministry, we are reaching out to frightened moms who feel hopeless and helpless by extending God's love and help to them and their babies. The Radiant Embrace Grace team has already rescued several babies and their mothers from Hell's abortion plans.

Embrace Grace comes alongside to rescue a terrified mother from making the most tragic decision of her life. The team does this with prayer and encouragement, along with making sure the mothers are well-equipped, prepared, and supplied with all the resources for taking care of their baby's needs. There is joy and excitement in our church as we welcome these moms and their babies into our hearts and our church family. We are committed to walking with them and being there for them throughout their journey.

When the George Floyd incident of police brutality occurred, it stirred fear, pain, and trauma in African American members of our congregation. Our congregation had a time of mourning and prayer and had some healthy dialogue. We again taught what the Scripture says about racism and denounced all forms of this evil. Then when BLM riots and the calls to defund the police broke out, we also decried lawlessness and social Marxism, based on the Word of God. We immediately came to the support of law enforcement. Radiant held monthly breakfasts for the local police department, and our Central Campus facility became a safe space for officers. We have continued as a close ally of our law enforcement community.

We have shared a few ways that three churches are engaged not only in the stream of revival but also in the stream of reformation. Can you imagine what would happen if most American churches would seriously pursue God's plan for revival and reformation? We would experience a Holy Rebellion and a Kingdom Revolution. Lord, may it be!

THE CRISIS IN EDUCATION

Though Kelly and I have always supported parents who homeschool their children and parents who send their children to private Christian schools, our conviction was to send our children to public schools. We knew our children would follow Christ if they were under our roof and under our influence. So, with limited funds, if we were going to invest in private education, it would not be for grammar school and high school, but rather for a Christian university. Even more significantly, we wanted them to be salt and light within their public school.

Throughout the past 17 years, that has been a good strategy for us. Our kids have been in a charter school within the public education system. They received a quality education, and they were a positive influence for Christ. Kelly volunteered in the classrooms and stayed engaged in what was being taught. There have been times that she had to have meetings with teachers about literature and teachings that opposed our convictions.

As with any organization that starts out on a right path, when compromise begins to occur, it is just a matter of time before the whole system is on a wrong path. Today parents can no longer send their kids to school (any school) and assume that they will be guided and instructed properly. Parents must be engaged, watching, and aware of what is being taught and encouraged in the schools their students attend.

Until last year, the teachers in our kids' schools were understanding and accommodating. Last year, we realized that our values and convictions were no longer accepted in the public system. Assignments were contrary not only to our values, but our daughter came to us distraught over the extreme blasphemy in the first few pages of a required reading. We went to the administration. Faith sincerely explained that seeing, reading, and hearing God's name taken in vain was painful to her. Of course, she understood that in the world we live in, it would be a reality from time to time. Yet, her concern was that as she was forced to read blasphemous terms *multiple* times, her heart would become calloused to it, and "it would no longer hurt her heart." Kelly researched the required literature for Faith's class and discovered that the reading material was packed full of blasphemy, profanity, sexual immorality, drunkenness, and corruption.

God's Word teaches us to guard our hearts above all else, because out of the heart flows the issues of life (Proverbs 4:23). As parents, we are responsible to guard our children's hearts and teach them to do the same throughout their lives. Therefore, we have taught our kids to guard their hearts by not subjecting themselves to dark, destructive, sinful, entertainment, media, music, and literature. When Kelly contacted the administration office with her concerns, she was told that our values would not be validated in the classroom and that our daughter would have to comply with the assigned reading. This is where parents must stand up, speak up and rebel against this hellish agenda. Parents do not comply with evil. We pulled Faith from that class last year and we now homeschool both of our children, using classical Christian homeschool curriculum. This may not be right for every family, but it was the right decision for our family.

Public Education in America began with God at the center and the Word of God being the basis for the instruction of our children. In recent decades, God was removed and has become banned from public education. Education has gone from being biblically based to blatantly opposing biblical truth and values. Morality has been replaced with immorality, and we are expected to comply and allow this agenda to replace our values and convictions. There is a demonic strategy to desensitize children to blasphemy, sin, corruption, perversion, and to lure them out of God's plan and onto the path of destruction.

Yet, we do not believe the church should abandon public schools. If you have the privilege of being in a good public or charter school, thank God for it, and fight to maintain it. For if you fail to, it will not continue to be. Radiant Church has partnered to help our public schools. We have provided various forms of help to under-resourced schools in our community, honored and celebrated the good teachers in our local schools, and assisted families in the schools who needed help around the holidays. In addition, we regularly pray for our schools and have been part of efforts to elect wise and godly leaders to serve on our local school boards to see essential changes.

Our education system needs a reformation. We support those creating parallel educational alternatives and policies that empower parents to have a real choice in their children's education. Radiant has hosted a homeschool co-op at one of our campuses and has encouraged private Christian school educators. Together, Holy Rebels will be part of the solution to the crisis in education. The Evil One's influence in the American education system has been a primary reason for America's turn from godliness and biblical values.

In this book, we have outlined a variety of practical steps individual believers and church leaders can take—led and empowered by the Holy Spirit — to push back or even displace the forces of evil that seek to enslave our children, strip us of our religious freedoms, and destroy our country. We also laid out vital steps that churches can take to inform, educate, motivate, and mobilize their congregations to effect positive changes in political and public policy arenas at the local, state, and federal level. There are some whose influence and affluence can allow them to make a bigger impact that others, but we all have our part to play.

FINAL CALL

We in the body of Christ must recognize that we are at war. It is not a physical battle, but a spiritual one that is between the kingdom of God and the kingdom of darkness. As our enemy rips through humanity, bringing devastation and massive casualties, much of the body of Christ is asleep. In recent years, Satanic forces have unleashed a shock and awe campaign on America, with outrageous casualties and horrific brutality. Yet, most of the church acts as if it is peacetime. They carry out ministry as usual, as if rearranging chairs on the deck of the Titanic as it approaches a massive iceberg. Many believers are living carnal lives of self-indulgence and worldly preoccupation. Worse, many who call themselves by the name of Jesus have defected from Christ's cause to betray biblical values and sabotage the work of God in these crucial hours.

We must rend our garments of complacency and apathy, and fall before our holy God in repentance, brokenness, and desperation. The hour is late and the need for action past due. If the sleeping giant of the church would arise to take its rightful place as the salt of the earth, the light of the world, and the slayer of demonic goliaths, this wicked madness would end. Individual believers — and especially pastors — must wake up, stand up, speak up, and push back against the demonic forces that threaten the innocence and safety of our children, the loss of our personal and religious freedoms, and the destruction of the very foundations on which our nation was founded and prospered for almost two and a half centuries.

Joe Biden said repeatedly during the last Presidential campaign, and he has continued to say, we are in a battle for the soul of our nation. Indeed, we are in a battle, but the side of the battle he, and most politicians, want to fight for, is antithetical to God and His word. Most of the major conflicts and controversies dividing and polarizing our nation are indeed a battle between good and evil. The problem for those of us who follow the God of the Bible is that on so many of these issues, the prevailing societal definition of what is good and what is evil has been flipped. Satan would have us fight for evil, using politicians, celebrities, and the media to convince us that evil is good. We are witnessing a living out of Isaiah 5:20, which says, "Woe to those who call evil good and good evil, who put darkness for light, and light for darkness." There are woeful and horrific consequences for people and nations who try to redefine the truth and the standards of God's Word.

In just the last few years, the pace of moral decline in America has accelerated to warp speed. It is not an overstatement to say that we are on the precipice of a total moral collapse and the potential destruction of our once strong Republic and beacon of light to the world.

It is past time for us, the body of Christ, to recognize that we are in a war for the hearts, minds, and eternal destiny of a nation of people, and that we must aggressively engage in this battle. The church of Jesus Christ cannot continue to sit silently on the sidelines—preoccupied with insignificant trivialities — as our society crumbles from within and our freedoms are swept away by godless and corrupt leaders. While this is primarily a spiritual battle that must be fought with prayer and spiritual weapons, believers also need to be engaged in warfare in the natural realm, including the political process, to bring about reformation.

As leading prophetic voices have been declaring, God has not forgotten America, nor the covenant our forefathers made with Him. America *can* be saved, but it will require the participation and faithful engagement of His people.

Let the enemy hear our war cry! May the hordes of hell feel the sting of the sword of our prophetic decrees and may the kingdom of darkness be shaken by the deep spiritual travail of our souls. May we stand with our Lord Jesus and God's other Holy Rebels across the millenniums, linking arms with Abraham, Moses, David, Elijah, Daniel, Esther, and other Old Covenant heroes of the faith, and joining with Paul and the rest of the Lord's Holy Rebel New Testament saints. Making a stand in our generation like Luther, Bonhoeffer, and Wilberforce did in theirs, and riding a wave of revival and awakening like Wesley, Whitefield, Evan Roberts, and William Seymour, we can thwart the evil that has encroached on our nation and bring about reformation and revival. It is our hour, and it is our time. If we will rebel against Hell's agenda with righteousness, holiness, and truth, we will destroy Satan's strongholds over our nation and usher in a tsunami of worldwide awakening that carries multiple millions into the kingdom of God. It is our time to be God's Holy Rebels for our generation.

MEET THE AUTHORS

TODD *and* KELLY HUDNALL are co-lead pastors of *Radiant Church*, a multi-campus church in Colorado Springs, CO. Both were raised in Kansas and have led Radiant Church since 2006, after serving churches in Kansas, Texas, and California. Having experienced an explosive wave of revival in their church in Texas, Todd and Kelly prayed and hungered for over 15 years for another mighty move of God, this time in Colorado. Over the years, they continuously urged their congregation to press in to God and cry out for revival.

Beginning in 2021, the fires of revival began to break out and sweep through Radiant Church. Desiring to see revival spread throughout their city and the surrounding region, Todd and Kelly began to pray for Mario Murillo to bring his tent crusade to Colorado Springs. Through a miraculous chain of events, God connected them to Mario and in July 2022, he brought his 3,000-seat tent to the grounds of a Radiant campus on the north side of the city. Every night for four days, the tent was filled to capacity, with up to 2,000 additional people watching from outside the tent. Over 3,500 people came forward for the salvation altar calls, and stunning healings and miracles took place as the Holy Spirit was poured out inside and outside the tent.

Like Mario Murillo, Todd and Kelly Hudnall are deeply concerned about the state of our nation and the need for pastors and individual believers to stand up and push back against the forces of evil that have taken over so much of our culture, our government, and other institutions–leading them to embrace and impose ungodly beliefs and practices through laws and regulations, employer mandates and cancel culture. They are particularly concerned that Christians do not remain silent about the continued slaughter of innocent lives through abortion; the redefinition of marriage and gender; ungodly and destructive indoctrination of our children and youth, and growing threats to our individual and religious liberty.

To get in touch with Todd and Kelly, or to view more of their teaching, use the following contacts:

Radiant Church Website: **RadiantChurch.org**
Holy Rebel Website: **HolyRebel.co**

Todd and Kelly's Blog: **blog.radiantchurch.org**
Radiant Church Youtube: **tinyurl.com/radiantchurch**
Holy Rebel for Teens: **tinyurl.com/holyrebelforteens**

Todd's Twitter: **@Todd_Hudnall**
Kelly's Twitter: **@khudnall1**

Email: **PastorTodd@radiantchurch.org**

ENDNOTES

1. Accessed November 6, 2021, https://www.christianpost.com/news/over-900000-christians-martyred-for-their-faith-in-last-10-years-report-173045/
2. Accessed November 6, 2021, https://efile.fara.gov/docs/6170-Informational-Materials-20210115-808.pdf
3. YouTube, 10 Questions: Religion in America, 2006, https://www.youtube.com/watch?v=35sGJrWKcmY, (accessed November 28, 2021)
4. Tony Evans, "Our Battle With Life's Strongholds," https://ezralivingfree.wordpress.com/2015/12/31/our-battle-with-lifes-strongholds/ (accessed November 12, 2021).
5. Ladd, George Eldon. The Gospel of the Kingdom: Scriptural Studies in the Kingdom of God (p. 48). Wm. B. Eerdmans Publishing Co. Kindle Edition.
6. H.G. Liddell, *A Lexicon: Abridged from Liddell and Scott's Greek-English Lexicon* (Oak Harbor, WA: Logos Research Systems, Inc., 1996), 239.
7. Ingram, Chip. The Invisible War: What Every Believer Need to Know About Satan, Demons, and Spiritual Warfare (p. 73). Baker Books, Grand Rapids, MI.
8. https://ms-my.facebook.com/SOScommunity/posts/4133019053460310 (Accessed November 21, 2021).
9. https://www.goodreads.com/author/quotes/5202174.Jonathan_Cahn (Accessed November 21, 2021).
10. https://www.goodreads.com/work/quotes/17626535-the-harbinger-the-ancient-mystery-that-holds-the-secret-of-america-s-f (Accessed November 21, 2021).
11. Morgan Chalfant, "Trump Likens Himself to a Wartime President Amid Coronavirus Pandemic," https://thehill.com/homenews/administration/488239-trump-likens-himself-to-a-wartime-president-amid-coronavirus-pandemic (Accessed November 11, 2021) .

12. Faithlife, LLC. "Logos Bible Software Bible Sense Lexicon." Logos Bible Software, Computer software. Bellingham, WA: Faithlife, LLC, December 11, 2021.

13. Bible Letter Bible, https://www.blueletterbible.org/lexicon/g3180/kjv/tr/0-1/ (Accessed December 9, 2021).

14. Sermon Index, https://www.sermonindex.net/modules/articles/index.php?view=article&aid=34452 (Accessed December 9, 2021).

15. Africa Freak, "10 Interesting Facts About Lions Eyes," https://africafreak.com/lion-eyes (Accessed December 10, 2021).

16. Jimmy Evans, "Battling Satan in the End Times, Tipping Point," https://www.youtube.com/watch?v=IUfCu9n-ADM&t=945s (Accessed November 30, 2021).

17. Megan Brenan, "American's Mental Health Ratings Sink to New Low," https://news.gallup.com/poll/327311/americans-mental-health-ratings-sink-new-low.aspx (Accessed November 30, 2021).

18. Barton, David, "Run to the Roar," https://www.youtube.com/watch?v=fgI-4IDXGunw&t=224s (Accessed November 30, 2021).

19. David Seal, "Satan," ed. John D. Barry et al., *The Lexham Bible Dictionary* (Bellingham, WA: Lexham Press, 2016).

20. Thayer's Greek New Testament, https://biblehub.com/greek/32.htm (Accessed December 10, 2021).

21. Revival Radio TV, "John Kilpatrick's Testimony," https://www.youtube.com/watch?v=MZqGHk704ho (Accessed December 11, 2021).

22. C. Keith Hansley, "Harald Hardrada Allegedly Conquered A Sicilian Town By Pretending To Be Dead," https://thehistorianshut.com/2018/06/30/harald-hardrada-allegedly-conquered-a-sicilian-town-by-pretending-to-be-dead/ (accessed December 4, 2021).

23. James Clark, "The Most Interesting War Tactics of all Time, According to the Internet," https://taskandpurpose.com/history/the-most-interesting-war-tactics-of-all-time-according-to-the-internet/ (accessed December 4, 2021).

24. Bible Hub, "methodeia," https://biblehub.com/greek/3180.htm (Accessed December 17, 2021).

25. Leonardo Blair, "Nearly 70% of Born-again Christians Say Other Religions Can Lead to Heaven: Study," https://www.christianpost.com/news/nearly-70-percent-of-born-again-christians-dont-see-jesus-as-only-way.html (accessed December 9, 2021).

26. Sam Alberry, "How Can I Know My Gender?" https://www.youtube.com/watch?v=2Kaex8EA2y4 (accessed December 14, 2021).

27. Rod Dreher. Live Not by Lies (p. 58-59). Penguin Publishing Group. Kindle Edition.

28. Edward E. Ericson Jr. and Daniel J. Mahoney, "The Solzhenitshyn Reader," https://www.solzhenitsyncenter.org/live-not-by-lies (accessed December 17, 2021).

29. Michael Reed, *Silence in the Face of Evil is Itself Evil*," https://www.

thestandardsc.org/michael-reed/silence-in-the-face-of-evil-is-itself-evil/ (accessed December 7, 2021).

30. R.K. Hudnut, *"A Sensitive Man and the Christ,"* https://www.wthrockmorton.com/wp-content/uploads/2016/11/Hudnut-speak-act-1971.png (accessed December 18, 2021).

31. Dutch Sheets, "The Sound of Redemption," https://www.youtube.com/watch?v=vDt8PBKhbsM (accessed June 20, 2022).

32. The Epic Battle of Thermopylae Remains One of the Most Stirring Defeats of All Time, Nathaniel Scharping, https://www.discovermagazine.com/planet-earth/the-epic-battle-of-thermopylae-remains-one-of-the-most-stirring-defeats-of.

33. Aleksandar Mishov, How Spartan Boys Were Turned Into Mighty Warriors, https://www.documentarytube.com/articles/how-spartan-boys-were-turned-into-mighty-warriors

34. Sparta, History.com Editors. https://www.history.com/topics/ancient-history/sparta

35. Msgr. Charles Pope, Is the Church a Cruise Ship or a Battleship, https://blog.adw.org/2018/05/church-cruise-ship-battleship/, May 17, 2018.

36. Barna, Changes in Worldview Among Christians Over the Past 13 Years, https://www.barna.com/research/barna-survey-examines-changes-in-worldview-among-christians-over-the-past-13-years, (Accessed December 15, 2021).

37. Ceslas Spicq and James D. Ernest, *Theological Lexicon of the New Testament* (Peabody, MA: Hendrickson Publishers, 1994), 344–353.

38. Engle, Lou. The Fast: Rediscovering Jesus' Pathway to Power (p. 33). Engle House Publishing . Kindle Edition.

39. A.T. Robertson, Word Pictures in the New Testament (Nashville, TN: Broadman Press, 1933), Jn 14:16.

40. Marvin Richardson Vincent, Word Studies in the New Testament, vol. 2 (New York: Charles Scribner's Sons, 1887), 244.

41. Smith, Malcolm. Holy Spirit Revealed. Unconditional Love. San Antonio, TX.

42. William Arndt et al., A Greek-English Lexicon of the New Testament and Other Early Christian Literature (Chicago: University of Chicago Press, 2000), 60.

43. D. A. Carson, "Matthew," in *The Expositor's Bible Commentary: Matthew, Mark, Luke*, ed. Frank E. Gaebelein, vol. 8 (Grand Rapids, MI: Zondervan Publishing House, 1984), 344.

44. Patricia Kasten, "What did Peter's Boat Look Like," The Compass, https://www.thecompassnews.org/2018/01/peters-boat-look-like/#, (Accessed May 5, 2022)

45. Wariboko, N., & Oliverio, L., Jr. (2020). The Society for Pentecostal Studies at 50 Years, *Pneuma*, 42(3-4), 327-333. doi: https://doi.org/10.1163/15700747-04203021 , (Accessed May 5, 2022)

46. Kenneth E. Hagin, The Art of Prayer (p. 28). Faith Library Publications. Kindle Edition.

47. John Wesley, Journal, August 15, 1750, The Works of John Wesley, vol. II (Grand Rapids, MI: Baker Book House, 1986), 204.

48. Craig S. Keener. Miracles Today: The Supernatural Work of God in the Modern World. Narrated by Mike Chamberlain (christianaudio.com, 2021).

49. Evangelism Statistics, Bible.org, Accessed August 26, 2022, https://bible.org/illustration/evangelism-statistics.

50. "Looking for Elijah," Steve Herzig, accessed June 9, 2022. https://israelmyglory.org/article/looking-for-elijah/.

51. G. A. Yee, "Jezebel (Person)," in David Noel Freedman, ed., The Anchor Yale Bible Dictionary, vol. 3 (New York: Doubleday, 1992), 848–849 with reference to Althayah Brenner-Idan, The Israelite Woman (Sheffield, England: Sheffield, 1985).

52. Allen R. Guenther, *Hosea, Amos*, Believers Church Bible Commentary (Scottdale, PA: Herald Press, 1998), 394.

53. Rashi's commentary to Jeremiah 7:31, as quoted in John Gill, "Commentary of Jeremiah 7:31," John Gill Exposition of the Entire Bible, accessed May 30, 2022. https://www.studylight.org/commentaries/geb/jeremiah-7.html.

54. "Bronze Bull," Center for Online Judaic Studies, http://cojs.org/bronze_bull-_c-_1200_bce/, accessed August 15, 2022.

55. "Over 63 million abortions have occurred in the US since Roe v. Wade decision in 1973," Kyle Morris and Sam Dorman, Fox News, accessed June 12, 2022. https://www.foxnews.com/politics/abortions-since-roe-v-wade.

56. "How Democrats Purged 'Safe, Legal, Rare' From the Party," Alexandra DeSancis, accessed June 12, 2022. https://www.washingtonpost.com/outlook/how-democrats-purged-safe-legal-rare-from-the-party/2019/11/15/369af73c-01a4-11ea-8bab-0fc209e065a8_story.html

57. "Abortion by the Numbers," Katie Jennings, accessed June 12, 2022. https://www.forbes.com/sites/katiejennings/2022/05/07/abortion-by-the-numbers/?sh=2d1711ef60a8

58. "Testimony of Brenda Pratt Shafer, R.N., Subcommittee on the Constitution," March 21, 1996, House Judiciary Committee Homepage, https://web.archive.org/web/19970430081149/https://www.house.gov/judiciary/215.htm.

59. Brown, Michael L.. Jezebel's War With America: The Plot to Destroy Our Country and What We Can Do to Turn the Tide (p.62). Charisma House. Kindle Edition.

60. "More Black Babies Aborted than Born in New York City," Alec Torres, accessed June 14, 2022. https://www.nationalreview.com/corner/more-black-babies-aborted-born-new-york-city-alec-torres/

61. "Teachers Across US Advocating Trans-ideology in classroom for 'Jazz & Frinds' Reading Day," Ryan Foley, accessed June 13, 2022. https://www.christianpost.com/news/teachers-across-us-advocating-transgenderism-in-classroom.html

62. LGBT Identification in U.S. Ticks Up to 7.1%, Jeffrey M. Jones, accessed June 12, 2022. https://news.gallup.com/poll/389792/lgbt-identification-ticks-up.aspx.

63. "John Hopkins Center Against Child Abuse Hired Allyn Walker, A Professor Who Defends 'Minor-Attracted Persons,'" Tyler O'Neil. Accessed June 16, 2022. https://www.foxnews.com/us/johns-hopkins-center-child-sexual-abuse-hires-professor-minor-attracted-persons

64. "Secular Intolerance of Christians' Views is Leading to Self-Censorship Report Warns," Anugrah Kumar, accessed June 13, 2022. https://www.christianpost.com/news/secular-intolerance-of-christians-is-leading-to-self-censorship-report.html?uid=*%7CUNIQID%7C*&utm_source=The+Christian+Post+List&utm_campaign=CP-Newsletter&utm_medium=email

65. "Lectures on Revival of Religion," Charles F. Finney, Lecture XV.

66. "The Summa Theologiae of St. Thomas Aquinas," New Advent, accessed June 11, 2022. https://www.newadvent.org/summa/3158.htm

67. "Letter to the American Church, Eric Metaxas," accessed September 14, 2022. https://www.youtube.com/watch?v=2MGvd1CVZwk.

68. Rod Dreher, "Live Not by Lies," (Penguin Publishing Group, 2020), 69.

69. All Authors, accessed August 3, 2022, https://allauthor.com/quotes/95449

70. Perry Stone, "When the Brook Goes Dry and the Birds Won't Fly," Perry Stone Hebraic Prophetic Study Bible: Old Testament (The Fedd Agency, 2019), 572

71. William Lee Holladay and Ludwig Köhler, *A Concise Hebrew and Aramaic Lexicon of the Old Testament* (Leiden: Brill, 2000), 294.

72. "American Worldview Inventory 2020," Cultural Research Center at Arizona Christian University, accessed May 30, 2022. https://www.arizonachristian.edu/wp-content/uploads/2020/04/CRC-AWVI-2020-Release-02_Faith-and-Worldview-1.pdf.

73. "Competing Worldviews Influence Today's Christians," Barna Research, accessed May 30, 2022. https://www.barna.com/research/competing-worldviews-influence-todays-christians/.

74. Malcolm Smith, *Faith's Challenge* (sermon, Growing in Dynamic Faith series).

75. James Swanson, *Dictionary of Biblical Languages with Semantic Domains : Hebrew (Old Testament)* (Oak Harbor: Logos Research Systems, Inc., 1997).

76. "What Blaise Pascal Saw In A November Night Of Fire That Inaugurated A Year Of Grace," Midge Fusselman, accessed June 6, 2022. https://thefederalist.com/2017/11/23/blaise-pascal-saw-november-night-fire-inaugurated-year-grace/.

77. "John Wesley's Heart Strangely Warmed," Dan Graves, accessed June 6, 2022, https://www.christianity.com/church/church-history/timeline/1701-1800/john-wesleys-heart-strangely-warmed-11630227.html.

78. Francis Brown, Samuel Rolles Driver, and Charles Augustus Briggs, *Enhanced Brown-Driver-Briggs Hebrew and English Lexicon* (Oxford: Clarendon Press, 1977), 929–930.

79. Christian History Institute, "Charles Grandison Finney: Father of American Revivalism," https://christianhistoryinstitute.org/magazine/article/charles-grandison-finney (Accessed July 2, 2022).

80. Richard Klein, "Charles Finney: An Nation's Character Redefined," https://www1.cbn.com/charles-finney-nations-character-redefined (accessed July 2, 2022).

81. Paul Reno, "Prevailing Prince of Prayer," https://www.hopefaithprayer.com/prayernew/prevailing-prince-prayer-daniel-nash (Accessed July 2, 2022).

82. Brown, Michael L.. Jezebel's War With America: The Plot to Destroy Our Country and What We Can Do to Turn the Tide. Charisma House. Kindle Edition.

83. Ortberg, John. *Who Is This Man?: The Unpredictable Impact of the Inescapable Jesus.* Zondervan. Kindle Edition.

84. Barton, David. "What is the Black Robe Regiment?," Accessed August 20, 2022. http://storage.cloversites.com/cornerstonefellowship1/documents/Black%20Robed%20Regiment.pdf

85. Barton, David. "America's Christian History." Accessed August 20, 2022. https://www.youtube.com/watch?v=ec8mGYcNOLo.

86. National Black Robe Regiment, Accessed August 20, 2022. https://nationalblackroberegiment.com/history-of-the-black-robe-regiment.